Jewish Interpretation
of the Bible

"In this masterful and nuanced survey, Karin Zetterhom argues that Judaism's ability to adapt to ever-changing circumstances can be traced to unique concepts and interpretative strategies developed in the period of the Talmudic rabbis—concepts and strategies that afforded a central place to human agency in the articulation of the divine law. Illustrating her arguments with numerous primary sources and drawing on the most recent scholarship, Zetterholm shows how this tradition of transformative Scriptural interpretation informed the early Jesus movement and—in a final chapter that vividly reminds us that much is at stake—how it continues to inform contemporary Jewish denominations struggling to balance fidelity to the past with adaptation to the present."

Christine Hayes | Yale University

Jewish Interpretation of the Bible

Ancient and Contemporary

Karin Hedner Zetterholm

Fortress Press

Minneapolis

To my parents
Ulla Hedner Bergentz and Pavo Hedner

JEWISH INTERPRETATION OF THE BIBLE
Ancient and Contemporary

Library of Congress Cataloging-in-Publication Data
Zetterholm, Karin.
Jewish interpretation of the Bible : ancient and contemporary / Karin Hedner Zetterholm.
p.   cm.
Includes bibliographical references (p.   ) and indexes.
ISBN 978-0-8006-9798-3 (pbk. : alk. paper) — ISBN 978-1-4514-2438-6 (ebook)
1. Bible. O.T.—Criticism, interpretation, etc., Jewish. 2. Bible. N.T.—Relation to the Old Testament. I. Title.
BS1186.Z48 2012
221.6088'296—dc23   2012011670

Cover image: *Black Fire on White Fire*, by Linda Berger Jacobs
Cover design: Laurie Ingram
Book design and typesetting: Josh Messner

The paper used in this publication meets the minimum requirements of American National Standard for Information Sciences—Permanence of Paper for Printed Library Materials, ANSI Z329.48-1984.
Manufactured in the U.S.A.

16 15 14 13 12 1 2 3 4 5 6 7 8 9 10

Contents

5. Continuity and Change in Contemporary Judaism   145

Movements within Contemporary Judaism • Revelation and Religious Authority in Contemporary Judaism • A Biblical Prohibition in Conflict with Modern Knowledge and Moral Sensibilities • When Bible and Tradition Offer No Guidance • The Legacy of Classical Rabbinic Judaism

Abbreviations

Agg. Ber.	*Aggadat Bereshit*
A.J.	*Antiquitates judaicae* (Josephus, *Antiquities of the Jews*)
b.	Babylonian Talmud
B. J.	*Bellum judaicum* (Josephus, *Jewish Wars*)
C. Ap.	*Contra Apionem* (Josephus, *Against Apion*)
Cels.	*Contra Celsum* (Origen)
Did.	*Didache* (in *Apostolic Fathers*)
Eccl. Rab.	*Ecclesiastes Rabbah* (in *Midrash Rabbah*)
Exod. Rab.	*Exodus Rabbah* (in *Midrash Rabbah*)
Frg. Targ.	*Fragmentary Targum*
Gen. Rab.	*Genesis Rabbah* (in *Midrash Rabbah*)
Gos. Thom.	*Gospel of Thomas*
Haer.	*Adversus Haereses* (Irenaeus)
Hom. Matt.	*Homiliae in Matthaeum* (John Chrysostom)
Jub.	*Jubilees* (in Pseudepigrapha)
L.A.B.	*Liber antiquitatum biblicarum* (Pseudo-Philo; in Pseudepigrapha)
Lam. Rab.	*Lamentations Rabbah*
Leq. Tov	*Leqah Tov*
Lev. Rab.	*Leviticus Rabbah* (in *Midrash Rabbah*)
m.	*Mishnah*
Macc.	*Maccabees* (in Pseudepigrapha)
Mekh. R. Ishmael	*Mekhilta de-Rabbi Ishmael*
Mekh. R. Shimon b. Yohai	*Mekhilta de-Rabbi Shimon bar Yohai*
Midr. ha-Gadol	*Midrash ha-Gadol*
Midr. Psalms	*Midrash Psalms*
Midr. Tannaim	*Midrash Tannaim*

Num. Rab.	*Numbers Rabbah*
Pirqe R. Eliezer	*Pirqe de-Rabbi Eliezer*
Pes. Rabb.	*Pesiqta Rabbati*
Pes. Rav Kah.	*Pesiqta de-Rav Kahana*
S. Eliahu Zuta	*Seder Eliahu Zuta*
S. Olam Rab.	*Seder Olam Rabbah*
Songs Rab.	*Song of Songs Rabbah* (in *Midrash Rabbah*)
t.	Tosefta
Tanh.	*Midrash Tanhuma*
Targ. Neof.	*Targum Neofiti*
Targ. Onq.	*Targum Onqelos*
Targ. Ps.-J.	*Targum Pseudo-Jonathan*
y.	Jerusalem/Palestinian (*Yerushalmi*) Talmud
Yalq. Shimoni	*Yalqut Shimoni*

TRACTATES (MISHNA, TOSEFTA, TALMUD)

Avod. Zar.	*Avodah Zarah*
B. Batra	*Bava Batra*
B. Kama	*Bava Kama*
B. Metzia	*Bava Metzia*
Bek.	*Bekhorot*
Ber.	*Berakhot*
Eduy.	*Eduyyot*
Eruv.	*Eruvin*
Gitt.	*Gittin*
Hag.	*Hagigah*
Hor.	*Horayot*
Ket.	*Ketubbot*
Meg.	*Megillah*
Menah.	*Menahot*
Rosh Hash.	*Rosh Hashanah*
Sanh.	*Sanhedrin*
Shabb.	*Shabbat*
Sot.	*Sotah*
Tem.	*Temurah*
Yad.	*Yadayim*
Yebam.	*Yebamot*

Illustrations

Fig. 1   The Bar'am Synagogue, Galilee, late fourth century C.E. Photograph by Anders Runesson.

Fig. 2   Sunrise at Mount Sinai, Egypt. Photograph by Anders Runesson.

Fig. 3   The Babylonian Rabbinic Academies. Map by Magnus Zetterholm.

Fig. 4   Page of the Babylonian Talmud, Vilna Edition (tractate *Taanit* 10a). Photograph by the Royal Library, Copenhagen. Used by permission.

Fig. 5   Details of a Page from the Biblia Hebraica. Photograph by Anders Runesson.

Fig. 6   Floor Mosaic from the Bet Alpha Synagogue, Israel.

Fig. 7   The Sea of Galilee. Photograph by Anders Runesson.

Fig. 8   Acropolis of Ancient Corinth. Photograph by Dieter Mitternacht.

Fig. 9   The Synagogue in Malmö, Sweden, built in 1903. Photograph by Stefan Hedner.

Fig. 10   Interior of the Hurva Synagogue, the Jewish Quarter of the Old City, Jerusalem. Photograph by Anders Runesson.

Preface and Acknowledgments

This book was originally written in Swedish with a general Swedish audience in mind, and to a large extent it has evolved around questions about Jewish tradition posed to me over the years by students and the public at large. These questions typically revolve around the ability of Jewish tradition to change and adapt while at the same time preserving a commitment to the Bible and its traditional interpretations. The combination of a seemingly free and at times even creative interpretation and reinterpretation of the Bible together with an insistence on the importance of and adherence to tradition within Judaism appears puzzling to many people whose background is in Protestant Christian tradition. How is it possible, for instance, to interpret away certain explicit biblical commandments but still insist on having separate dishes for meat and dairy products and to refrain from driving, writing, and knitting on the Sabbath—commandments and prohibitions that are *not* stated in the Bible?

This book addresses the ostensible paradox between commitment to the Bible and tradition on the one hand and the freedom in adapting them to present realities on the other. In order to comprehend this paradox, one needs to understand the underlying theology of revelation that, according to Jewish tradition, allows humans to be God's partners in interpreting his word. This idea of an ongoing dialectical process between divine revelation and human interpretation is the key, I believe, to understanding the character and development of Jewish tradition.

The aim of the original book was to provide an accessible introduction to these issues for readers with little access to scholarly literature in English. While such introductions are more easily available to readers of English, it is my hope that the unique combination of the various areas covered in this book will lead to new insights. The treatment of the strategies that the rabbis of the rabbinic period developed in order to adapt Jewish tradition to new circumstances and the underlying views of revelation that allowed them to do it (chapter 1), together with the ways that the various denominations of contemporary Judaism address legislation of new issues and reconsider laws and customs that conflict with modern moral sensibilities, highlight the imprint that classical rabbinic Judaism has left on its modern forms. By placing the early Jesus movement within a Jewish hermeneutic tradition emphasizing its Jewish character (chapter 4), I hope to demonstrate the ways in which knowledge of Second Temple Judaism and Jewish hermeneutics may contribute to our understanding of the beginnings of Christianity. Chapters 2 and 3 present the major works that make up rabbinic literature and focus on the ways that the rabbis of the rabbinic period understood and interpreted the Bible and tradition. This part can be used as an introduction to rabbinic literature. A glossary of key terms is provided at the end of the book.

Citations of biblical texts are taken from *JPS Hebrew-English Tanakh: The Traditional Hebrew Text and the New JPS Translation* (Philadelphia: Jewish Publication Society, 1988), although I have freely modified them when needed in order to make the rabbinic interpretations comprehensible. Unless otherwise indicated, translations of ancient sources are based on the English translations that appear in the bibliography, though at times I have modified them upon consultation with the original sources. Citations of stories from the Babylonian Talmud are taken from *Rabbinic Stories*, J. Rubenstein (New York: Paulist, 2002), and in the cases where the texts are not cited there, my translations are based on those that appear in *The Babylonian Talmud*, ed. I. Epstein (London: Soncino, 1935–1952). The transliteration of Hebrew is phonetic: ק=q, כ=kh, צ=ts, ח=h. When rendering common Hebrew terms I have not differentiated א from ע, ה from ח, or ס from ש. א and ע are indicated only in transliterations of Hebrew words that are not common terms.

I wish to thank Gunilla and Werner Guter's Foundation, Magnus Bergvall's Foundation and the Wenner-Gren Foundations for their financial support of the project of translating and reworking this book. For some time this was a side project while I enjoyed financial support from the Bank of Sweden Tercentenary Foundation and I wish to express my gratitude to them as well.

I am also grateful to the Department of Classics and Ancient Mediterranean Studies at Pennsylvania State University for arranging for me to do research and teach during the academic year of 2011–2012. I wish to thank David Eriksson for providing me with a preliminary translation of the Swedish version of the book. Although I eventually reworked and in the process also retranslated large portions of the book, I am very grateful for that first translation draft that saved me from having to start from scratch.

Although I have thoroughly enjoyed Pennsylvania State University and its library, it is sometimes difficult to work without access to one's own library. I want to express my gratitude to Eva-Maria Jansson of the Royal Library of Copenhagen who very kindly provided me with sources that I could not get hold of elsewhere, and when the situation demanded it, did so with extraordinary speed and efficiency! I am especially grateful to Elliot Dorff for his detailed reading and improvements on chapters 1 and 5, and to Anders Runesson for many helpful comments on chapter 4.

I wish to thank my family, and in particular my husband, Magnus, for his endless assistance in everything from computer problems to fruitful discussions on the detailed content of the book. The chapter on the early Jesus movement is based on what I learned from him and could not have been written without him. Finally, I want to thank my parents for their constant support and encouragement. This book is dedicated to them.

Timeline

B.C.E

586	Babylonian Exile begins
538	Persians permit the Jews to return to Judah
332	Alexander defeats the Persians; Hellenistic period begins
300–200	Land of Israel falls under the control of the Ptolemies of Egypt
200	Land of Israel falls under the control of the Seleucids of Syria
164	Maccabean victory; Maccabean period begins
63	Romans capture Jerusalem; Roman period begins

C.E.

70	The Jerusalem temple is destroyed; Tannaitic period begins (70–225)
132–135	Bar Kokhba Revolt
225	Redaction of the Mishnah; Amoraic period begins (225–550)
400	Redaction of the Palestinian Talmud
550–750	Redaction of the Babylonian Talmud

1

Continuity and Change in Rabbinic Judaism

Judaism, Christianity, and Islam share a common concern, namely how to preserve a connection and commitment to ancient Holy Scriptures and their traditional interpretations while at the same time adapting them to the present reality. Too much focus on preserving a literal understanding of Holy Scriptures and tradition leads to a situation where traditional laws and customs conflict with modern sensibilities, or appear irrelevant to the modern reality, whereas a complete abandonment of traditional texts and values may give rise to a sense of rootlessness and loss of identity. Trying to steer a middle course between these two extremes—and not leaving religion entirely in the hands of those who adhere to an extremist understanding of it—is also a concern shared by many Jews, Christians, and Muslims.

This book focuses on the ways in which Jewish tradition manages the balancing-act between continuity with the past and adaptation to the present. A key element in this project is the hermeneutic tradition that the Jewish leadership developed in the aftermath of the loss of the second temple when it was imperative to find ways to adapt to a life without a temple and ensure the survival of Judaism. The strategies developed then still play a significant role in the denominations of contemporary Judaism and highlight the connection between classical rabbinic Judaism and its modern expressions.

With its main focus on the rabbinic period, the book also provides an introduction to rabbinic Judaism and literature. Since the Jesus movement—the earliest stage of Christianity—was a Jewish phenomenon whose main figures, Jesus and Paul, engaged in the hermeneutics of their time in order to adapt the Bible to current realities and persuade people that their interpretation of Judaism was the correct one, a chapter on the Jesus movement and aspects of biblical interpretation in the New Testament has been included in this presentation of Jewish hermeneutical tradition.

The ways in which Jewish tradition understands the interaction between the word of God and human interpretation of it is intimately connected to the ways in which the rabbis envisioned the revelation of the Torah at Sinai, and it is to this issue that we will turn first. This first chapter of the book revolves around the rabbis' perceptions of the giving of the Torah at Sinai, the event at which Israel becomes God's special people and is appointed the guardians and interpreters of God's word. The ways in which this event was understood by the rabbis reveal how they understood their mandate to apply and develop the divine word entrusted to them. In order to put these ideas in a historical context, chapter 1 also includes a brief survey of the emergence of the rabbinic movement from Second Temple Judaism. The second chapter presents the results of the rabbis' mandate to apply and develop the divine word as preserved in the Mishnah and the Talmuds, two major works of rabbinic literature. Chapter 3 deals more specifically with rabbinic biblical interpretation and the approach to the Bible that gave rise to these interpretations, and with the relationship between biblical interpretation and rabbinic law and theology. Chapter 4 focuses on the Jewish character of the early Jesus movement and the ways in which knowledge of early Jewish hermeneutic tradition may contribute to our understanding of the beginnings of Christianity. The last chapter focuses on the ways divine revelation is perceived in contemporary Judaism and the balance between continuity with the past and adaptation to the present in the denominations of contemporary Judaism, as illustrated by the debates and procedures surrounding their decisions on issues of Jewish law.

Commitment to the Bible—Freedom of Interpretation

Jewish tradition is characterized by the constant tension between commitment to the Bible on the one hand, and a considerable freedom in interpreting and adapting its meaning on the other. When reading the laws of the Pentateuch, one finds relatively little correspondence between what is prescribed there and how modern Jews live. The law of retaliation, for example, as stipulated in Exod. 21:23-25 (parallels Lev. 24:17-21; Deut. 19:18-21)—"But if other damage ensues, the penalty shall be life for life, eye for eye, tooth for tooth, hand for hand, foot for foot, burn for burn, wound for wound, bruise for bruise"—is obviously not applied even by the most Orthodox Jews today. Nor are defiant sons punished by death as prescribed in Deut. 21:18-21: "If a man has a wayward and defiant son, who does not heed his father or mother and does not obey them even after they discipline him, his father and mother shall take hold of him and bring him out to the elders of his town at the public place of his community. They shall say to the elders of his town, 'This son of ours is disloyal and defiant; he does not heed us. He is a glutton and a drunkard.' Thereupon the men of his town shall stone him to death." By contrast, many religious Jews use different dishes for meat and dairy products, and refrain from driving, writing, knitting, and handling money on the Sabbath, commandments and prohibitions that are nowhere to be found in the Bible. Put bluntly, some biblical commandments do not seem to be kept at all, while other rules, which do not appear in the Bible, are scrupulously observed.

The solution to this ostensible paradox is found in the interpretive process that began the moment the Hebrew Bible was considered a normative text, and which reached its apex during the rabbinic period ca. 70–600 C.E. The Hebrew Bible was old and in need of clarification and interpretation already at the time of the destruction of the second temple in 70 C.E. when rabbinic Judaism began its formation. Some biblical words were no longer in use, others had taken on a different meaning, yet other expressions and phrases proved too vague and required interpretation in order to be applied in every day life.

For instance, the laws for the Sabbath (Exod. 20:8-11, 31:13-17) say that no work may be done on the seventh day of the week, and that no fire may be kindled (Exod. 35:1-3). No further details are given, and if one wishes to heed this prohibition a definition of the word "work" is imperative. Precisely which activities are referred to by the word "work" was established by the rabbis, ostensibly by means of scriptural exegesis, and in this way much of rabbinic tradition developed. In much the same way the tradition to use different sets of dishes for meat and dairy products developed based on Exod. 23:19. The verse simply states that it is forbidden to "boil a kid in its mother's milk," but it would eventually be understood to have a much broader meaning.

In other cases, a biblical passage required reinterpretation because the original meaning could not be reconciled with the worldview and ethics of a later time. This is the case both with the rules concerning the "defiant son" and the verses stipulating "eye for eye, tooth for tooth." It appears likely that the latter was originally an expression of the principle of retaliation, but already within the Hebrew Bible itself (Exod. 21:23-25 and Lev. 24:17-21) the emphasis is on compensation rather than retaliation. In rabbinic literature, the aspect of retaliation is completely interpreted away and the verses refer to economic compensation only.[1] In the case of the "defiant son," the rabbis introduced a series of impossible conditions that had to be met in order for this regulation to apply, effectually rendering the law nonfunctional.[2]

Developments and changes are the product of a combination of internal and external factors. Some grow out of ideas and principles inherent in Jewish tradition while others are primarily the result of outside influences. Some changes develop gradually and the need to justify them may occur only a long time after they have actually taken place, while other changes are more radical and deliberate. The process of interpretation and adaptation, especially in case of sudden and conscious innovations, involves a difficult balancing act. What some people consider legitimate and necessary adaptations, others perceive as unwarranted tampering with the Bible and tradition in order to suit modern secular sensibilities. To a large extent, it was disagreement over the pace of adaptation that led to the development of different Jewish denominations in the late nineteenth century. Pace aside, however, the ability to transform and adapt to new circumstances has proved instrumental for the vitality and survival of Judaism.

To be sure, there have been reactions against rabbinic interpretive tradition and the way it has transformed the Bible on various occasions throughout history. The best known is probably the Karaite movement, which emerged in the ninth century and which rejected the oral tradition of the rabbis and maintained that only the Bible was authoritative. Striving to adhere to the original meaning of the commandments of the Hebrew Bible, they rejected many rabbinic innovations. Over time the Karaites developed their own interpretive system, but it does not seem to have been as flexible as that of the rabbis, and while it enjoyed popularity during several centuries it eventually could not compete with rabbinic Judaism.

---

1. *Mekh. R. Ishmael* Nezikin 8 (Lauterbach vol. 3:62–69); *m. B. Kama* 2:6, 8:1–3; *b. B. Kama* 84b–84a. For a survey of the understanding of the principle of retaliation in ancient Near Eastern texts, biblical and Jewish tradition, see Larsson, *Bound for Freedom*, 162–67.
2. *b. Sanh.* 71a.

Interpretation as an Ideal

How is it possible, then, to reinterpret biblical texts, give them new meanings, and derive details not found there and still claim continuity between the Hebrew Bible and rabbinic Judaism and between rabbinic Judaism and contemporary forms of Judaism? How can one justify an interpretive process that at times completely transforms what appears to be the original meaning of the biblical text? A rabbinic parable has the following to say:

> By what parable may the question [of the difference between Scripture and oral tradition] be answered? By the one of a mortal king who had two servants whom he loved with utter love. To one he gave a measure of wheat and to the other he gave a measure of wheat, to one a bundle of flax and to the other a bundle of flax. What did the clever one of the two do? He took the flax and wove it into a tablecloth. He took the wheat and made it into fine flour by sifting the grain first and grinding it. Then he kneaded the dough and baked it, set the loaf upon the table, spread the tablecloth over it, and kept it to await the coming of the king. But the foolish one of the two did not do anything at all. After a while the king came into his house and said to the two servants, "My sons, bring me what I gave you." One brought out the table with the loaf baked of fine flour on it, and with the tablecloth spread over it. And the other brought out his wheat in a basket with the bundle of flax over the wheat grains. What a shame! What a disgrace! Need it be asked which of the two servants was the more beloved? He, of course, who laid out the table with the loaf baked of fine flour upon it.[3]

According to this parable, interpretation is an ongoing process that transforms the meaning of the biblical text. At first it may seem as if the servant who faithfully preserves what he was entrusted with is the one who acts in accordance with God's will, but it is the other one, the one who utterly transforms the wheat and flax, who is called wise. Thus, it becomes apparent that what God desires is active participation on the part of humans, resulting in a transformed, refined product. The wise servant understands God's intention and by means of his intellectual ability transforms what he was given into something new and useful. The text ends by

---

3. S. Eliahu Zuta 2.

saying: "The truth is that when the Holy One gave the Torah to Israel, He gave it to them as wheat out of which the fine flour of Mishnah was to be produced and as flax out of which the fine linen cloth of Mishnah was to be produced."[4]

In other words, the parable suggests that new interpretations of the biblical text are not only legitimate but desirable and even superior to the original product. According to this view, God expects humans to search for new meanings, develop and adapt the Bible to new circumstances. It is the one who engages in such a project who acts in accordance with God's will, not the one who safeguards the original meaning. The aim is not to establish the original or literal meaning of a given biblical passage, or attempt to reconstruct the circumstances in which it was composed, but rather to interpret and adapt it for contemporary times.

In Jewish tradition, the Bible is always read through its later interpretations. In order to learn how a given commandment should be performed, one consults the law codes, that is, the outcome of centuries of interpretation and application of the biblical commandment. As the Jewish philosopher Abraham Joshua Heschel (1907–1972) aptly put it: "Judaism is based on a minimum of revelation and a maximum of interpretation."[5] It is because of this tradition of interpretation that Judaism, already at the beginning of the Common Era, differed significantly from the Israelite religion of the Hebrew Bible, and the same interpretive tradition continues to shape Judaism today. Comprehending the way in which Jewish tradition itself justifies change while at the same time claiming continuity with the biblical text and the past is the key to understanding Judaism in both its ancient and contemporary forms.

What characterizes Judaism, perhaps more than anything else, and establishes continuity from the Hebrew Bible through rabbinic Judaism to modern Jewish denominations is the emphasis on the need for constant interpretation of the Hebrew Bible in order for it to remain relevant. In the view of the rabbis, this was an effect of the nature of revelation. Once the Torah was given to Israel at Sinai, God renounced his influence over its interpretation, as it were, and entrusted it to the rabbis who were convinced that they were given divine authority to develop and interpret it. "It [the Torah] is not in heaven" (Deut. 30:12), as they famously assert

---

4. Ibid.
5. Heschel, *God in Search*, 274.

in a story from the Babylonian Talmud.[6] The essence of Jewish tradition, then, can be characterized as an ongoing dialectical process between divine revelation and human creative interpretation.

THE SOURCES

The interpretations that developed as a result of a constant reading and explaining of the biblical text were at first transmitted orally, but as they continued to expand, it eventually became necessary to collect and redact them. The most important rabbinic works are the Mishnah, redacted in the early third century, the Jerusalem and Babylonian Talmuds, and collections of biblical interpretations, known as midrash. The Palestinian and the Babylonian rabbinic communities both commented and added material to the Mishnah, thus giving rise to two Talmuds: the Jerusalem Talmud (Yerushalmi), also called the Palestinian Talmud, which developed in the land of Israel between the third and fifth centuries, and the Babylonian Talmud (Bavli), which evolved in Babylonia between the third and the seventh centuries.

At first glance, one may get the impression that rabbinic literature is a rather homogenous collection of texts, since it contains a similar terminology and seems to share certain assumptions about the Bible and how it should be understood. But a closer look reveals a variety of genres, attitudes, and style. In addition, there are differences in concerns and attitudes between early rabbinic sages (*tannaim*) and later ones (*amoraim*), between Palestinian and Babylonian rabbis, as well as between legal and narrative texts (*halakhah* and *aggadah*).

The term for legal teachings, halakhah, is derived from the Hebrew root *halakh*, meaning "to walk," and is concerned with legal matters. It is sometimes briefly defined as "Jewish religious law," and accordingly deals with matters such as the eating of unleavened bread during Passover, keeping the dietary laws, fasting on the Day of Atonement, and the like. Halakhah establishes a minimal requirement and provides answers to questions such as "what," "when," and "how."

The term aggadah, derived from the Hebrew verb *lehagid* ("to tell"), is usually translated into English as "lore" or "storytelling" and refers

---

6. *b. B. Metzia* 59b.

to stories, legends, parables, homilies, theological reflections, and practical advice; in short, everything in rabbinic literature that is not halakhah. Aggadah often provides the rationale behind the commandments. The terms can also be said to distinguish between an external and an internal aspect of the word of God since a commandment often has both a legal, minimal aspect (halakhah) and an ethical, maximal aspect that cannot be measured (aggadah).[7] In Heschel's words:

> Agada deals with man's ineffable relations to God, to other men, and to the world. Halacha deals with details, with each commandment separately; agada with the whole of life, with the totality of religious life. Halacha deals with the law; agada with the meaning of the law. Halacha deals with subjects that can be expressed literally; agada introduces us to a realm which lies beyond the range of expression. Halacha teaches us how to perform common acts; agada tells us how to participate in the eternal drama. Halacha gives us knowledge; agada gives us aspiration. Halacha gives us the norms for action; agada, the vision of the ends of living. Halacha prescribes, agada suggests; halacha decrees, agada inspires; halacha is definite; agada is allusive.[8]

In spite of their differences, halakhah and aggadah are intimately connected, like two sides of the same coin. In comparing the relationship between them to that between ice and water, or a book of law to a book of poetry, Hayyim Nahman Bialik (1873–1934) emphasized the intimate relationship between the two. Halakhah is concerned with external things and aggadah with internal ones: "[halachah] is concerned with the shell, with the body, with actions; [aggadah] with the kernel, with the soul, with intentions."[9]

After this brief introduction, we now turn to a short survey of historical events and circumstances leading up to the emergence of rabbinic Judaism for the purpose of providing a context for the rabbinic ideas about divine revelation and its relation to human interpretation.

---

7. Larsson, *Bound for Freedom*, 190–92.
8. Heschel, *God in Search*, 336–37.
9. Bialik, *Halachah and Aggadah*, 9.

From Second Temple Judaism to Rabbinic Judaism

Second Temple Judaism

A major event that contributed to the emergence of rabbinic Judaism was the loss of the second temple, built by the returning exiles from Babylonia in the early sixth century B.C.E. and expanded by Herod the Great shortly before its destruction by the Romans in 70 C.E. Rabbinic Judaism developed from Second Temple Judaism, an era in Jewish history ranging from 538 B.C.E., when Cyrus of Persia allowed the Jewish exiles in Babylonia to return to their native land and rebuild the temple, through the reign of Alexander the Great and his successors until the destruction of Jerusalem by the Roman armies in 70.

In 332 B.C.E., Alexander the Great defeated the Persians, marking the beginning of a new era known as the Hellenistic period. After the death of Alexander in 323 B.C.E., his vast empire was divided between his most powerful generals. Judea was first controlled by the Ptolemaic dynasty, ruling over Egypt, and then, in 198 B.C.E., came under the power of the Seleucids, the rulers of Syria.

Alexander's conquest of the east produced a fusion of Greek and Oriental culture known as Hellenism, naturally also affecting the Jews. Through the Seleucid rule, the Jews in the land of Israel were exposed to Greek language, fashion, religious practices, and educational curriculum, including philosophy and physical training. The Jews were divided in their attitude toward Hellenistic culture and while many aristocrats, including members of the priesthood, were attracted by it, others vehemently opposed it.

In the mid-second century B.C.E., the Seleucid ruler Antiochus IV Epiphanes dedicated the temple in Jerusalem to pagan rites, provoking the outburst of an uprising that had long been in the making. In this rebellion, known as the Maccabean Revolt, the Jews of Judea, led by the priest Judah, managed to take control of the temple, purged it from the pollution of pagan rites, and re-inaugurated it—an event still commemorated by the celebration of Hanukkah. However, the uprising was not simply a Jewish protest against increasing Hellenization. The Maccabees were themselves attracted to Greek culture, and the Greek influence continued under the rule of the Maccabees. The Maccabees achieved political sovereignty in

142 B.C.E. and assumed the offices of both king and high priest; their kingdom lasted until 63 B.C.E., when the Romans conquered Jerusalem.[10]

The Maccabean period (164–63 B.C.E.) saw the emergence of a number of Jewish movements that were to play an important role during the final years of the Second Temple period. Some of these groups emerged in protest against the Maccabees' usurping the office of high priest, a hereditary office to which the Maccabees had no legitimate claim in the eyes of many Jews. One such group of separatists formed a settlement at Qumran by the Dead Sea, isolating themselves from what they considered the illegitimate and evil leadership of the temple. They seem to have been very particular about Sabbath and purity regulations and awaited an imminent final battle between the "Sons of Light" (their own community) and the "Sons of Darkness" (their enemies).

Another group was the Sadducees, of whom very little is known. They are typically portrayed as wealthy aristocrats with strong links to the priesthood who, according to the Jewish historian Josephus and the authors of the New Testament, denied the resurrection of the dead.[11] Recently, however, nearly every aspect of this standard picture has been challenged,[12] and accordingly our knowledge about the Sadducees appears to be even more scant than before.

A third group was the Pharisees, whose main characteristic appears to have been the belief in an oral tradition alongside the Bible. This oral tradition included laws about ritual purity and other details concerning oaths, Sabbath observance, and marriage. In addition there were other groups such as the Samaritans, who did not recognize the Jerusalem temple and had a temple of their own on Mount Gerizim. They also had a different version of the Pentateuch, and did not recognize the two other parts of the Jewish bible—the Prophets (*Nevi'im*) and the Writings (*Ketuvim*)—nor any oral tradition. In addition to these groups, several messianic movements emerged during the first century.

Since the sources are so few, usually later than the events they purport to describe and often tendentious, it is difficult to form an opinion about the various groups, the relationship between the different factions, and of the relationship between the factions and the common people who perhaps

---

10. Cohen, *From the Maccabees*, 35–45; Hengel, *Judaism and Hellenism*; Levine, *Judaism and Hellenism*, 3–32.
11. Matt. 22:23-33; Mark 12:18; Luke 20:27; Acts 23:8; *B. J.* 2.164–65.
12. Goodman, "Place of the Sadducees," 139–52.

did not belong to any group at all. It is generally acknowledged that Second Temple Judaism was very diverse, but how diverse is a matter of perspective. While it is customary to emphasize the sectarian nature of Second Temple Judaism, it is possible that a too narrow focus on the divisions and diversity in Jewish society may obscure the common denominators, such as belief in one God, the Torah, and the temple. Even if there were different views on the temple cult and different interpretations of the Torah, these likely still functioned as unifying factors.[13]

Some scholars suggest that the Sadducees and Pharisees are better understood as an integral part of the elite within mainstream Judaism rather than sectarian groups. The common scholarly emphasis on their distinctive features may have made the differences between them seem larger than they actually were. For the author of the Gospel of Matthew, for example, Sadducees were just another group of Jewish leaders alongside the Pharisees (Matt. 3:7, 16:1, 16:11-12). Given that they seem to have competed with each other and probably tried to appeal to the same segments of the Judean population, they presumably emphasized their differences. As a consequence, the sectarian divisions may have been important among priests, scribes, and others who belonged to one of these groups, especially in Judea, but their impact on Palestinian Jewish society as a whole was probably rather limited.[14]

The Roman-Jewish Wars

In 66 C.E., revolts against the Romans broke out in several Syrian cities, quickly developing into a war that ended with the destruction of the Jerusalem temple in 70 C.E. Although there was no mass expulsion of Jews, many fled the country and others were impoverished through confiscation of their lands. Judea became a Roman province and a punitive tax that had to be paid annually to the temple of Jupiter Capitolinus in Rome, known as the *fiscus iudaicus*, was imposed.

It is evident that the loss of the temple meant a reorientation of Judaism, but how dramatic that reorientation was remains a matter of scholarly debate. On the one hand, the temple was a religious center for Jews both in the land of Israel and in the Diaspora, ensuring the community's

---

13. Sanders, *Practice and Belief*; Schwartz, *Imperialism*, 49–99.
14. Schwartz, *Imperialism*, 91–99, Baumgarten, *Flourishing of Jewish Sects*; Goodman, "Place of the Sadducees," 147.

connection with the divine realm as well as playing a major role in the celebration of holidays, but on the other hand a majority of Jews lived outside of Jerusalem and had no daily contact with the temple. For the priests and ruling class who lost their power and influence, the loss of the temple was probably acutely felt, but the emergence of synagogues as a place where people gathered to pray and study the Scriptures during the late Second Temple period had to some extent prepared Judaism for an existence without the temple. Initially those aspects of religious life that did not require the temple, such as prayer, gained in importance, and eventually prayer was considered a replacement of sacrifices and by some even regarded as superior to them. Gradually a new leadership emerged based on learning rather than descent.[15]

Rabbinic sources seem careful not to pose a direct relationship between Second Temple Pharisees and post-temple period rabbis, but most scholars nevertheless believe that there is a strong connection between the two even if the two groups are surely not identical. Like the Pharisees, as they are described by Josephus and the New Testament, the rabbis followed an oral tradition and carefully observed laws of ritual purity, the Sabbath, and festivals. Rabban Gamliel I and his descendants, who according to Josephus and the New Testament were Pharisees, seem to have occupied a leading position within the rabbinic group around the year 100 c.e., further strengthening the tie between Pharisees and rabbis. Also, whenever rabbinic sources relate differences of opinion between the Pharisees and Sadducees, the rabbis always side with the Pharisees. However, the early rabbinic movement was likely made up of a variety of people and probably included priests and former Sadducees as well. Possibly, the reason for the reluctance of the early rabbinic movement to identify with the Pharisees was a wish to avoid sectarian division and present the rabbis as the leadership of all of Israel.[16]

The fact that Sadducees as a group lost their position of power after the fall of the second temple does not mean that individual priests immediately disappeared from their key positions in society. On the contrary, there is evidence that the priests remained interpreters of the Torah a long time after the temple had ceased to be the center of Jewish life, and they probably competed with the rabbis for power and influence. The rabbis eventually won the day, but this was likely a rather prolonged process.

---

15. Bokser, "Rabbinic Responses," 37–61; Bokser, "Wall," 349–74.
16. Cohen, "Significance of Yavneh," 31–41; Lapin, "Origins and Development," 208.

Along with the development of the rabbinic movement, a new office of leadership, known as the patriarchate, slowly emerged. The origin and exact nature of this office as well as the relationship between the patriarch and the rabbinic group is obscure and a matter of scholarly debate. According to earlier historical accounts, the patriarch was recognized as the leader of the Jews in the land of Israel both by the Jews and the Roman authorities already in the immediate post-temple era, enabling him to function as a link between the two. However, recent scholarship suggests that the patriarchate remained an informal and internal Jewish affair until the end of the fourth century, when the Romans legally recognized the patriarch as the leader of the Jews.[17]

A new uprising against the Romans broke out in 132 c.e., led by Bar Kokhba, believed to be the Messiah by some of his followers. The rebellion, which lasted for three years, took place primarily in Judea, and many Jews seem not to have participated or even supported the war. The circumstances surrounding the uprising are not altogether clear, but possible direct and indirect causes often mentioned are the unrest caused by the sizable Roman military presence in Judea, economic decline, influence from Jewish uprisings against Trajan in the Diaspora, a possible ban on circumcision, and the construction of a temple to Jupiter on the Temple Mount. The revolt was crushed and the Jews were expelled from Judea and Jerusalem and in its place the Roman city *Aelia Capitolina* was built. The province *Iudaea* was renamed *Syria Palaestina*, "Philistine Syria," to emphasize to the Jews that the land no longer belonged to them.[18]

Now the center of Jewish life shifted from Judea to the Galilee where the Mishnah, the Jerusalem Talmud, and the classical Midrash collections were subsequently compiled. Although the Christianization of the Roman Empire meant increasing hostilities against the Jews, Jewish life in the Galilee nevertheless continued to flourish also after the demise of the patriarchate in 425, as evidenced by the remains of large synagogue constructions from the fifth and sixth centuries. However, slowly a new Jewish center emerged in Babylonia, which would eventually replace the land of Israel as the center of Jewish life.

---

17. Goodblatt, *Monarchic Principle*, 131–231; Goodman, "Roman State," 127–39; Hezser, *Social Structure*, 405–49; Levine, "Status of the Patriarch," 1–32; Schwartz, "Patriarchs and the Diaspora," 208–22. For a survey of the scholarly debate, see Goodblatt, "Political and Social History," 416–23.
18. See Eshel, "Bar Kochba Revolt," 105–27; Schäfer, "Causes," 74–94.

Fig.1. The Bar'am Synagogue, Galilee, late fourth century c.e. Photograph by Anders Runesson.

The Emergence of Rabbinic Judaism

Rabbinic sources portray the reorientation of Judaism in the aftermath of the destruction of the second temple as a series of rapid reforms that took place in Yavneh, a place south of modern-day Tel Aviv, where, according to tradition, Rabban Yohanan ben Zakkai assembled the leading sages of his time to orchestrate necessary adaptations to a life without the temple, ensuring the survival of Judaism. For instance, customs once performed only in the temple and Jerusalem were decentralized and moved to synagogues and homes and performed throughout the country in commemoration of the temple (*m. Rosh Hash.* 4:3). New rituals were formed for festivals celebrated in the temple, such as Passover and the Day of Atonement. One gets the impression of a rabbinic movement that rapidly ascends to power, gaining a substantial influence over the Jewish population, establishing courts and ordaining disciples.

While earlier scholarship described the events in much the same way as rabbinic literature presents them, envisioning the rabbinic ascent to power and the reorientation of Judaism as a rapid and orderly process, and the rabbinic movement as having a substantial influence over the Jewish population already in the second century, a more critical reading of the sources has recently led to major revisions of this account. Scholars are now more inclined to regard the reforms after 70 c.e. and the adaptation to a life without the temple as a lengthy informal process and the rabbis as a small elite group with no central organization that only gradually gained power and influence. The historicity of the rabbinic assembly at Yavneh has also been questioned by some scholars, who argue that rather than being a historic event, it should be understood as a "foundation myth," in which later developments were retrojected back to the first century.[19]

In its initial stages, the rabbinic movement seems to have consisted of individual rabbis with no formal authority. They sometimes acted as judges, but most Jews probably handled their affairs through Roman courts. They seem to have met to study in private houses, in villages and towns throughout the country, but there seem to have been no formal rabbinic institutions. During the end of the fourth or beginning of the fifth century, more permanent and organized academies began to develop, but the great academies (*yeshivah* in Hebrew and *metivta* in Aramaic) that are described in the Babylonian Talmud with a fixed location and a distinct hierarchy seem to have emerged only in the amoraic or even post-amoraic period.[20]

Rabbinic influence over the synagogues was initially rather limited. Archeological remains, mainly from the Galilee, as well as early rabbinic sources seem to suggest that the synagogues were usually led by prominent or affluent members of the local community and frequented by ordinary people, whereas the rabbis and their disciples preferred their study houses. However, during the third and fourth centuries, as the rabbis sought to become the religious leaders of all Jews and gradually strengthened their position in general, their influence over the synagogues seems to have increased. A number of rabbinic texts from this time depict them as preaching and teaching in the synagogue before a lay audience.[21]

Thus, the rabbinic movement likely remained a loose-knit network, a self-proclaimed religious elite with loose ties both to other rabbis and to the population at large throughout the second century. This movement began to gain influence only in the third century, or even later in the view of some

---

19. See Boyarin, "Tale of Two Synods," 28–30.
20. Goodblatt, "Political and Social History," 423–27; Rubenstein, "Social and Institutional Settings," 58–74.
21. *Lev. Rab.* 32.7, 35.12; *y. Meg.* 3:1; Rubenstein, "Social and Institutional Settings," 64; Levine, "Sages and the Synagogue," 201–22.

scholars. Such a loose network of religious specialists, with only limited influence on people outside of their own circles, was hardly in a position to establish a common halakhah. The traditional scholarly account of a centralized rabbinic movement—in which unity was achieved either by excommunicating rabbis with deviant views, or by declaring disputes to be the ideal and all rabbinic views, however contradictory, to reflect the divine will[22]—has given way to a view of the early rabbinic movement as a loosely organized group fraught with internal divisions.[23] The rabbis eventually won the day, but probably never by attracting a large number of adherents; rather, they constructed an ideal of what Judaism should be like. Through rabbinic literature, those ideals helped shape all later forms of Judaism, eventually giving the rabbis a posthumous victory.

The main reason for the emergence of a new scholarly view is a more critical approach to rabbinic sources. The earlier reconstruction was to a large extent based on sources from the Babylonian Talmud that describe events and conditions in the land of Israel several hundred years earlier. There is now a heightened awareness that these accounts are colored by the concerns and ideology of a later period, and they are no longer taken as reliable evidence of events in the land of Israel during the two first centuries. Scholars are now very careful to distinguish between early and late sources and between Palestinian and Babylonian texts when trying to reconstruct the early rabbinic period. There is also a greater awareness that rabbinic literature, being the product of the religious elite, is likely to exaggerate rabbinic importance and influence and that common people did not necessarily share their particular concerns and interests.

---

22. *m. Eduy.* 5:6, *b. B. Metzia* 59b. In an often-cited article from 1984 ("Significance of Yavneh," 27–53), Cohen argues that the rabbis achieved hegemony by consensus building rather than expelling people with whom they disagreed. According to this view, the rabbis promoted a society that tolerated and even encouraged vigorous debate, a grand coalition of different groups and parties that agreed to disagree.

23. For a survey of the development of the rabbinic movement, see Hezser, *Social Structure*; Hezser, "Social Fragmentation," 234–51; Rubenstein, "Social and Institutional Settings," 58–74; Boyarin, *Border Lines*, 151–201; Goodblatt, "Political and Social History," 423–27; Lapin, "Origins and Development," 213–18; Schwartz, *Imperialism*, 103–28. Other scholars take a middle ground, arguing that, although the rabbinic movement was not as powerful and influential as earlier scholarship maintained, it also was not as marginal as some have argued recently. See Miller, for example, *Sages and Commoners*; Levine, "Sages and the Synagogue," 201–22.

The realization that the rabbinic movement was not as powerful and uniform as was previously believed also has consequences for the understanding of rabbinic literature. Whereas scholars of an earlier period tended to harmonize or explain away contradictory rabbinic viewpoints and contradictions within or between different sources, there is now a greater readiness to acknowledge the possibility that the sources contradict each other and possibly reflect views of different rabbinic constellations and ideologies. We turn now to the significance the rabbis attributed to the giving of the Torah at Sinai and the different ways in which they envisioned it.

THE REVELATION AT SINAI

Exodus 19–24 describes how God descends on Mount Sinai and makes a covenant with Israel, giving them the Torah. It is this event that creates the special relationship between God and Israel and shapes their self-understanding. Accordingly, the giving of the Torah is seen, together with the exodus from Egypt, as the most important event in the history of the people of Israel and the biblical account of these events is the subject of numerous commentaries.

The Bible tells us that God begins his conversation with Moses by reminding the Israelites of what he has done for them, "You have seen what I did to the Egyptians, how I bore you on eagles' wings and brought you to me" (Exod. 19:4). The foundation of the covenant is God's unconditional saving act of bringing his people out of Egypt, and only when he has introduced himself in this way does he ask for a response from the Israelites. As a sign of their acceptance of the covenantal relationship that God is offering them, they are asked to embrace the commandments of the Torah: "Now then, if you will obey Me faithfully and keep My covenant, you shall be My treasured possession among all the peoples [mi-kol ha-'amim], for all the earth is Mine. You shall be to Me a kingdom of priests and a holy nation [goy qadosh]."[24] The original meaning of the Hebrew word qadosh, translated as "holy," is actually "separate," and accordingly, a holy people is a people set apart from other peoples. Translated literally the Hebrew text says that Israel is God's treasured possession "from all other peoples." Unfortunately, the phrase is sometimes translated, "you shall be a special

---

24. Exod. 19:5-6.

treasure to me above all people,"[25] reflecting the understanding that a holy people is better than others. Such a rendering misses the point that holiness is a matter of separateness rather than excellence. This aspect of holiness is actually illustrated by the Jewish wedding ritual, in which the groom says to the bride, "Behold you are sanctified/separated (*qeddushah*) for me through this ring." This obviously does not mean that the bride is better than other women, only that she is set apart for the groom.[26]

The biblical text presents the election of Israel as an act of grace and the holy people as a people set apart for a particular purpose, a purpose that is hinted at in the reason God gives for making Israel his special people, "for all the earth is mine." The text seems to be saying that God also has the other nations in mind when he chooses Israel to be his special people. Election implies obligations rather than advantages, and this is the common understanding of what it means to be God's chosen people in Jewish tradition.[27]

The covenant between God and Israel creates a special bond between them, a relationship that rabbinic literature often describes as a marriage.[28] In some texts, the Torah represents the marriage contract,[29] while in others Israel is portrayed as being married to the Torah.[30] Many of these texts seem to be saying that to be God's chosen people is like being married to God, which means separation from other peoples with all the difficulties that such isolation entails.

The isolation and sometimes hostility from their neighbors give rise to ambivalent feelings about being God's chosen people, feelings that are often expressed in parable form in which God is represented as a king and Israel as his wife. The image of a king who forbids his wife to have anything to do with her neighbors and then leaves her alone for extended periods of time without giving any explanation for his absence illustrates the way Israel sees her relationship to God. The long absences makes the wife fear that her husband has left her for good, but as she remains married

---

25. See, for example, the New King James Version.

26. See also Lev. 20:26, "You shall be holy to me, for I the Lord am holy, and I have set you apart from other peoples to be mine," where the "setting apart" appears to be a synonym of "holy."

27. See Larsson, *Bound for Freedom*, 126–33.

28. See, for example, *Mekh. R. Ishmael* Bahodesh 3 (Lauterbach vol. 2:219); *Pirqe R. Eliezer* 40 (Friedlander, 41).

29. *Lam. Rab.* 3.21.

30. *Sifre* Deut §345.

to him she cannot remarry or even have a friendly daily relationship with her neighbors.[31]

God's giving of the Torah at Mount Sinai was accompanied by thunder and lightning according to Exod. 20:15: "And all the people saw the thunder [ha-qolot] and the flames [ha-lapidim]." The word qol (plural qolot), translated as "thunder," can also mean "voice," so an alternate rendering would be that God's voice was heard at the moment of revelation. The somewhat awkward use of a single verb "see" with regard both to the lightning and the thunder/voice was noted by the rabbis and gave rise to the question of how a sound can be seen. A number of rabbinic sources explain this irregularity to mean that God's words emerged as tongues of fire, which could be seen by the people, an exegesis that also explains the plural form "flames." Accordingly, God's words were understood to be both audible and visible. This understanding is probably also informed by the description of God's revelation of the Torah in Deuteronomy where the word "fire" occurs time and again (Deut. 5:4, 22, 23, 24, 25, 26). The connection between God's word and fire is expressed also in Jer. 23:29, "Behold, My word is like fire—declares the Lord—and like a hammer that shatters rock!"[32]

Another peculiarity in the verse is the plural form "voices" (qolot), which some rabbinic sources explain to mean that God's voice was divided into many voices, each one speaking a different language.[33] This interpretation of "voices" can be understood against the background of an early Jewish tradition according to which God offered the Torah to all the peoples of the world, only giving it to Israel after the other peoples had rejected it on the grounds of its content. Israel, however, immediately accepted it with the words, "All that the Lord has spoken we will faithfully do!" (Exod. 24:7).[34] Thus, this tradition explains and justifies Israel's position as God's special people. God offered to give the Torah to all the nations of the world and accordingly they have only themselves to blame

---

31. See, for example, Lam. Rab. 1.56, 3.21; and Stern, Parables in Midrash, 56–62, 79–82.

32. Mekh. R. Ishmael Bahodesh 9 (Lauterbach, 2:266); Sifre Deut §343; Pirqe R. Eliezer 41, and Larsson, Bound for Freedom, 135; Fraade, "Hearing and Seeing," 250–54; idem, Tradition, 45.

33. b. Shabb. 88b; Exod. Rab. 5.9, 28.6; Midr. Psalms 92.3. Cf. Acts 2:1-11.

34. Mekh. R. Ishmael Bahodesh 5 (Lauterbach, 2:234–37); Sifre Deut §343; b. Avod. Zar. 2b–3a; Exod. Rab. 27.9; Lev. Rab. 13.2. See also Fraade, Tradition, 28–48; and Larsson, Bound for Freedom, 135–36.

for their current status outside of the covenant. Their refusal to accept the Torah affects their relationship with Israel's God, and according to at least one rabbinic source it makes them subject to the Torah's judgment.[35] According to Jewish tradition, God made this covenant not only with the Israelites who were physically at Sinai but with all future generations as well (Deut. 29:10-15).

However, rabbinic literature also contains a different tradition about the giving of the Torah at Sinai, according to which Israel did not voluntarily accept it. According to Exod. 19:17 (cf. Deut. 4:11), the people were standing "at the foot of the mountain," but as the Hebrew preposition could be understood to imply that they were actually standing *under* Mount Sinai, some sources claim that God held Mount Sinai above the Israelites, threatening to drop it on top of them if they did not accept the Torah.[36] According to this tradition, election is definitely not seen as a privilege.

Fig. 2. Sunrise at Mount Sinai, Egypt. Photograph by Anders Runesson.

DIVINE REVELATION AND HUMAN INTERPRETATION

The Torah that was revealed at Mount Sinai was by the rabbis understood to include not only the Hebrew Bible but also oral instructions about its interpretation and application. Although the term "Torah" in its most restricted sense refers to the five books of Moses, its sense gradually

---

35. See, for example, *Exod. Rab.* 5.9.
36. *b. Shabb.* 88a. See also *Mekh. R. Ishmael* Bahodesh 4 (Lauterbach, 2:219).

expanded to include all of the Hebrew Bible, referring also to the parts known as the Prophets and the Writings. Eventually, "Torah" came to be used also to designate the explanations, interpretations, and applications that according to the rabbis accompanied the Bible, and the idea arose of a dual Torah, one written (the Hebrew Bible) and one oral (interpretations of the Written Torah), both originating at the moment of revelation. Thus, Torah in its most expanded sense refers to the entire revelation in both its written and oral forms. Accordingly, "instruction" would be a better rendering of "Torah" than the rather common translation "law," since the word "law" normally refers to obligations and requirements only.

The revelatory event is envisioned in slightly different ways in rabbinic literature with early sources tending to portray humans as playing an active role as interpreters of God's word. *Sifre*, a third-century midrash to Deuteronomy, describes it as follows: "*He cared for him* [Deut. 32:10]. With the Ten Commandments. This teaches that when [each] utterance [commandment] went forth from the mouth of the Holy One, blessed be He, Israel would see and understand it and would know how much interpretation [*midrash*] could be inferred from it, how many laws [*halakhot*] could be inferred from it, how many *a fortiori* arguments could be inferred from it, how many arguments by verbal analogy could be inferred from it."[37]

Another early source, *Mekhilta de-Rabbi Ishmael*, a commentary on the book of Exodus, likewise emphasizes the role of humans as interpreters of God's word: "Rabbi says: This is to proclaim the excellence of the Israelites. For when they all stood before Mount Sinai to receive the Torah they interpreted the divine word as soon as they heard it."[38] These texts envision revelation as consisting of two parts: God's giving of the Torah on the one hand, and Israel's reception of it on the other, making the latter an active participant in the revelatory event.[39] According to this view, interpretation is not a belated exercise aiming at reconstructing the original meaning of God's word, but an ongoing process contained in revelation itself. Accordingly, human interpretation is part of divine revelation, a

37. *Sifre* Deut. §313.Translation based on Fraade, *Tradition*, 60–61.
38. *Mekh. R. Ishmael* Bahodesh 9 (Lauterbach, 2:267).
39. In Fraade's words: "Thus, even at the very moment of revelation, the people of Israel were not simply passive *receivers* of the divine word, but already empowered by God as the active *perceivers* of its multiple hermeneutical (and performative) potentialities," Fraade, *Tradition*, 62.

view that enabled the rabbis to derive from the biblical text laws that are not explicitly stated there and through analogy to formulate laws for new phenomena that are not mentioned there at all.

The rabbis saw themselves as participating in the process of developing the meaning of the Torah, exposing what is hidden in it and making explicit what is implicit there. Thus, they preserved transmitted traditions while at the same time subtly transforming them, as illustrated by the chain of Torah transmission in the Mishnah: "Moses received Torah from Sinai and transmitted it to Joshua, and Joshua to the elders, and the elders to the prophets, and the prophets transmitted it to the men of the Great Assembly. They said three things: Be thorough in judgment, raise up many disciples, and make a fence around the Torah. Simeon the Just was among the last of the Great Assembly. He used to say: . . . Antigonus of Sokho received [Torah] from Simeon the Just."[40]

The chain of tradition continues with five pairs of teachers, each of whom adds their own teaching to what he has received and then transmits the transformed Torah to the next link in the chain. The last pair is that of Hillel and Shammai, pre-70 sages and immediate predecessors of the rabbis, who pass on what they have received and taught to Rabban Yohanan ben Zakkai (*m. Avot* 2:8), who according to tradition established the rabbinic academy of Yavneh. In this way the rabbis stand in direct continuity with Sinai. Each generation in this chain, beginning with Moses, transforms as it transmits tradition and that which is added is no less Torah than that which precedes it, since it all in some form originated at Sinai.[41]

The rabbis saw themselves as the present-day extension of the biblical elders, who accompanied Moses onto Mount Sinai (Exod. 24:1, 9) and were appointed leaders and judges by him (Num. 11:16-25). It is in part their link to these elders that allowed them to claim both to have inherited the authority to transmit the Torah received at Sinai and to be its authoritative interpreters.[42] As the immediate successors of the men of the Great Assembly, the rabbis saw themselves as heirs of the biblical prophets, the former messengers of the divine will. As prophets no longer existed, according to rabbinic historiography, they had in effect replaced the prophets, claiming that the gift of prophecy had been taken from the prophets and given to them: "R. Avdimi from Haifa said: 'Since the day

---

40. *m. Avot* 1:1–3. My translation.
41. Fraade, *Tradition*, 69–70.
42. Ibid.

when the Temple was destroyed, prophecy has been taken from the prophets and given to the Sages.'"[43] Thus, religious authority that had formerly belonged to the prophets was transferred to the rabbis.

These rabbinic claims to authority were in all likelihood part of the rabbis' attempt to establish themselves as the legitimate custodians and heirs of biblical tradition. Palestinian Judaism in the first century C.E. consisted of a number of competing religious groups, such as the Samaritans, remnants of the Pharisees and Sadducees, various groups of Jesus disciples, and the emerging rabbinic movement, each of whom claimed to be the sole and authentic heir of biblical tradition. The rabbis probably also faced competition from the priests, who in Second Temple times had the authority to teach and to adjudicate laws and traditions and whose status and authority most likely continued to be a factor long after 70 C.E. It is significant that all mention of priests is omitted in the chain of tradition in tractate *Avot*, but this almost certainly does not mean that they had disappeared from the political and religious arena. Rather, it appears to be a conscious effort by the rabbis to eliminate them as a link in the chain of tradition from Sinai and an attempt to establish the sole legitimacy of the rabbis and their oral tradition.[44]

A number of texts show that the rabbis were aware that their interpretations at times produced an understanding of the biblical text that was radically different from its original meaning. In addition to the parable of the wheat and flax, there is the well known story from the Babylonian Talmud about Moses' visit to R. Aqiva's study house:

> Rav Yehudah said that Rav said: At the time when Moses ascended on high [to receive the Torah] he found God sitting and attaching crowns to the letters. He said to Him, "Master of the Universe! who stays your hand [from giving the Torah now, without the crowns]?" He said to him, "There is a certain man who will live a few generations into the future, and Aqiva b. Yosef is his name. He will derive heaps and heaps of laws from all the tips [of the crowns of the letters]." He said to him, "Master of the Universe! Show him to me." He said to him, "Turn around." He [Moses] went and sat at the back of eighteen rows of students [among the most inferior students], but he did not understand what they were

---

43. *b. B. Batra* 12a. Compare *S. Olam Rab.* 30; *y. Avod. Zar.* 2:7.
44. See Fraade, *Tradition*, 69–75; Boyarin, *Border Lines*, 77–86; Stern, *Midrash and Theory*, 32.

saying. His strength failed him. When they came to a certain matter, his [Aqiva's] students said to him, "Master, how do you know this?" He said to them, "It is a law [given] to Moses at Sinai." His [Moses'] [peace of] mind was restored.[45]

During the many centuries that separate R. Aqiva from Moses, the laws of the Torah had been interpreted and adapted so much that even Moses, to whom the Torah was first entrusted, does not recognize it and accordingly feels ill at ease. From the decorations of the letters and the details of the text, generation after generation of interpreters have derived heaps and heaps of laws in the course transforming its meaning. Moses' unease at not understanding R. Aqiva's teaching reflects the rabbis' awareness that their interpretations had transformed the Torah beyond recognition and, perhaps, their concern that their teachings may not be a legitimate continuation of biblical tradition.

However, Moses is comforted as soon as he realizes that the Torah that R. Aqiva is teaching is the very same Torah that he received at Mount Sinai. It is the same Torah that is studied and taught even though centuries of interpretation have transformed it beyond recognition. Through the portrayal of God as R. Aqiva's partner, the rabbis seem to want to convince themselves and others that in spite of all that seems to separate their teachings from those of the Bible, there is continuity between them. Moses' realization that the law taught by R. Aqiva, in spite of its thorough transformation, is the same one with which he was entrusted at Sinai finally comforts him. This conveys the message that as long as the biblical text is taken seriously, being quoted and grappled with, new understandings of it are legitimate. As in the parable about the wheat and the flax, this story expresses the idea that as long as there is a commitment to the Bible, rethinking its meaning is legitimate and even desirable.

ORAL TORAH

During the amoraic period, a slightly different perception of revelation developed, according to which the entire rabbinic oral tradition with all its details was revealed to Moses already on Mount Sinai:

---

45. *b. Menah.* 29b. Translation and explanatory comments from Rubenstein, *Rabbinic Stories*, 216–17.

R. Levi bar Hama said in the name of R. Shimon ben Laqish: What is the meaning of the verse, [The Lord said to Moses], *Come up to the mountain and wait there, and I will give you the stone tablets with the teachings and commandments which I have inscribed to instruct them* [Exod. 24:12]? "Tablets" [*luhot ha-'even*] means the Ten Commandments, "teachings" [*ha-torah*] the Five Books of Moses, "commandments" [*ha-mitzvah*] the Mishnah, "which I have inscribed" the Prophets and the Writings, and "to instruct them," the Talmud. This teaches that they were all given to Moses at Sinai.[46]

R. Hiyya bar Abba said in the name of R. Yohanan: What is the meaning of the verse, *And the Lord gave me the two tablets of stone, inscribed by the finger of God, with the exact words that the Lord had addressed to you on the mountain* [Deut. 9:10]? It teaches us that the Holy One, blessed be He, showed Moses the details of the Torah and the details [that would be taught] by the Scribes, and the innovations that would be introduced by the Scribes.[47]

According to these texts, revelation took the form of a body of set teachings, including even later rabbinic interpretations, such as the Mishnah and the Talmud. Such as view gives humans a much more passive role as the transmitters of a body of set and detailed teachings, rather than active participants in shaping the content of revelation. According to the most radical formulation of this position, God revealed all future interpretations and applications of the Written Torah to Moses at Sinai.[48]

The idea that rabbinic tradition in its entirety was revealed in all its details to Moses at Sinai is not known to have existed in the tannaitic period and seems to have developed in rabbinic circles sometime during the mid- to late fourth century. Rather than understanding rabbinic laws and interpretations as a legitimate *human* contribution to the divinely revealed word, these texts envision rabbinic interpretations and innovations as having been divinely revealed at Mount Sinai. The term "Oral Torah" as a designation for rabbinic interpretation that appears for the first time around this time reflects this development.[49]

---

46. *b. Ber.* 5a.
47. *b. Meg.* 19b.
48. *y. Peah* 2:6; *y. Hag.* 1:8; *y. Meg.* 4:1. See also *Lev. Rab.* 22.1, and Halivni, *Peshat and Derash*, 112–19; Halivni, "Reflections," 50–76.
49. Kraemer, *Mind*, 117–18.

Tracing rabbinic tradition in its entirety back to the revelatory moment at Sinai leads to a view according to which rabbinic innovations are in fact no innovations at all, since they were all given at Sinai alongside the Written Torah and transmitted in detail from generation to generation. Accordingly, humans actually never invent anything but rather gradually unveil what is implicit in the Written Torah. Thus, rabbinic innovations would not be seen as human innovations but as divinely revealed laws. By contrast, the idea of revelation in the texts from the tannaitic period represents innovations as a legitimate but human interpretation of the divine word.

A concrete example may illustrate these different ways of reasoning. Those who see rabbinic tradition as having been revealed in its entirety, together even with future interpretations at Sinai, would argue that the meaning of the law of retaliation ("eye for eye" in Exod. 21:24 with parallels) is, and has always been, monetary compensation in accordance with the interpretation of the Talmud. The rabbinic interpretation is the divinely intended meaning, but humans only gradually disclose it. By contrast, those who emphasize the active role of humans in revelation would maintain that monetary compensation is a human reinterpretation of the law of retaliation but that such a rethinking of its meaning is in accordance with God's will. A potential weakness of the latter position is that it hinges on the recognition of the authority of the interpreters. If their authority is contested, their interpretations and legislation may be disputed too.

Such a challenge to rabbinic interpretive authority may have come from groups within the Jesus movement in Mesopotamia whose identity formation and consolidation of interpretive authority reached its peak in the fourth century. Adherents of the Jesus movement read the same Bible as the rabbis but interpreted it differently, rejecting both rabbinic tradition and rabbinic interpretive authority. Claiming direct access to the divine through Jesus, who was considered a prophet, they developed a different interpretive authority with the life and death of Jesus as a hermeneutic key.[50]

---

50. For instance, the author/redactor of the third century Syrian *Didascalia Apostolorum* and the Pseudo-Clementine writings, *Homilies* and *Recognitions*, redacted in Syria in the fourth century. For the construction of an interpretive tradition in distinction from rabbinic Judaism by the *Didascalia*, see Fonrobert, "Didascalia Apostolorum," 483–509.

A common language, and the well-documented close relationship and blurred boundaries between Jews and non-Jews and between Jews and various forms of the Jesus movement in fourth century Syria,[51] make it likely that the various communities were relatively familiar with one another's claims and responded to them. The fact that some of these groups seem to have had a Jewish, albeit non-rabbinic identity and shared rabbinic hermeneutic techniques would only have made things worse from a rabbinic point of view, since that would make their arguments potentially persuasive and appealing to rabbinic Jews. Claims by such Jewish communities to be in possession of prophetic authority and a tradition transmitted without human interpretation or intervention from Jesus via Peter to the community would likely be perceived by the rabbis as a challenge to rabbinic tradition.

Thus, it seems very likely that the idea that rabbinic tradition was wholly divine and revealed at Sinai developed in response to the rejection of rabbinic tradition and interpretive authority by non-rabbinic Jewish groups. Faced with their competing claims to be the true heirs of biblical tradition, the rabbis may have felt the need to strengthen their tradition by asserting that it, too, derived in its entirety directly from God, rather than being the outcome of human interpretive activity. The early rabbinic view that interpretation was inherent in the revelatory event at Sinai and that rabbinic tradition developed through constant human interpretation may have paled when confronted with these claims by non-rabbinic Jews to possess a new understanding of the Bible directly revealed by God. The idea that rabbinic tradition was divinely revealed as a body of set teachings to Moses at Sinai developed in the fourth century, coinciding with the construction and consolidation of interpretive authority by groups within the Jesus movement throughout Mesopotamia. This fact seems to suggest a connection.

The idea of a wholly divine Oral Torah may have served the purpose of bolstering rabbinic tradition and defending it against claims from competing groups, but it also raised the problem of multiple contradictory rabbinic interpretations. If rabbinic tradition was revealed as a body of set teachings, the existence of contradictory rabbinic views would seem to suggest that rabbinic tradition was not correctly transmitted. The serious problem that the view of rabbinic tradition as a body of wholly divine teachings creates, together with the relatively few traces it has left

---

51. For instance, Drijvers, "Syrian Christianity," 124–46.

in rabbinic literature, seem to suggest that it developed in a polemical context in response to a particular challenge. A number of post-fourth-century texts continue to assume the early view that human interpretation is part of the divine revelation, such as the story of R. Aqiva's visit to Moses' academy and the parable about the wheat and the flax. A passage from *Exodus Rabbah*, a late midrash to the Book of Exodus, even seems to argue against the idea that the oral tradition was given in the form of a body of set teachings by stating explicitly that only interpretive principles were revealed to Moses: "Could Moses have learned the whole Torah [on Mount Sinai]? Of the Torah it says: *Its measure is longer than the earth and broader than the sea* [Job 11:9]. No, it was only the principles thereof which God taught Moses."[52]

JEWISH LAW AND DIVINE TRUTH

The rabbis maintained that when God gave the Torah to Israel, he also gave them the right and responsibility to interpret it, a claim that they based on Deut. 17:8-11: "If a case is too baffling for you to decide . . . you shall promptly repair to the place that the Lord your God will have chosen, and appear before the levitical priests, or the magistrate in charge at that time, and present your problem. When they have announced to you the verdict in the case, you shall carry out the verdict that is announced to you from that place that the Lord chose, observing scrupulously all their instructions to you. You shall act in accordance with the instructions given you and the ruling handed down to you; you must not deviate from the verdict that they announce to you either to the right or to the left."

The key phrase here is "the magistrate in charge at that time" (*shofet* = NRSV, "judge"), which in the rabbis' view entrusts the right of interpretation to the religious authority of every generation, a principle that is also embraced in modern Judaism. The authorities of later times have the same right as authorities of earlier generations to make decisions for their time, making it possible to innovate and adapt Jewish law. This permission is granted even if earlier authorities were greater in wisdom.[53]

The verse, "you must not deviate from the verdict that they [the judges] announce to you either to the right or to the left," is in the *Sifre* interpreted

---

52. *Exod. Rab.* 41.6.
53. See *Eccl. Rab.* 1:4; *b. Rosh Hash.* 25b.

to mean: "Even if it appears to you that [what the religious leadership says is] right is [actually] left and [what they say is] left is [actually] right, you shall obey them."[54] According to this interpretation, rabbinic authority knows no bounds. As the sole authoritative interpreters of the meaning of the Torah, the Torah means whatever the rabbis say it means.[55]

The rabbis maintained that in extraordinary circumstances they even had the authority to annul a biblical commandment. Based on Ps. 119:126, "It is time to act for the Lord, for they have violated Your teaching," they asserted that "to act for the Lord" could, in particular circumstances, involve the violation of the letter of a commandment in order to preserve its intention.[56] However, this principle was applied with great caution and usually only used to justify innovations that had already taken place.

A judge or an interpreter must depend on his own reasoning and intellect, and not rely on divine revelations or earlier authorities. According to Maimonides (1135–1204), the one who opposes tradition and appeals to divine inspiration is a false prophet, even if he supports his arguments with miracles. The classic story establishing rabbinic authority to legislate and interpret according to majority view even when it runs counter to God's will appears in the Babylonian Talmud. It portrays a conflict between R. Eliezer Hyrcanus and other rabbis concerning the ritual purity of an oven. R. Eliezer presents all possible arguments to support his view, and when he still fails to convince the others, he appeals to miracles and finally asks God to intervene on his behalf:

It was taught: On that day R. Eliezer responded with all the responses in the world, but they did not accept them from him. He said to them, "If the law is as I say, let the carob [tree] prove it." The carob tree uprooted itself from its place and went one hundred cubits—and some say four hundred cubits. They said to him, "One does not bring proof from the carob." The carob returned to its place. He said to them, "If the law is as I say, let the aqueduct prove it." The water turned backward. They said to him, "One does not bring proof from water." The water returned to its place. He said to them, "If it [the law] is as I say, let the walls of the academy prove it." The walls of the academy inclined to fall. R. Yehoshua rebuked them. He said to them, "When sages defeat each other

---

54. *Sifre* Deut §154. My translation.
55. Roth, *Halakhic Process*, 125–26.
56. Berkovits, *Not in Heaven*, 64–67.

in law, what is it for you?" It was taught: They did not fall because of the honor of R. Yehoshua, and they did not stand because of the honor of R. Eliezer, and they are still inclining and standing. He said to them, "If it is as I say, let it be proved from Heaven." A heavenly voice went forth and said, "What is it for you with R. Eliezer, since the law is like him in every place?" R. Yehoshua stood up on his feet and said, "*It is not in Heaven* [Deut 30:12]." What is, "It is not in Heaven"? R. Yirmiah said, "We do not listen to a heavenly voice, since you already gave it to us on Mount Sinai and it is written there, *Incline after the majority* [Exod. 23:2]." R. Natan came upon Elijah. He said to him, "What was the Holy One doing at that time?" He said to him, "He laughed and smiled and said, 'My sons have defeated me, my sons have defeated me.'" At that time they brought all the objects that R. Eliezer had ruled were pure and burned them and voted and banned him.[57]

Here the rabbis boldly assert their authority over God. Miracles, along with a heavenly voice stating explicitly that the law is in accordance with R. Eliezer's view, fail to make an impression on them. R. Yehoshua simply refutes the legitimacy of both, citing God's own words and using them against him. God himself, in the act of revelation, handed over the authority to interpret and legislate to humans, or more precisely to the rabbis, and accordingly he no longer has any influence over Jewish law. Halakhah is now to be established by means of human reasoning following majority opinion, and God accepts the result of such human decision-making whatever its outcome. Halakhah must somehow be agreed upon in order to prevent chaos and sectarianism, but being based on majority opinion, such decisions are to some extent arbitrary and do not necessarily reflect divine truth. Ultimately, it is the rabbis' own interpretation of the Torah that validates their right to interpret and defines the scope of that right, even to the point of an apparently erroneous understanding of the divine will. The assumption underlying these claims is that the development of Jewish law is providentially guided. Since the rabbis are guarded from error, even an apparent miscarriage of the divine will is in accordance with God's will.[58]

---

57. *b. B. Metzia* 59b. Translation from Rubenstein, *Rabbinic Stories*, 82–83.
58. For a more comprehensive discussion of these issues, see Berkovits, *Not in Heaven*, 47–70; Elon, *Jewish Law*, 240–61; Halbertal, *People*, 81–89; Roth, *Halakhic Process*, 115–52.

In refusing to concede to majority opinion and by overruling the normal legal process with his appeal to miracles and direct intervention from heaven, R. Eliezer not only endangers the unity of the rabbinic movement but also challenges the very foundation of rabbinic ideology and authority. By appealing directly to God, R. Eliezer implicitly denies the rabbis' role as intermediaries of God's word and their right to interpret and legislate that, according to rabbinic understanding, was given to them at Sinai. Such denial poses a threat to rabbinic legitimacy and authority and is likely the reason for his excommunication, a punishment that may at first seem out of proportion to his offense.

Possibly the story also reflects a conflict between the rabbis and the Jesus movement. R. Eliezer is portrayed elsewhere in rabbinic literature as having close relations to Jewish disciples of Jesus and in view of the fact that miracles and heavenly voices were associated with Jesus, it has been suggested that the rabbis have modeled R. Eliezer along the lines of Jesus, another charismatic figure who challenged the Pharisees, the religious authority of his time, and the spiritual forebears of the rabbis. The fact that R. Eliezer, a highly respected rabbi, is portrayed as being closely associated with disciples of Jesus may indicate that there were close relationships between Jewish disciples of Jesus and some members of the rabbinic movement, an intimacy that the rabbis found disturbing.[59]

In spite of their confident rejection of the heavenly voice, the rabbis, paradoxically, still seem to feel the need for direct affirmation from God, as evidenced in the Elijah episode at the end. Here the prophet Elijah appears in what seems to be a postscript to the story, providing assurance that God laughs happily at being overruled and delights in human independence. As in response to the heavenly voice that intervened on behalf of R. Eliezer, Elijah, acting as a direct messenger from God, asserts that the rabbis are right to ignore the heavenly voice and that the rabbinic way of independently interpreting and legislating is indeed in accordance with the divine will.

It is evident, then, that decisions concerning Jewish law are not understood to reflect divine truth but rather are seen as pragmatic decisions in order to safeguard the unity of rabbinic Judaism. This means, at least

---

59. Boyarin, *Border Lines*, 168–74; Schäfer, *Jesus in the Talmud*, 49–51. For further analyses of this story, see, for instance, Rubenstein, *Talmudic Stories*, 34–63; Berkovits, *Not in Heaven*, 64–67; Elon, *Jewish Law*, 261–63; Halbertal, *People*, 48–50; Roth, *Halakhic Process*, 123–24.

theoretically, that halakhic decisions can be altered. Perhaps it may also in part explain why the Mishnah and the Talmuds often preserve minority opinions along with the majority view and the Talmud's predilection for pursuing minority opinions. If halakhic decisions are not divinely inspired but simply reflect the view of the majority of rabbis, the divine will may just as well be enshrined in a rejected minority position. In another time period, under different circumstances, the rejected opinion may theoretically become halakhah.

According to another view, God does not have an opinion on specific matters of halakhah but goes along with whatever decision is made by humans: "For three years there was a dispute between the schools of Shammai and Hillel, the former asserting, 'Halakhah agrees with us,' and the latter contending, 'Halakhah agrees with us.' Then a voice from heaven went forth saying: 'Both [opinions] are the words of the living God.'"[60] The story then explains that the reason why Hillel's position was to become halakhah was that his followers were peaceful and humble, teaching Shammai's point opinion along with their own. Accordingly, two conflicting views may both reflect the will of God, and the decision to follow one of them is merely pragmatic. This text reflects the idea that the Bible is an essentially open text having no determinate sense. God's word is susceptible to multiple interpretations, even contradictory ones, and neither one is necessarily more true or false than the other. Perhaps this position also reflects the insight that truth, in the sense of divine will, is unattainable, and that different perspectives should therefore be respected. Hillel's position did not become halakhah because it was more correct than Shammai's, but only because of the humble and conciliatory nature of Hillel and his disciples.[61]

The Babylonian Talmud also elsewhere emphasizes the importance of showing respect for others, and a concern to avoid embarrassing or shaming other rabbis. The atmosphere in the Babylonian academies at times seems to have been quite hostile, the animosity deriving from the intensity with which the rabbis debated points of law. In the highly structured academies with numerous students, where rank depended on ability of argumentation, respect and politeness may easily have given way to fierce competition and violence of debate. The ability of dialectical argumentation was considered

---

60. *b. Eruv.* 13b.
61. Kraemer, "Rabbinic Sources," 139–56; Roth, *Halakhic Process*, 129–30; Stern, *Midrash and Theory*, 21–22.

the highest form of intellectual acumen, and failure to respond to an objection was perceived as humiliating.[62]

A literary analysis of the R. Eliezer story actually reveals a subtle criticism of the rabbis' treatment of R. Eliezer in this regard. The rabbis are portrayed as treating him rather harshly, "surrounding him with words," suggesting that they spoke with cunning and guile, and they punished him unnecessarily harshly by burning all the items he had proclaimed pure, eventually leading to disaster and the death of Rabban Gamliel. The story affirms the rabbis' right to debate, legislate and interpret, but criticizes the insensitive way in which they exercised this right, hurting R. Eliezer's feelings and dignity.[63]

SEVENTY FACES OF THE TORAH

The confident assertion that multiple conflicting opinions are all valid expressions of the divine will may actually betray a sense of unease as expressed in the following midrash on a verse from Ecclesiastes:

[What does the phrase] *the sayings of the wise are like goads, like fixed nails are the masters of assemblies* [Eccl. 12:11] mean? "Masters of assemblies" are the disciples of the wise who sit in manifold assemblies and occupy themselves with the Torah, some pronouncing impure and others pronouncing pure, some prohibiting and others permitting, some declaring unfit and others declaring fit. Someone might say, "How in these circumstances shall I learn Torah?" Therefore Scripture says, *All of them are given from one shepherd.* One God gave them, one leader [that is, Moses] uttered them from the mouth of the Lord of all creation, blessed be He, as it is written, *God spoke all these words* [Exod 20:1]. Therefore make your ear like the hopper and acquire a perceptive heart to understand the words of those who pronounce impure and the words of those who pronounce pure, the words of those who prohibit and the words of those who permit, the words of those who declare unfit and the words of those who declare fit.[64]

---

62. Rubenstein, *Culture*, 67–79.
63. Rubenstein, *Talmudic Stories*, 34–63.
64. *b. Hag.* 3b. See also *t. Sot.* 7:12; *Num. Rab.* 15.22.

If every verse of the Torah can be subject to numerous contradictory interpretations, what then is the point of studying it, and if the rabbis disagree on practically everything, how can they claim to be its sole authentic interpreters? Such doubts possibly underlie the question voiced in the text, "How in these circumstances shall I learn Torah?" The issue here is not how to establish halakhah but rather what the true meaning of Scripture is. The Karaites considered the existence of multiple contradictory interpretations within rabbinic Judaism as a sign that rabbinic tradition was a human invention, but given the rabbis' awareness of having adapted and transformed the Bible, the question was bound to have arisen even before the Karaite movement gave explicit expression to this charge.

The problem of multiple interpretations is solved in the story by the assertion that all rabbinic interpretations and opinions are part of the Torah and the result of a single revelation. They were all spoken by the mouth of one shepherd, Moses, who received them all from one God, as it says, "God spoke *all these* words" (Exod. 20:1), that is, contradictory views and interpretive possibilities were included in the Torah from the moment of its revelation. To preclude any possibility of error in rabbinic tradition, revelation is portrayed as not fully determined, including contradictory interpretations. According to one opinion voiced in the Jerusalem Talmud, the Torah was not given in the form of clear-cut unambiguous laws, but rather for each and every word that God spoke Moses was given forty-nine arguments for declaring something pure and forty-nine arguments for declaring it impure.[65] God intentionally included in the Torah many potential meanings and left it to humans to disclose them and choose which one to apply in each and every individual case. Thus, multiple interpretations of the same biblical verse are not a consequence of later interpreters' inability to understand the text but the outcome of God's deliberate choice to imbue the Torah with multiple meanings. Hence, the famous rabbinic expression that there are "seventy faces [or aspects] of the Torah."[66]

The idea that every biblical verse carries many different meanings is explicitly stated in the following passage from the Babylonian Talmud: "Abbaye said: 'For Scripture says, *One thing God has spoken; two things have I heard* [Ps. 62:12]. One biblical verse may convey several meanings, but a single meaning cannot be deduced from different Scriptural

---

65. *y. Sanh.* 4:2. See also *Num. Rab.* 2.3; *Midr. Psalms* 12.4; *Pes. Rabb.* 21.
66. *Num. Rab.* 13.15.

verses.' In the School of Rabbi Ishmael it was taught: *Behold, my word is like a fire—declares the Lord—and like a hammer that shatters rock!* [Jer. 23:29]. Just as [the rock] is split into many splinters [when the hammer strikes it], so also one biblical verse conveys many meanings."[67] God's word is like fiery sparks produced by a hammer when it strikes a rock; the many senses that are inherent in each and every verse are released when hit by the interpretive hammer. Thus, when God gave the Torah to Israel, he also gave them the ability to discover the multiple meanings enshrined in it.[68]

The Babylonian Talmud (*b. Sanh.* 88b) includes another view, according to which conflicting views are a sign of decline and failure to correctly adhere to tradition, but this notion does not seem to have been widespread in the rabbinic period. During the Middle Ages, however, it was discussed by a number of philosophers who understood the halakhic process as the transmission from generation to generation of a divinely revealed body of halakhah that was originally complete and perfect but had begun to erode as a result of carelessness in transmission. From this perspective, the multiplicity of interpretations was seen as attempts to reconstruct, through argumentation, the original and true interpretation. Medieval philosophers, such as Yom Tov Ishbili (Ritba) and Nissim Gerondi (Ran), however, further developed the rabbinic view that controversy was rooted in revelation and the body of knowledge transmitted to Moses open-ended. Accordingly, they held that it was left to the court of each generation to constitute halakhah, and in this way tradition becomes more definitive over time as each generation decides the norms out of the multiplicity of options transmitted to them.[69]

STUDY AS FELLOWSHIP WITH GOD

Just as the Torah can have many different meanings, the rabbis envisioned God as possessing many countenances and appearing to Israel in various ways:

---

67. *b. Sanh.* 34a. See also *b. Shabb.* 88b; *Mekh. R. Ishmael* Bahodesh 7 (Lauterbach, 2:252); *Midr. Psalms* 92.3.
68. Berkovits, *Not in Heaven*, 51–53; Halbertal, *People*, 45–54; Stern, *Midrash and Theory*, 15–38.
69. See, Halbertal, *People*, 54–72.

[T]he Holy One appeared to Israel at the Red Sea as a mighty man waging war, and appeared to them at Sinai as a pedagogue who teaches the day's lesson and then again and again goes over with his pupils what they have been taught, and appeared to them in the days of Daniel as an elder teaching Torah, and in the days of Solomon appeared to them as a young man. The Holy One said to Israel: "Come to no false conclusions because you see me in many different guises, for I am He who was with you at the Red Sea and I am He who is with you at Sinai." . . . R. Hanina bar Papa said: "The Holy One appeared to Israel with a stern face, with a neutral face, with a friendly face, with a joyous face." . . . R. Levi said: "The Holy One appeared to them as though He were a statue with faces on every side, so that though a thousand men might be looking at the statue, they would be led to believe that it was looking at each one of them. So, too, when the Holy One spoke, each and every person in Israel could say: 'The divine word is addressing me.'"[70]

In the view of the rabbis, God and the Torah were intimately linked to one another, and for them studying the Torah was a way of communicating with God. Accordingly, studying for its own sake (*torah lishma*) is considered far more important than the outcome of the interpretation of individual legal cases or verses. After the destruction of the temple, the Torah became the most important sign of the continued existence of the covenantal relationship between God and Israel, and the study of Torah became the principal way of preserving that relationship. Biblical interpretation became, in David Stern's words, "a kind of conversation the Rabbis invented in order to enable God to speak to them from between the lines of Scripture . . . [t]he multiplication of interpretations in midrash was a way, as it were, to prolong that conversation."[71]

Just as the rabbis found a diversity of legitimate interpretations in the Bible, rabbinic literature preserves multiple, often contradictory opinions voiced by rabbis. As was mentioned above, this practice may reflect the recognition that absolute truth is unattainable, and that God's will may just as well be enshrined in the minority opinion as in the one determined to be halakhah, but it is likewise possible that the preservation of multiple opinions was also part of a strategy to legitimize rabbinic Judaism. Instead of creating unity by excluding certain views, rabbinic literature creates

---

70. *Pes. Rav Kah.* 12.24–25.
71. Stern, *Midrash and Theory*, 31.

unity, or at least an impression of unity, by including all opinions as long as they are voiced by rabbis.

The result is an idealized image of the rabbinic academies where everyone disagrees, but a friendly atmosphere nevertheless prevails. Different opinions in questions of interpretation are portrayed as enriching, and disputes are either resolved agreeably or maintained peacefully. However, this representation may be a literary construction, created by the editors of rabbinic literature in an attempt to overcome the divisions and discord within rabbinic society.[72] Even if it probably does not reflect reality, the image of a rabbinic society that tolerates and encourages debate and differences of opinion has nevertheless influenced Jewish tradition by constituting a model for ideal conduct. We will now turn to the rabbinic texts in which these ideas and ideals are expressed.

STUDY QUESTIONS

1. In what ways have a more critical approach to rabbinic sources affected scholarly reconstructions of the early history of rabbinic Judaism?

2. Describe the different rabbinic theologies of revelation. How do they impact the perception of adaptations and innovations and the justification for them?

3. What is the relation between Jewish law and divine truth in the rabbinic texts discussed above?

SUGGESTIONS FOR FURTHER READING

The Emergence of the Rabbinic Movement
Lapin, H. "The Origins and Development of the Rabbinic Movement in the Land of Israel." In vol. 4 of *The Cambridge History of* Judaism, edited by Steven T. Katz, 206–29. Cambridge: Cambridge University Press, 2006.
Hezser, C. *The Social Structure of the Rabbinic Movement.* Tübingen: Mohr Siebeck, 1997.

---

72. Ibid.

Interpretive Tradition and Rabbinic Authority
Berkovits, E. *Not in Heaven: The Nature and Function of Halakhah.* New York: Ktav, 1983.
Dorff, E. N. *For the Love of God and People: A Philosophy of Jewish Law.* Philadelphia: Jewish Publication Society, 2007.
Dorff, E. N., and A. Rosett. *A Living Tree: The Roots and Growth of Jewish Law.* Albany: SUNY Press, 1988.
Elon, M. *Jewish Law: History, Sources, Principles.* Philadelphia: Jewish Publication Society, 1994.
Halbertal, M. *People of the Book: Canon, Meaning, and Authority.* Cambridge: Harvard University Press, 1997.
Roth, J. *The Halakhic Process: A Systemic Analysis.* New York: Jewish Theological Seminary of America, 1986.

The Giving of the Torah at Sinai
Fraade, S. *From Tradition to Commentary: Torah and Its Interpretation in the Midrash Sifre to Deuteronomy.* Albany: SUNY Press, 1991.
Larsson, G. *Bound for Freedom: The Book of Exodus in Jewish and Christian Traditions.* Peabody: Hendrickson, 1999.

2

Tradition in the Making—
The Mishnah and the Talmuds

The Mishnah is one of the earliest rabbinic works and as such a very important one. It is primarily a collection of legal traditions attributed to rabbis who lived during the first two centuries C.E. According to tradition, it was edited by Yehudah ha-Nasi (Yehudah the Patriarch) at the beginning of the third century. Although most of the material is halakhic, the Mishnah also includes some non-legal material.

THE MISHNAH

The word *mishnah* is derived from the Hebrew root *shanah*, meaning "to repeat," and refers to the process of orally repeating traditions in order to memorize them. A rabbinic sage during Mishnaic times was called a *tanna* (plur. *tannaim*), which is the Aramaic equivalent of the Hebrew *shanah*, and this term has lent its name to the earliest era of rabbinic Judaism, the tannaitic period. During later times, the rabbis were referred to as *amoraim* (sing. *amora*) from the root *'amar* ("to say"), and the era known as the amoraic period (ca. 225–550).

The Mishnah does not reveal anything about its origins, and major historical events such as the destruction of the second temple and the Bar Kokhba Revolt are mentioned only in passing. Apart from the political and social consequences of these events, they must have raised theological questions, but the Mishnah is remarkably reticent about these matters. The continued validity of the covenant between God and Israel and the question of whether God had abandoned his people are discussed in post-seventy apocalyptic literature, but do not seem to interest the rabbis of the Mishnah. Instead, they are devoted to discussions of the temple and its cult and debates about detailed halakhic matters that no longer had any bearing on everyday life. It is possible that the rabbis behind the Mishnah were confidently awaiting the restoration of the temple, or believed that because the temple cult had been ordained by God the study of its regulations was now the equivalent of their implementation, but it has also been suggested that the rabbis were attempting to create in their minds an ideal and perfect world to which they could escape from the calamities in the world around them. According to this view, the Mishnah represents an early rabbinic vision of a redeemed world where the temple was restored.[1]

The rabbis saw themselves as the custodians of the Torah, and by studying and observing the commandments they were endeavoring to imitate God. In their view, studying the Torah extended to all areas of life and a devout student would attempt to imitate his teacher even concerning trivial details of everyday life. Rabbinic literature often presents the biblical patriarchs and other important biblical characters as observing the Torah according to its rabbinic interpretation. Even God is portrayed as a rabbi studying the Torah and donning *tefillin*, the small black cubic boxes containing scrolls of parchment inscribed with biblical verses that are attached to the forehead and arm of observant Jewish men during weekday morning prayers in accordance with Deut 6:8. This is undoubtedly a way of asserting that rabbinic Judaism was the legitimate heir and continuation of biblical tradition, but it may also suggest that this form of Judaism was the ideal one in the eyes of the rabbis.[2]

Structure and Content

Basically, the Mishnah is organized topically and contains six major orders or divisions (*sedarim*, sing. *seder*), which in turn are divided into sixty-three tractates (*massekhtot*, sing. *massekhet*). These tractates are then divided into chapters (*peraqim*, sing. *pereq*) and *mishnayot* (sing. *mishnah*), the *mishnah* being the smallest unit.

---

1. Cohen, *From the Maccabees*, 218–21; Kraemer, "Mishnah," 311–13.
2. See Gafni, "Rabbinic Historiography," 295–312.

Zeraim (seeds) mainly contains laws pertaining to agriculture but this order also includes the tractate *Berakhot* (benedictions) that deals with regulations for prayer.

Moed (appointed times or Festival Days) contains laws concerning the Sabbath and festivals. Tractate *Pesahim*, for example, includes regulations for the celebration of Passover, and tractate *Sukkah* instructions for how to build a *sukkah* (booth).

Nashim (women) mainly contains laws concerning marriage, marriage contracts and divorce, as well as vows and their cancellation.

Nezikin (damages or civil law) includes, among other things, laws covering damages and torts, laws regulating conduct of business, labor and real estate transactions, and criminal penalties.

Qodashim (holy things) mainly contains laws of sacrifices in the temple.

Toharot (purities) contains laws of ritual purity, or rather laws defining the way people and things contract or eliminate ritual impurity.[3]

The Mishnah is characterized by a terse style, which seems to assume that the reader is familiar with the topics discussed. No background information is offered and one gets the impression of being thrown into the middle of a discussion between well-informed people who communicate by means of key words. Most likely, the Mishnah was not aimed at ordinary people but rather compiled by rabbis for rabbis and their students. The debates take the form of detailed concrete examples and only rarely are general rules formulated. It can hardly have been easily accessible even in its own time, and for modern people who do not share the worldview and basic assumptions of rabbinic Judaism, it is even more difficult to understand. An example from tractate *Berakhot* will illustrate some of these characteristics:

From what time do we recite the *Shema* in the evening? From the hour that the priests enter [their homes] to eat their heave-offering, until the end of the first watch. This is the view of R. Eliezer, but the rabbis say, "Until midnight." Rabban Gamaliel says, "Until the rise of dawn." It happened once that his sons returned from a banquet and said to him: "We have not yet recited the *Shema*." He told them: "If it is not yet dawn you should recite it." And not only in this case but in all cases where

3. For a more detailed survey of the content of the Mishnah, see Stemberger, *Introduction*, 110–18.

the rabbis say "until midnight," the obligation persists until the rise of dawn . . . If so, why did the rabbis say "until midnight"? In order to keep humans away from transgression.

From what time do we recite the *Shema* in the morning? From the hour that one can distinguish between blue and white. R. Eliezer says, "Between blue and green." And one must complete it before sunrise. R. Yehoshua says, "By the third hour, because it is the habit of royalty to rise by the third hour." One who recites later has not lost [anything], for he is as one who reads from the Torah.[4]

One need not understand all the technical details of the text to see that it takes a lot for granted. The reader is expected to know what "reciting the *Shema*" means, agree that it is to be read twice a day, and be familiar with terms such as "heave-offering" and "first watch." No effort is made to explain the meaning of these concepts and terms. Another typical feature of the Mishnah is that disagreements are not resolved. Different opinions stand side by side and there is no hint as to which one should be followed. The Mishnah is the earliest canonical text that preserves tradition in the form of disputes. Moreover, the various opinions in the Mishnah are usually stated without reference to Scripture, and although occasional quotations from the Bible do occur, the Mishnah generally appears to take its own authority for granted.[5]

During the tannaitic, period there seems to have been two ways of organizing halakhah; thematically as in the Mishnah, or according to biblical verses as in the collections of midrash. The relationship between these two modes has been the subject of a long-standing scholarly debate in which some scholars maintain that the method of deriving laws from Scripture (midrash) is the older, while others hold that the earliest oral tradition developed independently of the Bible (Mishnah) and was only later buttressed through a connection to a biblical verse. Those who believe the midrash method to be the older claim that Scripture was an integral part of the process of shaping new laws and that many legal decisions are derived through the interpretation of a biblical verse. Yet other scholars maintain that the two methods

---

4. *m. Ber.* 1:1–2. My translation.
5. For a more detailed description of the Mishnah's content and characteristics, see Goldberg, "Mishna," 227–33; Goldenberg, "Talmud," 131–34; Kraemer, "Mishnah," 299–311; Neusner, *Invitation to the Talmud*, 28–37; Stemberger, *Introduction*, 110–18.

existed side by side and whereas some laws really seem to be the result of interpretation of a verse, others appear to have been created independently of Scripture and only later corroborated by linking them to a biblical verse.[6]

Purpose and Redaction

As mentioned above, the Mishnah was redacted in the early third century but it also contains earlier traditions. Rabbinic tradition unanimously regards Rabbi Yehudah ha-Nasi, also known simply as Rabbi, as the redactor of the Mishnah, and while it is clear that numerous additions were made after his time, scholars agree that as long as we suppose that for a time the text retained a certain flexibility, Rabbi can be seen as the main figure under whose authority the Mishnah was edited. The Mishnah contains traditions from different time periods, and purportedly some even go as far back as the Second Temple period, but scholarly opinion differs as to the extent of later reworking of these traditions. A much-debated issue is whether it is at all possible to reconstruct earlier periods based on these traditions, or whether they have been reworked so much that they rather reflect the time of their redaction.

Traditionally, traditions from four different periods have been discerned in the Mishnah:

The Second Temple period
The Yavneh period (ca. 70–135)
The Usha period (135–170)
The time of the final redaction (ca. 225)

Although attributions to individual rabbis cannot be taken at face value, most scholars agree that traditions can be assigned with reasonable confidence to a particular time period. In addition to views attributed to named rabbis, the Mishnah also contains anonymous opinions, traditionally considered to reflect the view of the redactor. However, in many cases these anonymous teachings do not correspond to the opinion of Rabbi as attested elsewhere. While it is possible that Rabbi changed his opinion, or chose to include teachings with which he did not agree in order to make the Mishnah acceptable to as many as possible, it may also be the case

---

6. Safrai, "Halakha," 146–63. For a discussion of the shift in scholarly consensus, see Halivni, *Midrash*, 18–21.

that the Mishnah was simply not consistently redacted in accordance with Rabbi's views. Many rabbinic texts have undergone this kind of redaction where the redactor in some cases has reworked the sources in accordance with his view but in others preserved earlier traditions intact even if they did not conform to his opinion.

Another issue that is subject to scholarly debate is the purpose of the Mishnah. Is it to be understood as an authoritative law code, an anthology of legal sources, or a legal teaching manual? This question has important implications for how the Mishnah should be understood and employed for the history of Judaism, both rabbinic and pre-rabbinic. Since it mainly includes legal sources, it seemed natural to assume that it was intended to be a law code. But it has been argued that the many repetitions and contradictions—as well as the fact that it often fails to make clear which one of the many cited opinions is valid halakhah—undermines this view. In addition, the view of the Mishnah as a legal code leaves unexplained the parts that legislate practices or presume institutions that were no longer functioning after the destruction of the temple. The view of the Mishnah as a guide for teaching is a mediating position according to which the redactor made a selection of available material but also chose to include traditions with which he himself did not agree in the attempt to create a universally acceptable summary of halakhah.[7]

Recently a modification of this view has been suggested according to which the function of the Mishnah was indeed pedagogical, but, rather than conveying halakhic norms as the traditional view would have it, its purpose was to impart to its students a way of thinking. The cases preserved in the Mishnah were meant to develop the intellectual skills of the students and teach them to apply the norms of the legal system. The Mishnah's function, then, was primarily pedagogical but since it also conveys information about the standards and norms of the legal system it may also have served as an authoritative source of normative law.[8]

If the primary aim of the Mishnah was to train students in various modes of legal analysis, it would explain its disproportionate interest in improbable cases and circumstances as well as borderline cases. Situations that involve a pigeon found exactly half-way between two domains (*m. B. Batra* 2:6) or the man who tithes doubtfully-tithed-produce while naked (*m. Dem.* 1:4) were not likely to occur but would be of interest to the Mishnah because

7. For a survey, see Stemberger, *Talmud and Midrash*, 133–39.
8. Shanks Alexander, *Transmitting Mishnah*, 167–73.

the disparate circumstances involved in each invoke or allude to a different legal principle. By creating such scenarios, the Mishnah could bring competing principles into conflict, thereby compelling the student or audience to consider how diverse and competing legal concerns interact with one another. In a similar way, the ambiguities inherent in borderline cases would encourage students and listeners to reflect on how to apply appropriate legal principles, promoting sophisticated analytic thinking.[9]

The extent to which the Mishnah underwent an intentional redaction is a much-debated question. Most scholars would agree that the Mishnah displays structuring principles and creates coherence and meaning through various linguistic patterns and literary devices such as repetitions, inclusios (words, themes, or sounds from the beginning of a literary unit that are repeated, with some alteration, at the end of the unit), and enchainments (the linking of one *mishnah* to the next by means of a repeated phrase or word). A number of recent studies focusing on these features and techniques argue that they are not random, natural recurrences of language nor features introduced to ease memorization but rather the intentional product of a redactor who was responsible for selecting and imposing coherence on the material. These literary devices employed by the redactor may be understood not only to provide coherence and unity but also to convey ethical and theological meanings.[10]

Oral Transmission

The Mishnah is very much associated with orality and its succinct style and mnemonic features are commonly taken as evidence of oral recitation and transmission. According to traditional accounts, oral transmission of mishnaic traditions were formulated with great precision and consisted of a fixed verbal content that was transmitted primarily through rote memorization. The Mishnah was even considered to have undergone an oral publication process before it was finally written down.[11] The assumption underlying the traditional view is that the orally transmitted text looked very much like the text as it was later written down and while written notes may have existed, only the oral version of the Mishnah would have been authoritative.[12]

---

9. Ibid.
10. Walfish, "Mishnah," 153–189
11. See Lieberman, *Greek/Hellenism in Jewish Palestine*, 83–99.
12. See, for example, Goldberg, "Mishna," 211–51.

However, recent scholarship on oral transmission in diverse cultures has shown that oral transmission does not necessarily start with a fixed text and that oral performance does not automatically aim for word for word reproduction. Rather, texts in oral settings tend to be fluid and the transmission process an active one where the performer does not passively transmit traditions verbatim but rather interprets and shapes them. This insight has influenced the view of the development of the Mishnah and has led some scholars to view the mishnaic material as compositional building blocks from which traditions could be constructed in various ways in different performative settings rather than an orally transmitted fixed text.[13]

It is also increasingly recognized that oral transmission and literary composition coexist and interact in a variety of ways. A written text can interact with oral performance even after it is written down and is not necessarily fixed. It is not only a record of past performative events but can also serve as a script for future performative events. Rather than seeing oral traces in the mishnaic text as an aid to rote memorization, they can be understood as a script for an oral performative event. The transmission process may have consisted of different phases where the earlier ones were characterized by a large degree of fluidity while the later ones more closely resembled the model of oral recitation as rote memorization.

Also, rather than implying an exclusively oral transmission, the notion of Oral Torah, of which the Mishnah formed a part, may have been designed to distinguish the part of revelation that was given orally at Mount Sinai from the one given in writing. To retain both the oral and the written components of the Torah and distinguish between the two may have been a way of reenacting the original revelation and preserving not only the content of revelation but also the mode.[14]

Even though the Mishnah was not originally considered a binding law code, later generations regarded it as such. This view of the Mishnah as an authoritative text led to attempts at harmonizing contradictory views and to reinterpretations in order to make the Mishnah agree with contemporary understandings of halakhah. The rabbis of the post-mishnaic period also devoted themselves to clarifying passages that seemed obscure, expanding the discussions, and extracting general principles of action from the particular rules of the Mishnah, and thus the commentaries grew. The first generation discussed the Mishnah, the second generation continued

13. Shanks-Alexander, *Transmitting Mishnah*, 1–76.
14. Fraade, "Literary Composition," 33–51; Jaffee, "Oral Tradition," 3–32.

this discussion while also adding comments on sayings by their predecessors, the third generation added comments on both sets of earlier commentaries as well as discussions on their relationship to one another, and thus the Talmuds took form.

THE TOSEFTA

Before presenting the Talmuds, however, mention should be made of the Tosefta, another rabbinic compilation whose main content originates from approximately the same time as the Mishnah. The Aramaic word *tosefta* means "addition" and until recently there was a scholarly consensus that the Tosefta was an addition to, or continuation of, the Mishnah. In recent years, however, scholars have noted that the relationship between the Mishnah and the Tosefta seems to be more complex and a number of different theories have been suggested.

The structure of the Tosefta is identical to that of the Mishnah, its language is mishnaic Hebrew, and the rabbis mentioned in the Mishnah are also found in the Tosefta. The Tosefta also covers the same topics but it is approximately three times the size of the Mishnah. Where the Mishnah only cites a few different opinions, the Tosefta often develops the subject more extensively and includes more rabbinic opinions. Sometimes it also formulates rules that significantly differ from those found in the Mishnah concerning the same subject. In addition to the material that the two works have in common, the Tosefta also contains traditions from rabbis that lived a generation or several generations after the latest ones cited in the Mishnah.[15]

Close comparisons between the Mishnah and the Tosefta have given rise to contradictory theories concerning their relationship. While some Tosefta passages give the impression of being a commentary and a continuation of the Mishnah, others seem to predate their parallel version in the Mishnah. This has led some scholars to suggest that some Tosefta passages may actually predate their mishnaic parallels even if the redacted form of the Tosefta postdates the Mishnah. Others have proposed that the relationship varies from tractate to tractate, so that some tractates

---

15. For a survey of the Tosefta, see Goldberg, "Tosefta," 283–302; Neusner, *Invitation to the Talmud*, 70–95; Stemberger, *Introduction*, 149–63; Mandel, "Tosefta," 316–35.

of the Mishnah are earlier than their counterparts in the Tosefta while others are later.[16]

Recently, it was suggested that the Tosefta is a commentary on an earlier version of the Mishnah, a kind of "Ur-Mishnah." Both this Ur-Mishnah and the Tosefta served as sources for our present Mishnah, which means that the Tosefta may in some instances be the source of the Mishnah, while in others a commentary on it. The Ur-Mishnah was sometimes incorporated into our present Mishnah without being reworked, and in these cases, the Tosefta looks like a commentary to the Mishnah. According to this view, the fact that the Tosefta cites rabbis from a later time than the Mishnah—often cited as evidence that the final redaction of the Tosefta took place later than that of the Mishnah—means only that the redactor of the Mishnah in certain cases chose not to include these later traditions. Either they were not considered as authoritative as the earlier traditions, or they were, in some cases, incorporated without attributing them to named rabbis.[17]

THE TALMUDS

During the amoraic period, two other rabbinic compilations emerged: the Palestinian or Jerusalem Talmud (Yerushalmi), whose final redaction took place in the land of Israel circa 400 C.E., and the Babylonian Talmud (Bavli), composed by rabbis who lived in Babylonia from the third through the seventh or eighth century. The word "Talmud" is derived from the Hebrew verb *lamad*, which means "to study." Alongside the Bible, the Babylonian Talmud is the most important Jewish text, and it has exerted a tremendous influence on Jewish tradition from late antiquity until the present.

The two Talmuds emerged in very different cultural contexts: the Palestinian Talmud in the land of Israel, which was under Roman rule and influenced by Greco-Roman culture, and the Babylonian Talmud in the Sassanian Persian Empire, a religiously diverse region populated by Zoroastrians and Christians of various stripes. Under the Sassanians, the Jews enjoyed limited self-rule and were represented by the exilarch, the Babylonian counterpart to the patriarch.

---

16. For a survey of the relationship between the Mishnah and the Tosefta, see Hauptman, *Rereading the Mishnah*, 14–16; Fox and Meacham, *Introducing Tosefta*.

17. Hauptman, *Rereading the Mishnah*, 1–30.

In spite of their development in different milieus, the Palestinian and the Babylonian Talmud exhibit many basic similarities. They are both continuations of the debates in the Mishnah and share much of their content. There seems to have been close contacts between the rabbinic centers in the land of Israel and Babylonia, and the rabbis often traveled back and forth sharing learning and exchanging traditions. The Babylonian Talmud, however, continued to develop a few centuries after the redaction of the Palestinian Talmud and is therefore much more extensive. It has certain unique traits, which can be explained by cultural conditions specific to Babylonia and the fact that it in part reflects a later time period.

During the amoraic period, the Jewish center slowly moved from the land of Israel to Babylonia, where the rabbinic community gained in importance and self-esteem, emerging as a rival to the one in the land of Israel. A veritable competition developed between these two rabbinic centers, in which the Babylonian rabbinic community claimed to be the equal of the one in the land of Israel and according to some, even superior to it: "We consider ourselves in Babylonia as being in the land of Israel, from the day Rav came to Babylonia."[18] Redefining "Zion" as the rabbinic academy rather than a geographical place, the Babylonian rabbis were able to reinterpret biblical references to Jerusalem as referring to Torah learning in Babylonia, even to the point of strongly dissuading emigration to the land of Israel.[19] In response, the Palestinian rabbis began emphasizing the importance of living in the land of Israel, even asserting that this was the equivalent to fulfilling all the commandments in the Torah.[20] With the shift of center to Babylonia, the Babylonian Talmud gained influence at the expense of the Yerushalmi. From the eighth century onward, it almost completely replaced the Palestinian Talmud, and the Mishnah was practically studied only through the Babylonian Talmud.

---

18. *b. Gitt.* 6a.

19. *b. Ket.* 110b–111a. The contemporary anti-Zionist Satmar hasidim appeal to this passage in order to deter Jews from moving to the modern State of Israel.

20. *t. Avod. Zar.* 5. Similarly in *Pirqe R. Eliezer* 8: "Even when there are Sages and righteous outside the land, and only a shepherd or a herdsman in the land, it is the shepherd or the herdsman who is to declare the New Year. And even if you have prophets outside the Land of Israel, and commoners in the Land, authority to proclaim the calendar rests with the commoners in the Land of Israel." On the competition between the land of Israel and Babylonia, see Gafni, *Land, Center*.

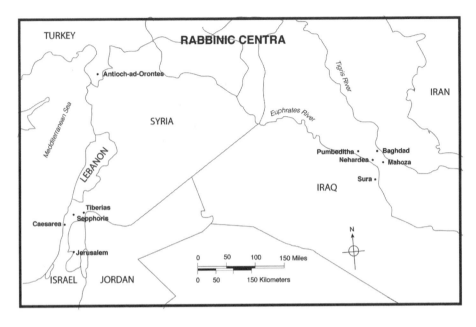

Fig. 3. The Babylonian Rabbinic Academies. Map by Magnus Zetterholm.

In addition to the halakhic material from the Mishnah, the Talmuds—
the Babylonian one in particular—contain large amounts of aggadic
material such as legends, folk tales, scriptural interpretations, magical
incantations, and observations about theology, medicine, astronomy,
and medicine. As much as a third of the Babylonian Talmud consists of
aggadah, parts of which consists of commentary on Scripture. The Jerusalem Talmud is more narrowly focused on law and Mishnah commentary, which is likely due, at least in part, to the fact that in the land of
Israel scriptural interpretations were compiled in special collections that
circulated independently (midrash). Both Talmuds develop and expand
the debates in the Mishnah, but they also contain a large amount of additional material that is only loosely, or not at all, connected to the Mishnah. They both developed during a very long time and therefore contain
material from different time periods. In addition to the text of the Mishnah itself, they also include material from the tannaitic period that was
not included in the Mishnah, known as *baraitot* (sing. *baraita*), as well as
traditions from the amoraic and post-amoraic periods.

The Babylonian Talmud

The content of a tractate in the Babylonian Talmud is organized loosely
around a specific topic, creating a literary unit known as *sugya* (pl. *sugyot*) in Hebrew. A *sugya* is typically comprised of traditions from different time periods, with the oldest material dating from the tannaitic
period and the latest from the post-amoraic period. Sayings from the
post-amoraic period are unattributed and transmitted anonymously
(*stam* in Hebrew), giving no hint as to their date. Traditions from the
tannaitic period are transmitted in Hebrew, the amoraic sayings appear
in a mixture of Aramaic and Hebrew, and the anonymous layer is almost
entirely in Aramaic.

The unattributed sayings are characterized by a certain terminology
as well as specific literary features and usually provide an interpretive
framework for tannaitic and amoraic sayings, only rarely making independent assertions of their own. It is for this reason that the anonymous
layer is commonly considered later than the others, even if shorter anonymous additions may have originated already in the amoraic period.[21]

---

21. That the anonymous layer postdates the amoraic sayings was suggested by David
Weiss Halivni and Shamma Friedman independent of each other in the 1970s. A sum-

The anonymous layer is quite thin in the Palestinian Talmud, but makes up as much as fifty percent of the Babylonian Talmud.

Below is the Babylonian Talmud's expansion of the mishnaic passage at the beginning of tractate *Berakhot*. The citations from the Mishnah appear in capital letters and the citations from the Bible in italics:

> On what does the Tanna base himself when he says: FROM WHAT TIME [IS THE *SHEMA* RECITED]? Furthermore, why does he deal first with the evening [*Shema*]? Let him begin with the morning [*Shema*]! The tannaitic rabbi bases himself on Scripture, where it is written [*Recite them . . .*] *when you lie down and when you get up* [Deut. 6:7] and he teaches thus: When does the time of the recital of the *Shema* of lying down begin? When the priests enter to eat their *terumah* [heave-offering]. And if you like, I can answer: He learns [the precedence of the evening] from the account of the creation of the world, where it is written, *And there was evening and there was morning, a first day* [Gen. 1:15] . . . FROM THE TIME THAT THE PRIESTS ENTER TO EAT THEIR TERUMAH. When do the priests eat *terumah*? From the time of the appearance of the stars.[22]

Without going into all the technical details, several observations concerning the Talmudic commentary (*gemara*) can be made on the basis of this brief passage. While the Mishnah merely states that one should recite the *Shema*, the *gemara* fills in background details perceived to be missing, such as the reason why the *Shema* should be recited at all and why the recitation of the Shema in the evening is mentioned before the recitation of the Shema in the morning. One might think it more logical to begin with the recitation of the morning *Shema*, so why does the Mishnah begin with the evening? After asking these questions, the *gemara* answers them by providing prooftexts from the Bible. The rabbi in the Mishnah bases his teaching on Deut. 6:7, where the recitation of the *Shema* is prescribed, and the reason for mentioning the evening *Shema* first is that it appears in this order in the biblical verse: "when you lie down" is mentioned before "when you rise." The *gemara* then provides additional support for mentioning the evening *Shema* first, citing Gen. 1:5 in which evening precedes morning.

---

mary of Halivni's hypothesis in English appears in *Midrash*, 76–104, and the latest revision of his dating of the anonymous layer is found in "Aspects," 339–60.
22. *b. Ber.* 2a.

The structure of a traditional page from the Babylonian Talmud was established at the time of its first printing in 1520–1523. Subsequently, more commentaries were added, but the appearance of the page has changed very little. The edition that served as the model for all later editions is the Vilna edition, printed in 1880–1886. The next pages depict a traditional page of the Babylonian Talmud together with an explanation of the most important commentaries appearing on the page.[23]

The Layout of a Talmud Page

1. The number of the page in Hebrew letters. Every sheet (double page) is numbered and the first side of the sheet is called a, and the second side is called b. The standard practice when referring to a page of the Talmud is to cite the name of the tractate, the number of the sheet, and the side, for instance, *Taanit* 10a. To indicate which Talmud is meant, the letters *y* (Yerushalmi) or *b* (Bavli) is placed before the tractate, for instance, *b. Taanit* 10a.

2. The name of the tractate.

3. The main text on a Talmud page, consisting of the Mishnah and gemara.

4. Abbreviation of the word *matnitin*, indicating the beginning of a quotation from the Mishnah.

5. Abbreviation of the word *gemara*, indicating the beginning of the amoraic commentaries on the Mishnah.

6. Commentary by Rashi (R. Shlomo Yitzhak 1040–1104), found on the inner side of the page closest to the binding in all traditional editions of the Talmud. Rashi lived in Troyes, France, and his explanations are the most famous and widely read commentary to the Talmud. He explains the text, sometimes translating into French (and occasionally German), words or expressions that were no longer familiar to people of his time. In order to separate it from the main text, Rashi's commentary appears in "Rashiscript," a script that is slightly different from the regular Hebrew characters.

---

23. For surveys of the Babylonian Talmud, see Goldberg, "Babylonian Talmud," 323–66; Goldenberg, "Talmud," 129–75; Goodblatt, "Babylonian Talmud," 257–336; Halivni, *Midrash*, 66–104; Kalmin, "Formation and Character," 840–76; Neusner, *Invitation to the Talmud*, 96–270; Stemberger, *Introduction*, 164–224.

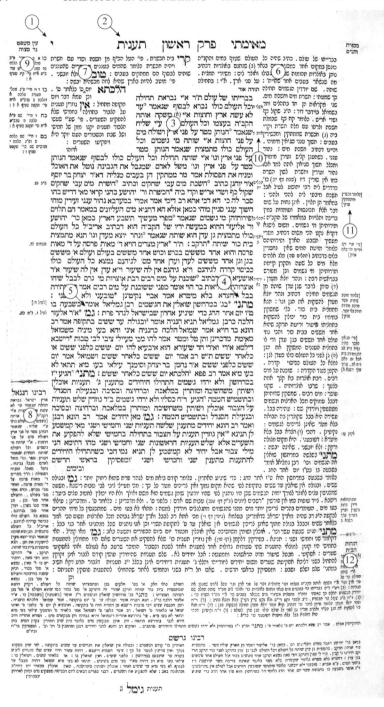

Fig. 4. Page of the Babylonian Talmud, Vilna Edition (tractate *Taanit* 10a). Photograph by the Royal Library, Copenhagen. Used by permission.

7. Tosafot (literally "additions"), appear in the outer column of the page (also in Rashi-script). They began as additions to Rashi's commentary by his disciples and descendants, but developed into an independent interpretation of the gemara.

8. Commentary by Rabbenu Hananel (990–1055), one of the earliest commentaries on the Talmud.

9. *Ein mishpat ner mitzvah*. References to the main law codes dealing with the same topic as the gemara. The law codes most commonly referred to are *Mishneh Torah* by Maimonides (1138–1204), *Sefer Mitzvot Gadol* by Rabbi Moses of Coucy (first half of the thirteenth century), *Arba'ah Turim* by Rabbi Jacob ben Asher (ca. 1270–1340), and *Shulhan Arukh* by Rabbi Joseph Caro (1488–1575).

10. References to biblical passages.

11. *Masoret ha-Shas*. Cross-references to parallel passages elsewhere in the Talmud.

12. *Haggahot ha-Bah*. Proposed emendations in the text of the gemara, Rashi's commentary, and the Tosafot, by Rabbi Yoel Sirkes (seventeenth century).[24]

The Anonymous Layer

As mentioned above, much of the Babylonian Talmud consists of anonymous discussion characterized by a discursive style. While amoraic sayings are often brief, stating viewpoints without explaining the reasoning behind them, the anonymous layer explores the logic, reasons, and consequences underlying these statements, producing long dialectical debates in which various opinions and possibilities are compared, analyzed, and explained, with equal attention to minority opinions, which have no bearing on practical law. In contrast to the rabbis from an earlier period who seem to have considered analysis and argumentation as merely a means to reach a conclusion and not worthy of preservation, the rabbis behind the anonymous layer seem to have valued analysis and argumentation as ends in and of themselves. Sometimes it seems that they even created debates by juxtaposing statements that originally had no connection to each other, presenting them in question and answer form.[25]

It has been suggested that the willingness to engage in argumentation and the interest in preserving different, sometimes contradictory viewpoints and pursuing their underlying rationales and consequences reflects a recognition that a single undisputed divine truth is unobtainable. The

---

24. For a more detailed description, see Steinsaltz, *Reference Guide*, 48–59.
25. Halivni, *Midrash*, 86–92.

rabbis maintained that after the cessation of prophecy, the only way to seek out God's will was through interpretation of the Torah, an activity that gives humans a crucial role in establishing God's will. However, humans are, by definition, imperfect, and therefore human interpretation will also be imperfect and incomplete. Being dependent on human interpretation, the divine message is available only in a multiplicity of human interpretations. Because any single interpretation encompasses only part of the truth, preserving many alternate interpretations becomes a way of grasping as many aspects of the divine truth as possible. Accordingly, a minority view is no less a reflection of an aspect of God's will than the majority opinion.[26]

The reason why the rabbis behind the latest Talmudic layer chose to be anonymous is the subject of scholarly debate. A common view is that they did so in order to distinguish their additions, which they considered less authoritative, from the teachings of the amoraim. Presumably, they regarded their work as a restatement and clarification of what to earlier generations was self-evident, and believed that they were adding nothing new. According to this view, transmitting their comments anonymously was a way of acknowledging the supremacy of earlier generations.[27]

Layers in the Talmud

Anonymous/Redactional layer
Dialectical discussions of the
tannaitic and amoraic material

Amoraic layer
comments on mishnayot and baraitot

Tannaitic layer
mishnayot
baraitot

Redaction
In the view of David Weiss Halivni, the father of source-critical analysis of the Talmud, it is these anonymous commentators who were responsible for the redaction of the Babylonian Talmud during a period ranging from the middle of the sixth century to the middle of the eighth.[28] These redactors arranged, interpreted, and discussed the material, weaving together

---

26. Kraemer, *Mind*, 99–139.
27. Halivni, *Midrash*, 87.
28. Halivni, "Aspects," 346.

amoraic sayings with *baraitot*, as well as adding their own comments. In Halivni's opinion, the *sugya* is essentially the creation of the redactors.[29] Other scholars are reluctant to assign redactional activity to a specific time period and have suggested that the features typical of the anonymous layer are characteristics of redactional activity rather than traits typical of a distinct historical era.[30]

Recently, Judith Hauptman has proposed a modification of Halivni's model, arguing that the *sugya* developed gradually in chronological order. According to her theory, the *baraitot* commenting on the *mishnah* constitute the oldest redacted stratum of the *sugya*, to which rabbis from the amoraic period added their comments. Finally, the redactors added their comments and interpretations, tying everything together and providing an interpretive framework.[31]

In recent years Jeffrey Rubenstein, a student of Halivni's, has argued that the redactors of the Talmud also authored or reworked many of the Bavli's lengthy and complex stories. Developing an approach to the study of Talmudic stories that combines literary analysis with source and form criticism, he maintains that a close study of Bavli narratives reveals that they were composed by means of creative reworking of earlier sources with methods and techniques of composition akin to those exhibited in legal *sugyot*, as described by Halivni and others. This similarity in methods and technique, together with the fact that many of the complex stories express admiration for skill in dialectic argumentation, an activity highly valued by the redactors of the legal material, led him to conclude that the redactors were responsible not only for the structure of the legal material but also for the stories. Since many typically Babylonian motifs and concerns, common in Bavli stories but absent from their Palestinian parallels, appear primarily in narratives that exhibit redactional techniques of composition, he argues that these specific Babylonian motifs should be attributed to the redactors rather than to the rabbis from the amoraic period. If he is correct, the lengthy and complex stories may be dated as late as the sixth and seventh centuries rather than to the third and fourth.

The idea of the redactors as the main authors of the Bavli stories has been challenged by other scholars who either maintain that the contribution of the redactors cannot be clearly separated from that of the amoraim,

---

29. Halivni, *Midrash*, 76–92.
30. See for instance Friedman, "Good Story," 71–100.
31. Hauptman, *Development*, 227–50.

or believe that the stories should be attributed mainly to the amoraim. In any event, whether or not Rubenstein's theory of the redactors as authors of the stories is embraced, there is general agreement that his studies demonstrate important differences between Palestinian and Babylonian rabbinic culture and have greatly enhanced our understanding of both the stories and culture of the Babylonian Talmud.

In Babylonia, Torah study was esteemed as the highest value, even at the expense of other parts of religious life, and based on a number of stories in the Babylonian Talmud, Rubenstein argues that rabbinic culture in the post-amoraic period was elitist, with rabbinic interests revolving around matters connected to the academy, such as legitimate leadership and the proper way of conducting debates. In his view, many specifically Babylonian rabbinic concerns can be explained against the background of the large academies that had developed in Babylonia with a strict hierarchy and a competitive, even hostile atmosphere.

Students sat in rows according to their status, the best students in the front, and the more inferior ones in the back. At the top of the hierarchy was the head of the academy who was appointed based on proficiency in Torah and eminent ancestry, the latter a significant concern in Sassanian culture. In this milieu, a particular rabbi's place in the academic hierarchy was largely dependent on his ability to excel in argumentation. Failure in this regard would lead to demotion and humiliation, and accordingly, dialectical ability came to be considered the most exalted and valued form of learning. Success in the academy was a delicate business that depended on a rabbi's ability to defeat his opponents with clever arguments while at the same time taking care to avoid insulting or embarrassing his colleagues.[32]

Because these large rabbinic academies were located in the cities, students had to spend extended periods of time away from their homes and families, creating a tension between marriage and study, and between studying and earning a living. Such tensions underlie a number of Bavli stories, and may explain the view of wives as an obstacle to Torah study that appears in some stories.[33]

---

32. Rubenstein, *Stories*; Rubenstein, *Culture*; Rubenstein, *Talmudic Stories*.
33. For the tension between Torah study and marriage, see *b. Yebam.* 62b–63a; *b. Ket.* 61b–64a, and Boyarin, *Carnal Israel*, 142–66; Satlow, *Jewish Marriage*, 3–41; Rubenstein, *Culture*, 102–22. On the tension caused by the ideal to study Torah on the one hand and the need to earn a living on the other, see *b. Taanit* 21a, and Licht, *Ten Legends*, 181–206; Rubenstein, *Stories* 41–61, and also *b. Shabb.* 33b–34a, and Rubenstein, *Talmudic Stories*, 105–38.

Another scholarly debate concerns the extent to which the redactors
have reworked their sources, a question that has ramifications for the possibility of using the Talmud as a source for historical reconstruction. If the
Talmud preserves sources from the different time periods of its development, transmitted without too much interference from the redactors, it can
be used as a historical source for the period prior to its final redaction, but
if the redactors have altered them beyond recognition in adapting them to
the concerns and values of a later period, it can only be used as a historical
source for the time of its redaction.

Jacob Neusner is the primary proponent of the latter view, claiming that
the Talmud is basically a creation of its final redactors. While acknowledging that the Talmud contains sources from earlier periods, he maintains
that they have been reworked beyond recognition by the final redactors.[34]
A majority of scholars, however, believe that it is possible to distinguish
different layers from different time periods based on grammar, terminology, and style. While acknowledging that earlier sources are reflected
through the concerns and values of the redactors' time, they maintain that
they are neither thoroughly nor consistently reworked. The freedom of
reworking seems to vary and in general the redactors seem to have been
more restrained with regard to halakhic material than with aggadah.

These scholars point out that the Babylonian Talmud itself calls attention to its various sources by citing traditions in the names of different
rabbis, by the use of different citations formulae, and by the alternation
between Hebrew and Aramaic. Even if it cannot be ascertained that a saying attributed to R. Aqiva really goes back to him, most scholars maintain
that it is possible to draw some general distinctions between Babylonian
and Palestinian rabbis, and between tannaim and amoraim. It is true that
the sophisticated literary character of stories in the Talmud diminishes
their value as sources for historical events, but although they do not always
yield information about historical facts, they nevertheless reflect rabbinic
values and attitudes. Most scholars agree that cultural-historical information can be obtained from rabbinic texts provided they are read critically.
Such a critical reading involves recognition of the important roles of the
redactors in transforming earlier sources, as well as attention to the special
literary characteristics of the text,[35] a topic to which we will return shortly

---

34. See, for instance, Neusner, *Making the Classics*.
35. Hayes, *Between the Talmuds*, 9–17; Kalmin, *Sages*, xiii–17; Kalmin, "Formation
and Character," 843–52; Kraemer, *Mind*, 20–25.

The Palestinian Talmud

The Palestinian Talmud, also known as the Talmud Yerushalmi (Jerusalem Talmud), is the commentary on the Mishnah produced by the rabbinic community in the land of Israel during the third and fourth centuries. In spite of its name, it was not produced in Jerusalem but in various locations in the Galilee. A *sugya* in the Palestinian Talmud is generally simpler than a Bavli *sugya* and typically consists of tannaitic material, briefly commented upon. Only occasionally do longer dialectic debates occur.

The development and redaction of the Palestinian Talmud have drawn much less scholarly attention than studies of the Babylonian Talmud and many conclusions are yet tentative. The Palestinian Talmud seems to have developed through accumulation of additional layers of commentaries with the passing of time without much redactional intervention. The fact that similar terminology and modes of reasoning are used throughout the whole work, and the same rabbis quoted in all of its parts, suggests that it underwent a single uniform redaction. Most scholars assume that the final redaction was minimal and simply the last stage of the accumulation of traditions. In contrast to the anonymous material in the Babylonian Talmud, the Yerushalmi's anonymous material does not differ substantially from the attributed traditions. Accordingly, it has been argued that there is no compelling reason to attribute this material to later redactors, or for assuming that they played a significant role in the formation of the Palestinian Talmud.[36]

The relationship between the two Talmuds is a matter of scholarly debate. On one hand, they share much of their content, but on the other, they are also very different. The similarities have commonly been explained by the extensive exchange of material that took place when the rabbis travelled back and forth between the land of Israel and Babylonia and brought their respective traditions along, but until recently there was a relative consensus that the redactors of the Babylonian Talmud did not know the redacted form of the Palestinian Talmud. While they may have had access to an early version of the Yerushalmi, which both they and the redactors of the Palestinian Talmud may have used as a base for their respective compilations, most scholars believed that the redacted form of the Yerushalmi was unknown to them.

---

36. For a survey of the Palestinian Talmud, see Bokser, "Palestinian Talmud," 139–256; Goldberg, "Palestinian Talmud," 303–22; Moscovitz, "Formation and Character," 663–77.

However, a recent study of tractate *Avodah Zarah* has demonstrated that there are significant structural similarities between the two Talmuds in this particular tractate, raising the possibility that the Babylonian redactors did in fact know a Yerushalmi version that closely resembles the present one. The author argues that the similarities are so striking that they can hardly be explained by a common source of traditions, but rather seem to be a result of a Babylonian revision of a completed Palestinian version.[37] This raises the possibility that the Babylonian redactors had access to a redacted version of the Jerusalem Talmud for other tractates also, although this has yet to be demonstrated.

The differences between the Palestinian and the Babylonian Talmuds are likely the result of both cultural and chronological factors. While the Palestinian Talmud was redacted around 400 C.E., the Babylonian Talmud continued to develop for several hundred years. Scholars differ over whether the differences should be attributed primarily to the rabbis of the amoraic period, or whether they are the outcome of later reworking by the Babylonian redactors.

Rabbinic Literature as a Source for Historical Reconstruction

As mentioned above, most scholars maintain that rabbinic sources can be used to obtain some historical information, although the view of the kind of data they are believed to yield has changed considerably during the last fifty years. A general skepticism to rabbinic traditions, an awareness of the role of redactors in reworking earlier material, and the recognition that rabbinic narratives are literary artifacts have thoroughly changed the prospect of using rabbinic literature as a source for historical reconstruction.

At the beginning of the academic study of Judaism in the nineteenth century, scholars treated rabbinic literature as a relatively reliable source of historical information. It was presumed that rabbinic stories conveyed something that actually had happened and that they reflected a historical reality. Although scholars recognized their exaggerated and legendary elements, they believed that it was possible to get behind the text and isolate a "historical kernel" through critical analysis. By excluding the supernatural elements and harmonizing different sources, detailed reconstructions of rabbinic history and biographies of individual rabbis were produced.

---

37. Gray, *Talmud in Exile*.

Jacob Neusner vehemently criticized this approach starting in the early 1970s. He demonstrated that many traditions in different rabbinic compilations, and sometimes even within the same compilation, contradict each other and that later texts often rework earlier ones so that there is no way to distinguish historical descriptions from fiction. While earlier scholarship tended to consider all divergent versions of an event as essentially reliable, Neusner showed that later versions were often not independent historical testimonies but rather the result of transformations of earlier sources in the course of transmission, or deliberate reworkings of an earlier source. He also questioned the accuracy of attributions of sayings to individual rabbis and promoted a generally skeptical attitude toward historical accuracy of traditions in general, since they are often recorded long after the events they purport to describe.[38]

With Neusner, scholarly focus essentially shifted from the historical context of the characters within a story to that of the storytellers behind the story. A certain skepticism to rabbinic traditions in general is now prevalent among most scholars. For instance, traditions attributed to early Palestinian rabbis that appear only in the Babylonian Talmud are no longer automatically considered to convey accurate information about the conditions in the land of Israel at the time when these rabbis lived. Rather, most scholars at least consider the possibility that these traditions reflect later Babylonian conditions that have been projected back to earlier centuries. The same applies to purportedly tannaitic traditions in the Babylonian Talmud that lack parallels in tannaitic compilations. Although it is possible that they indeed date from tannaitic times but happen to be preserved only in the Bavli, one must consider the possibility that they originated with amoraic or post-amoraic rabbis.

The recognition that rabbinic stories are literary creations told for didactic purposes and not intended to record historical events has significant ramifications for the view of their potential to reveal historical facts. Rather than trying to get behind the stories to a historical reality, scholars have turned their attention to the message of the story and developed methods to determine the meaning of the extant text. An important proponent of a literary approach to rabbinic stories is Jonah Fraenkel, who developed a method of close reading of narratives with careful attention to wording, structure, and plot. He rejects all approaches that consider

---

38. See for instance Neusner, *Development of a Legend*; Neusner, *Rabbinic Traditions*. See also Green, "What's in a Name?" 77–96.

rabbinic stories as historical sources, arguing that to treat them as such is a misunderstanding of their genre. Rabbinic stories are fiction, he maintains—reflecting the spiritual world of the storytellers, not the real world of the characters—whose meaning emerges through a close reading that identifies the structure, determines the plot, describes the characters, and analyzes literary devices.[39]

However, even narratives that are made up and told for didactic purposes reveal something about their authors' values and concerns, and although they may not yield much information about specific historical events or details of individual rabbis' lives, they may provide a window to rabbinic attitudes and ideas. Provided they are read critically, taking into account their sophisticated literary character, rhetorical features, and the role of the redactors in transforming the sources, most scholars agree that rabbinic sources can be used for reconstructions of the history of rabbinic ideas and attitudes.[40]

The well-known story of the deposition of Rabban Gamliel in *b. Ber.* 27b–28a may serve to illustrate which kind of information can be derived from rabbinic sources:

Our sages have taught [in a *baraita*]: Once a certain disciple came before R. Yehoshua. He said to him: "The evening prayer—optional or obligatory?" He said to him: "Optional." He came before Rabban Gamliel. He said to him: "The evening prayer—optional or obligatory?" He said to him: "Obligatory." He said to him: "But did not R. Yehoshua say to me 'optional'?" He said to him: "Wait until the shield-bearers [the sages] enter the academy."

When the shield-bearers entered,[41] the questioner stood up and asked: "The evening prayer—optional or obligatory?" Rabban Gamliel said to him: "Oligatory." Rabban Gamliel said to the sages: "Is there anyone who disagrees on this matter?" R. Yehoshua said to him: "No." Rabban Gamliel said to him: "But did they not say to me in your name, 'Optional'?" He said to him: "Yehoshua! Stand on your feet that they may bear witness against you."

---

39. See Fraenkel, *Darkhe haaggadah*.
40. See Goodblatt, "Rehabilitation" 31–44; Kalmin, "Rabbinic Literature," 187–99; Kraemer, "Rabbinic Sources," 201–12.
41. Metaphors of war are often used to describe rabbinic debates over Torah. See Rubenstein, *Culture*, 59–64.

R. Yehoshua stood on his feet and said: "If I were alive and he [the student] dead—the living could contradict the dead. Now that I am alive and he is alive—how can the living contradict the living?" [that is, how can I deny that I said this?].

Rabban Gamliel was sitting and expounding while R. Yehoshua stood on his feet, until all the people murmured and sait to Huspit the *turgeman* [the interpreter]: "Stop!" and he stopped. They said: "How long will he [Rabban Gamliel] go on distressing [R. Yehoshua]? He distressed him last year on Rosh Hashanah.[42] He distressed him in [the matter of] the firstling, in the incident involving R. Zadoq.[43] Now he distresses him again. Come, let us depose him. Whom will we raise up [in his place]? Shall we raise up R. Yehoshua? He is involved in the matter. Shall we raise up R. Aqiva? Perhaps he [Rabban Gamliel] will harm him, since he has no ancestral merit. Rather, let us raise up R. Eleazar b. Azariah, for he is wise, and he is wealthy, and he is tenth [in descent] from Ezra. He is wise—so that if anyone asks a difficult question, he will be able to answer it. He is wealthy—in case he has to pay honor to the emperor. And he is tenth in descent from Ezra—he has ancestral merit and he [Rabban Gamliel] will not be able to harm him."

They said to him: "Would our Master consent to be the head of the academy?" He said to them: "Let me go and consult with the members of my household." He went and consulted his wife. She said to him: "Perhaps they will reconcile with him and depose you?" He said to her: "There is a tradition, One raises the level of holiness but does not diminish it [*m. Menah.* 11:7]."[44] She said to him: "perhaps he [Rabban Gamliel] will harm you?" He said: "Let a man use a valuable cup for one day even if it breaks on the morrow." She said to him: "You have no white hair." That day he was eighteen years old. A miracle happened for him and he was crowned with eighteen rows of white hair . . .

---

42. By telling him to appear before him with his staff and money on the day that according to Rabbi Yehoshua was Yom Kippur (*b. Rosh Hash.* 25a and *m. Rosh Hash.* 2:8–9).

43. This refers to a similar story in which R. Yehoshua and Rabban Gamliel answer R. Zadoq's question about a blemished firstling in opposite ways, and the people tell Huspit to stop (*b. Bek.* 36a).

44. R. Eleazar applies this principle of temple law—that once an object or sacrifice takes on a certain level of holiness, it cannot be reduced to a less holy state—to his situation. Once he has been promoted to the position of head of the academy he will not be demoted.

It was taught [in a *baraita*]: That day they removed the guard of the gate and gave students permission to enter. For Rabban Gamliel had decreed: "Any student whose inside is not like his outside may not enter the academy." That day many benches were added. R. Yohanan said: "Abba Yosef b. Dostenai and the sages disagree. One said, 'Four hundred benches were added.' And one said: 'Seven hundred benches were added.'"

Rabban Gamliel became distressed. He said: "Perhaps, God forbid, I held back Torah from Israel." They showed him in a dream white casks filled with ashes.[45] But that was not the case, they showed him [the dream] only to put his mind at ease [but he really had held back Torah].

It was taught [in a *baraita*]: They taught [Tractate] *Eduyyot* on that day (and anywhere that it says "on that day" [in the Mishnah]—[refers to] that day [when R. Eleazar was appointed head of the academy]. And there was not a single law pending in the academy that they did not resolve . . .

Rabban Gamliel said: "I will go and appease R. Yehoshua."[46] When he arrived at his house, he saw that the walls of his house were black. He said to him: "From the walls of your house it is evident that you are a smith." He said to him: "Woe to the generation whose chief you are, for you do not know the distress of the scholars, how they earn a living and how they subsist." He said to him: "I apologize to you. Forgive me." He [R. Yehoshua] paid no attention to him. [Rabban Gamliel said,] "Do it for the honor of my father's house." He said to him: "You are forgiven" . . .

They said: "What shall we do? Shall we depose him [R. Eleazar b. Azariah]? There is a tradition, "One raises the level of holiness but does not diminish it" [*m. Menah.* 7:11]. "Shall this master expound on one Sabbath and that master on the next? He [Rabban Gamliel] will not accept that since he will be jealous of him." Rather, they ordained that Rabban Gamliel would expound three Sabbaths and R. Eleazar b. Azariah one Sabbath. (This explains the tradition, "Whose Sabbath was it? It was [the Sabbath] of R. Eleazar b. Azariah" [*t. Sotah* 7:9]. And the student [who asked the original question] was R. Shimon bar Yohai.)[47]

---

45. The casks with ashes symbolize unworthy students whose insides (personal character) are as worthless as ash.

46. Apparently he realizes that the presence of numerous students helps to resolve disputes and problems of law and therefore resolves to change his ways.

47. Translation and explanatory comments are taken from Rubenstein, *Rabbinic Stories*, 99–103. For analyses of the story, see Goldenberg, "Deposition," 167–90; Steinmetz, "Must the Patriarch," 163–90; Rubenstein, *Stories*, 77–90.

Whereas in the pre-Neusner era this narrative would essentially have been taken at face value (with the exception of the supernatural detail about Rabbi Eleazar b. Azaria's hair turning white), and considered a story from tannaitic times about a conflict between rabbis of the immediate post-temple times, scholars today are more skeptical as to its provenance and more restrained in drawing detailed historical conclusions from it. While it is purportedly a tannaitic tradition (*baraita*) featuring Palestinian rabbis, it seems to reflect particular Babylonian conditions of a later period, such as large academies, concern over matters related to the leadership of the academy, and the view of wives as an obstacle to a career within the academy.[48] Furthermore, cross-references to and quotation of other rabbinic sources seem to indicate redactional authorship or reworking.[49]

While no longer understood to reflect a historical dispute between Rabban Gamliel and R. Yehoshua in the first century, most scholars would understand it to reflect Babylonian rabbinic culture of a later period, taking it as evidence of a tendency toward dynastic succession in the appointment of head of the academy and an internal rabbinic concern over the leadership style and general policy of the academies. The motif of guards and their removal from the entrance of the academy may be understood to reflect a conflict over whether Torah study should be accessible to all or restricted to a limited number of worthy students. From the deliberations regarding whom to appoint as head of the academy in place of Rabban Gamliel may be deduced that wealth, learning, and ancestral merit were considered important qualifications for leadership in the Babylonian academy.

Following this presentation of the rabbinic understanding and development of biblical tradition as evidenced in the Mishnah and the two Talmuds, we will now turn to the rabbis' interpretation of the Bible and the assumptions that underlie it.

---

48. Rubenstein, *Stories*, 77–90.
49. Rubenstein, *Culture*, 102–21.

STUDY QUESTIONS

1. What are the characteristics of the Mishnah and how have scholars explained them?

2. Explain the different scholarly theories about the purpose and function of the Mishnah.

3. In what ways has recent scholarship on orality influenced the view of how the Mishnah developed and was transmitted?

4. Describe the characteristics and particular concerns/motifs of the Babylonian Talmud as compared to the Mishnah and the Palestinian Talmud.

5. What are the problems involved in using rabbinic sources for the purpose of historical reconstructions?

SUGGESTIONS FOR FURTHER READING

The Mishnah and Tosefta
Shanks Alexander, E. *Transmitting Mishnah: The Shaping Influence of Oral Tradition.* New York: Cambridge University Press, 2006.
Kraemer, D. "The Mishnah." In *The Cambridge History of Judaism, Volume 4: The Late Roman-Rabbinic Period*, edited by Steven T. Katz, 299–315. Cambridge: Cambridge University Press, 2006.
Mandel, P. "The Tosefta." In vol. 4 of *The Cambridge History of Judaism: The Late Roman-Rabbinic Period*, edited by Steven T. Katz, 316–35. Cambridge: Cambridge University Press, 2006.

The Palestinian Talmud
Bokser, B. M. "An Annotated Bibliographical Guide to the Study of the Palestinian Talmud." In *Aufstieg und Niedergang der römischen Welt* 19.2, edited by H. Temporini and W. Haase, 139–256. Berlin: de Gruyter, 1979.
Moscovitz, L. "The Formation and Character of the Jerusalem Talmud." In vol. 4 of *The Cambridge History of Judaism: The Late Roman-Rabbinic Period*, edited by Steven T. Katz, 663–77. Cambridge: Cambridge University Press, 2006.

The Babylonian Talmud
Goodblatt, D. "The Babylonian Talmud." In *Aufstieg und Niedergang der römischen Welt* 19.2, edited by H. Temporini and W. Haase, 257–336. Berlin: de Gruyter, 1979.
Kalmin, R. L. "The Formation and Character of the Babylonian Talmud." In vol. 4 of *The Cambridge History of Judaism: The Late Roman-Rabbinic Period*, edited by Steven T. Katz, 840–76. Cambridge: Cambridge University Press, 2006.
Rubenstein, J. L. *Talmudic Stories: Narrative Art, Composition, and Culture*. Baltimore: Johns Hopkins University Press, 1999.
———. *Stories of the Babylonian Talmud*. Baltimore: Johns Hopkins University Press, 2010.

History and Culture of Babylonian Jewry
Gafni, I. "Babylonian Rabbinic Culture." In *Cultures of the Jews: A New History*, edited by D. Biale, 223–65. New York: Schocken, 2002.
———. "The Political, Social, and Economic History of Babylonian Jewry." In vol. 4 of *The Cambridge History of Judaism: The Late Roman-Rabbinic Period*, edited by Steven T. Katz, 792–820. Cambridge: Cambridge University Press, 2006.
Rubenstein, J. L. *The Culture of the Babylonian Talmud*. Baltimore: Johns Hopkins University Press, 2003.

3

Rabbinic Biblical Interpretation—Midrash

The rabbis' expansions on the Bible always take as their point of departure something in the verse that appeared problematic to them. Such problems could be anything from a textual detail—an unusual word, grammatical form, or spelling, a repetition, omission, or a contradiction between two verses—to wide-ranging theological problems caused by actions by the biblical characters or by God not in keeping with the moral code of the rabbis. For instance, the story of the sacrifice of Isaac in Genesis 22 raises the theologically difficult question of why a good and omniscient God would test Abraham by commanding him to kill his beloved son, Isaac, thus necessitating interpretation. A completely different kind of difficulty—but nevertheless one that needed to be addressed in the eyes of the rabbis—is the reality of the different rules for the preparation of the Passover lamb in Exodus and Deuteronomy. According to Deut. 16:7, it should be boiled, whereas Exod. 12:9 says that it should be roasted over fire, thus creating a contradiction that needed to be solved.

While a modern reader of the Bible may likewise be troubled by the theological problem raised by God's command to sacrifice Isaac, he or she is unlikely to be bothered by repetitions and contradictions between different parts of the Bible or by odd wordings and unusual spellings. Most modern readers would simply attribute these things to the fact that the Bible consists of a number of different sources that date from different time periods and to the change that language naturally undergoes over time.

ASSUMPTIONS ABOUT THE BIBLICAL TEXT

It is evident, then, that the difficulties perceived in the biblical text are dependent on the reader's understanding of the Bible and his or her expectations of it. In spite of the great variety of styles, genres, and interpretive methods of ancient biblical interpreters, a common approach nevertheless seems to underlie their interpretations and they seem to share a common set of assumptions about the biblical text, as observed and described by James Kugel. He identifies four fundamental assumptions about the Bible that underlie all ancient biblical interpretation. First, ancient exegetes seem to take for granted that the Bible is a fundamentally cryptic document, that is, they assume that behind the apparent meaning there is some hidden esoteric meaning. Even though it says X, what it really means is Y, or while Y is not openly stated, it is hinted at or implied in X. When Isaac says in Gen. 27:35 that Jacob "came with deceit" and took the blessing that rightly belonged to his brother Esau, it really means that he acted with wisdom (*Gen. Rab.* 67.4). The belief that it had been God's will all along that Jacob gain his father's blessing justifies Jacob's conduct since he was only doing what was necessary to carry out the divine plan. The same assumption that the Bible is a cryptic document allowed early Christian interpreters to claim that the suffering servant in Isaiah 52 alludes to Jesus.

The second assumption is that the Bible is a fundamentally relevant text. It is not primarily a book about Israel's ancient history but speaks to its readers' present situation and was written down for later generations to learn moral lessons from it. The patriarchs are held up as models of conduct, and their lives considered a source for inspiration. It is this view of the lives of the patriarchs as models of conduct that necessitated the reinterpretation of Jacob's taking of the blessing and his lying to his father. The idea that all of the Bible could be applied to the present made even prophecies and genealogies relevant to the rabbinic present.

The third assumption is that the Bible is perfect and perfectly harmonious. This means that it contains no mistakes (anything that might look as a mistake is only an illusion and will be clarified by proper interpretation) or inconsistencies between its various parts and that any biblical passage might illuminate any other. Taken to its extreme, the idea of the Bible as perfect led to the view that every detail of the text was significant. Nothing is said in vain or for rhetorical flourish and there is divine intention behind every detail. Accordingly, unusual words or grammatical forms, repetitions or omissions, and juxtapositions of one event to another were understood as potentially significant and deliberately placed there by God as an invitation to interpretation.

For instance, the fact that only Abraham is mentioned in Gen. 12:11, even though it is clear that he and Sarah were travelling together, calls for an explanation: "When he was about to enter Egypt, he said to his wife, Sarai, 'I know that you are a beautiful woman.'" Assuming that the Bible is perfect and that there is divine intention behind every detail, the verse should have read: When *they* were about to enter Egypt. Accordingly, the fact that only Abraham is mentioned led the rabbis to suggest that Abraham had hidden Sarah in a box (*Gen. Rab.* 40.5). Similarly, when the Israelites' departure from Egypt is mentioned for the third time in Exod. 32:11 in the passage about the sin with the Golden Calf, it cannot merely be a piece of information. Rather, Moses mentions it here in order to remind God that Israel has only recently left Egypt where calf worship is common, and accordingly he must understand that he cannot immediately expect impeccable behavior from the Israelites (*Exod. Rab.* 43.9). Ultimately, the perfect nature of the Bible also included the conduct of biblical heroes and the content of its teachings, so that they were assumed to be in accordance with the interpreter's own ideas and standards of conduct.

The fourth assumption is that the Bible in its entirety is divinely inspired: that is, not only the parts that contain divine speeches introduced with "And the Lord spoke to Moses, saying . . ." or prophecies, but also the parts that may appear to be of human fashioning, such as the intrigues in King David's court, or supplications directed to God, are actually divinely inspired. Even if Moses or King Solomon are said to be the authors of this or that biblical book, they are merely a human conduit of the divine word.

As a consequence of these assumptions, ancient biblical interpreters scrutinized every detail of the biblical text in search of hidden meaning. Any apparent contradiction, superfluous detail or repetition, any action by God or by a biblical hero not in accordance with the rabbis' expectations, were seen by them as an invitation from God to look deeper into the text and discover its true meaning intended by God.[1]

This common set of assumptions about the biblical text was not unique to the rabbis but shared by all ancient interpreters, including the Christians. If the Christian interpreters often reached different conclusions from

---

1. For the assumptions underlying ancient biblical exegesis, see Kugel, *Bible as It Was*, 1–36.

those of the rabbis this is because they were driven by a different set of anxieties. While the Jews were anxious to find evidence in the Bible that they remained God's chosen people in spite of Christian claims to the contrary, the Christians needed to defend their status as God's chosen people and demonstrate that the New Testament was the key to understanding the Hebrew Bible.[2]

The assumptions about the biblical text outlined above did not originate with the rabbis and Christian interpreters in the first centuries c.e. but underlie much of earlier interpretation as well. The oldest form of biblical interpretation is found within the Bible itself where biblical authors frequently revised earlier texts in order for them to remain relevant or better conform to the worldview of later times. A classic example is 1 and 2 Chronicles, whose author retells the books of Samuel and Kings and reshapes them by omitting some things and adding others. In a similar fashion, the author of Genesis 20 essentially retells the story of Abraham and Sarah in Egypt (Gen. 12:10-20), but places it in Gerar, removing or glossing over elements that seemed offensive to him. In chapter 12, for instance, Abraham asks Sara to lie and tell the Egyptians that she is his sister rather than his wife because he is afraid that they will otherwise kill him, a behavior not fitting a patriarch and a model of conduct. As a result, Sarah is "taken into Pharaoh's palace," and in return Abraham is given sheep, oxen, camels, and slaves. In chapter 20, by contrast, Sarah is saved from becoming the wife of the king of Gerar through direct intervention from God, who reveals to him that Sarah is Abraham's wife. To make sure nobody gets the wrong impression of Abraham, chapter 20 also adds that in addition to being Abraham's wife, Sarah was also his sister.

As with Chronicles, interpretation here takes the form of a retelling of a biblical story where elements perceived as troublesome or offensive are simply replaced, a practice that developed into a genre known as "rewritten" Bible. This practice can operate on the level of a single word, whereby a term whose meaning had shifted and was no longer widely understood is replaced by a more common word, or on the level of a whole phrase, whereby an ideologically problematic phrase such as "with deceit" as a description of Jacob's actions was replaced with the more acceptable "with wisdom." This practice of substitution or replacement rather than openly

---

2. Stern, "Midrash and Jewish Interpretation," 1863–75.

commenting on a biblical verse produces an interpretation that is barely discernable. Only someone who is very well acquainted with the Bible would recognize the somewhat odd expression in 2 Chron. 35:13, "They cooked the Passover lamb with fire," as a subtle harmonization of Exod. 12:9, stating that the Passover lamb should be roasted over fire, and Deut. 16:7, saying that it should be boiled.

Likewise, the passage from the *Wisdom of Solomon* (first or second century B.C.E.), "She [Wisdom] brought them over the Red Sea, and led them through the deep waters; but she drowned their enemies and cast them up from the depth of the sea," may be recognized as a harmonization of the contradiction created by the statement in Exod. 15:5, "They [Pharoh's army] went down into the depths like a stone," and Exod. 14:30, "Israel saw the Egyptians dead on the shore of the sea." Since both statements must be true, the *Wisdom of Solomon* explains that the Egyptians at first sank to the bottom of the sea and were then thrown back up on the shore.[3] Rabbinic interpretation of the Bible, however, only rarely took the form of such "rewritten Bible." Typically, the rabbis would compile interpretive comments and attach them to biblical verses in a way that made their comments easily distinguishable from the biblical verse.

The approach to the biblical text that produces these kinds of interpretations is often referred to as *midrash*, a word derived from the Hebrew root *darash* whose basic meaning is "to seek out" the will of God. In the early parts of the Bible, it is often used in the sense of asking God, or exploring his will through consulting Moses or a prophet (Gen. 25:22; Exod. 18:15). In later times, when prophecy was believed to have ceased,[4] there was a shift in focus to interpreting the text of the Bible, which was then considered the only place where God's will was to be found. In this broad sense of biblical interpretation, midrash includes pre-rabbinic interpretations (such as, for instance, the *Wisdom of Solomon*) as well as the early Aramaic translations of the Bible (targumim). In addition to interpretive activity, the term *midrash* also denotes the corpus in which these interpretations are preserved as well as the smallest interpretive unit in such a corpus.[5]

---

3. Kugel, *Bible as It Was*, 16–34. Translation from Kugel, *Bible as It Was*, 16.
4. According to the common rabbinic view, prophecy ceased after the last biblical prophets Haggai, Zechariah, and Malachi (*t. Sot.* 13:3; *y. Sot.* 9:13; *b. Sot.* 48b; *b. B. Batra* 14b; *S. Olam Rab.* 30.
5. Kugel, *Bible as It Was*, 1–36; Shinan and Zakovitch, "Midrash on Scripture," 257–77.

Textual Problems

Although biblical interpretation was by no means an invention of the rabbis, it reached its peak during the rabbinic period. Rabbinic biblical interpretation often goes beyond the simplest solutions to the difficulties perceived in the biblical text and commonly involves the reconstruction of events and conversations between biblical characters. For instance, literally translated, Gen. 4:8 reads: "Cain said to his brother Abel . . . and when they were in the field, Cain set upon his brother Abel and killed him," an odd wording that suggests something is missing. What Cain said to Abel is somehow omitted, and assuming that the text was deliberately fashioned in this way to invite interpretation, the rabbis reconstructed the omitted conversation, explaining the reason for Abel's murder by suggesting that a quarrel between the brothers preceded it:

> *Cain set upon his brother Abel [and killed him]* [Gen. 4:8]. About what did they quarrel? "Come," said they, "let us divide the world." One took the land and the other the movables. The former said: "The land you stand on is mine," while the other retorted: "What you are wearing is mine!" One said: "Strip!" the other retorted: "Fly" [off the ground]. Out of this quarrel *Cain set upon his brother* . . . Rabbi Joshua of Siknin said in Rabbi Levi's name: Both took land and both took movables, so what did they quarrel about? One said: "The temple must be built in my area," while the other claimed: "It must be built in mine!" For it is written, *And when they were in the field* [Gen. 4:8]. Now, "field" refers to the Temple, as you read, *Zion* [that is, the temple] *shall be plowed as a field* [Micah 3:12]. Out of this argument *Cain set upon his brother* . . . Judah b. Rabbi said: Their quarrel was about the first Eve. Rabbi Aibu said: The first Eve had returned to dust, so what, then, was their quarrel about? Rabbi Huna said: An additional twin was born with Abel, and each claimed her. The one claimed: "I will have her, because I am the firstborn," while the other maintained: "I must have her, because she was born with me."[6]

At first glance, the suggestion that Cain and Abel quarreled over the temple—which did not yet exist in their time—may seem naïve, but because the rabbis were mainly interested in the timeless truths and moral lessons that could be drawn from the biblical text, they did not shy away from

---

6. *Gen. Rab.* 22.7.

blatant anachronisms. They also tend to employ very specific examples, and sometimes it is necessary to translate them into more general categories in order to make sense of them. If "land and movables" is taken to represent property in general, the temple as symbolizing power or career, and "the first Eve" as women in general, their suggestions appear less naïve and even insightful. Being common, timeless issues of contention between people, a quarrel over them appears as an altogether plausible reason behind the murder of Abel.

Fig. 5. Details of a page from the Biblia Hebraica. Photograph by Anders Runesson.

Theological Problems

At other times, the biblical text raised problems of a theological nature precipitating interpretation. For instance, in the story about Cain and Abel in Gen. 4:1-10, God accepts Abel's sacrifice but rejects Cain's for no obvious reason, making God appear arbitrary or outright unjust. This difficulty provoked various interpretations, some of which attempt to justify God while others do not hesitate to criticize him. Focusing on a slight difference in wording in the Bible's description of their respective sacrifices in Gen. 4:3-4, the rabbis suggest that Cain's sacrifice was indeed inferior to Abel's, because it says that Abel sacrificed the "choicest of the firstlings of his flock"(Gen. 4:4) whereas Cain simply offered a sacrifice. "Cain brought an offering to the Lord," obviously not bothering to give the best to God. As a consequence, God's rejection of Cain's sacrifice was neither arbitrary nor unjust but completely justified.[7] Another interpretation, however, does not shy away from the idea that God shares the responsibility for Abel's death:

> When the Holy One, blessed be He, asked Cain: *"Where is your brother Abel?"* He said: *"I do not know. Am I my brother's keeper?* [Gen. 4:9]. You are the one who watches over all living beings, and you ask this of me!" This can be compared to a thief who stole things at night and got away. In the morning the gatekeeper caught him and asked: "Why did you steal these things?" The thief replied: "I stole but I did not neglect my job. But you whose job it is to keep watch at the gate, why did you neglect your job? And now, you speak to me like this!" Similarly, Cain said: "Yes, I killed him, but you created the evil inclination in me. You are the keeper of everything and yet you let me kill him! It is you who killed him, for had you accepted my sacrifice as you accepted his, I would not have been jealeous of him."[8]

Rather than defending God's actions by claiming that Cain's sacrifice was of inferior quality, the rabbis, through a parable, play with the idea that God is to blame for Abel's death. In order to shift the blame away from himself to God, Cain advances three arguments: First, God created the evil inclination, making him ultimately responsible for all evil actions that humans do; second, he did not prevent him from killing his brother; and third, he bears responsibility for the conflict between the brothers because he accepted the sacrifice of one but not of the other.

Cain argues cleverly and may at first sight appear to have a point, but by comparing him to a thief the author of the parable hints at a flaw in his logic. A criminal can hardly be excused by arguing that he is a skilled criminal, and his argument that the watchman alone is responsible for everything that happens does not hold up either. Relieving all the city's inhabitants of any responsibility whatsoever and placing it all on the gatekeeper is not reasonable. Each individual person cannot do whatever he feels like doing and then argue that he is blameless because the gatekeeper did not prevent him from doing what he did. To argue that the world

---

7. *Gen. Rab.* 22.5.
8. *Tanh. Bereshit* 9. My translation.

would have been better had God created humans without an inclination to do evil may have some validity as a philosophical argument, but given our existence as it is, humans must accept responsibility for their actions. Nevertheless, Cain's arguments seem to reflect doubts on the part of the author of the parable, and the claim that God is to blame—because his rejection of Cain's sacrifice made Cain feel rejected and angry—remains unanswered. The parable is ambiguous, struggling with the problem of human evil and divine responsibility rather than giving a clear-cut answer.[9]

A similar, even-more-daring example, which illustrates that the rabbis did not hesitate to criticize God, is the parable about the two athletes wrestling before the king:

> *The Lord said to Cain, "Where is your brother Abel?"* [Gen. 4:9]. It is difficult to say this and it is impossible to utter it plainly. It can be compared to two athletes wrestling before the king. Had the king wished, he could have separated them, but he did not and one overcame the other and killed him. The dying man cried: "Let my cause be pleaded before the king!" Similarly, *the voice of your brother's blood cries out against Me from the ground!"* [Gen. 4:10].[10]

Instead of reading Gen. 4:10 as God's reproach against Cain, the Hebrew preposition *'elai,* "to me" is read as *'alai,* "against me" (replacing the Hebrew letter *alef* with *ayin*), transforming it into an accusation against God, "your brother's blood cries out *against* me [God] from the ground!"

Another interpretation evolves around the peculiar fact that the word "blood" and the verb "cry" that goes with it appear in the plural, "your brother's bloods are crying" (*qol deme ahikha tsoaqim*). Since "blood" does not usually appear in the plural in Hebrew, the rabbis felt the need to explain it and suggest that the verse does not refer only to Abel's blood but also to the descendants he would never have:

> Rabbi Judan, Rabbi Huna and the [other] rabbis commented [on the plural form]: Rabbi Judan said: It is not written, "your brother's blood [sing.] [*dam 'ahikha*], but your brother's bloods [plur.] [*deme 'ahikha*], that is, his blood and the blood of his descendants."[11]

---

9. See Holtz, "Midrash," 194–97.
10. *Gen. Rab.* 22.10. In Soncino's English translation it appears in 22.9.
11. *Gen. Rab.* 22.9.

According to this interpretation, Cain may be considered guilty of murdering not only Abel but also the descendants that the latter never would have.

Another example of a theological difficulty is the problem raised by God's decision to test Abraham in Gen 22:1. That God would test the righteous Abraham by commanding him to sacrifice his beloved son, Isaac, seemed cruel and offensive to the rabbis who were convinced that God was both good and omniscient. Since God would know in advance how Abraham would act, there was no need for such a cruel test, a test that also involves the innocent Isaac. Accordingly, some of the rabbinic explanations of this passage claim that the intention of the test was not to prove to God that Abraham would obey, but to demonstrate to others Abraham's obedience and loyalty.[12] According to others, the test was caused by Satan's insinuation that Abraham loved his son more than he loved God, thus making it necessary for God to test Abraham in order to refute Satan's slander.[13]

However, in most rabbinic interpretations of the story, it is not Abraham but Isaac who is the hero of the story and the one to provoke the test. The phrase that introduces the story, "After these things, God tested Abraham," can also be taken to mean "after these words," providing the rabbis with the opportunity to introduce another quarrel, this time between Abraham's sons, Isaac and Ishmael. The brothers brag and both try to portray themselves as the one most beloved by God:

> Isaac and Ishmael were engaged in a controversy: the latter argued: "I am more beloved than you, because I was circumcised at the age of thirteen," while the other retorted, "I am more beloved than you, because I was circumcised at eight days." Said Ishmael to him: "I am more beloved, because I could have protested, yet did not." At that moment Isaac exclaimed: "O that God would appear to me and ask me to cut off one of my limbs! Then I would not refuse." Said God: "Even if I ask you to sacrifice yourself, you will not refuse."[14]

According to this interpretation, God initiates the test in direct response to Isaac's words, thus solving or at least mitigating the problem of why a good and omniscient God would demand such a horrible sacrifice.

---

12. *Gen. Rab.* 55.1.
13. *b. Sanh.* 89b.
14. *Gen. Rab.* 55.4. See also *Targ. Ps.-J.* Gen 22.1.

Exegesis or Ideology?

One may legitimately ask whether these interpretations really evolved in response to difficulties in the biblical text, or whether they were rather generated by some outside concerns. Indeed, earlier scholarship on rabbinic midrash tended to focus precisely on its ideological side, assuming that the interpretations were generated by the rabbis' political views or political agenda, or regarding it as bits of free-floating popular folklore that had more or less randomly been attached to a given biblical verse. Jacob Neusner, for instance, views rabbinic interpretation as wholly dictated by ideology with the biblical verse merely serving as a pretext. His approach to midrash as a source for the reconstruction of the development of rabbinic Judaism makes him focus on the redaction of each midrashic collection and the ideology and worldview that they in his opinion reveal, largely ignoring the interpretive aspects.[15]

In recent years, however, increasing attention has been given to the exegetical nature of midrash, leading to the view that rabbinic interpretations are indeed the outcome of the rabbis' grappling with the biblical text. This approach is influenced by insights from modern literary theory, according to which meaning of a text is established in the encounter between text and reader, and is at least in part due to the encounter between midrash and modern literary theory that occurred as a result of an increasing interest in midrash as the subject of university studies in the 1980s. Literary theorists describe literary works as consisting of bits and fragments that are pieced together in the process of reading whereby the reader, consciously or unconsciously, fills in any implicit or missing detail about an event, motive, or causal connection.[16] Such filling in of gaps perceived in the text ranges from an automatic filling in of small details, which are obvious from the context, to adding more complex lines of argument based on information from other parts of the story. If modern texts contain gaps, it is all the more true of the biblical text that was composed by many different authors over a long period of time.[17]

Inspired by this insight, an increasing number of scholars of midrash argue that rabbinic interpretations were generated by interaction between

---

15. Neusner, *Comparative Midrash*; Neusner, *Judaism and Scripture*; Neusner, *Midrash in Context*.
16. Fish, *Text*; Iser, *Act of Reading*.
17. Sternberg, *Poetics of Biblical Narrative*.

the biblical text and the rabbinic reader with a specific set of assumptions about the Bible. While not denying the role of ideological, theological, and political factors in generating biblical interpretation, midrash was increasingly understood to be the outcome of the rabbis' attempts to make sense of the biblical text and to fill in gaps that they perceived in the text.[18] The material with which the rabbis filled the gaps derives from other parts of the Bible and from the rabbis' own experiences, background, and worldview, their "ideological code," in Daniel Boyarin's words.

Thus, the rabbis' experience told them that conflicts between people often concern property, power, and women, so in response to the gap in Gen 4:8 they constructed an argument between Cain and Abel over these things, supplying the information that seems to be missing from the biblical text. In a similar process, the attempt to solve the theological problems that the rabbis perceived in Genesis 22, together with close attention to the details of the biblical text, produced the idea that God's commandment to sacrifice Isaac was the result of a provocation from Isaac. Because of their belief that God was good and omniscient, the rabbis found his commandment to sacrifice Isaac offensive, and in the introduction to the story, "it happened after these things," they found an irregularity that hinted at the problem's solution. Reading with the assumption that every detail is significant, the phrase, "after these things," may appear somewhat odd and one may wonder, after which things? The phrase could be understood to refer back to the events described in the previous chapter, but the Hebrew word for "thing" (*davar*) can also mean "word," and from this sense the idea of a quarrel between Isaac and Ishmael arose, giving a rationale for the test while exonerating God.

At other times, the rabbis used material from other parts of the Bible to solve difficulties that they perceived in the biblical text, letting verses from different parts of the Bible shed light on one another. For instance, the idea that Laban was an archenemy of Israel who attempted to kill Jacob, expressed in a large number of midrashim and targumim,[19] but perhaps best known from the Passover Haggadah, is very likely the outcome of such an intertextual reading where a number of verses from different parts of the Bible were juxtaposed: "Go and learn what Laban the Aramean

---

18. Boyarin, *Intertextuality*; Fraade, *Tradition*; Kugel, *Potiphar's House*; Kugel, *Bible as It Was*; Stern, *Midrash and Theory*.
19. Targs. *Onq; Neof; Neof* (marg.); *Ps.-J.*; *Sifre; Midr. Tannaim* on Deut 26:5; *Tanh.* Eqev 5 (ed. Buber); *Midr. Psalms* 30.4.

attempted to do to our father Jacob! Pharaoh decreed only against the males but Laban attempted to uproot everything, as it is said, *An Aramean destroyed my father. Then he went down to Egypt"* [Deut. 26:5]. Modern Bible translations usually render the quote from Deut. 26:5, "My father was a wandering Aramean," but the Haggadah and all targumim and early midrashim understand it to mean that Laban attempted to kill Jacob. While the phrase *'arami 'oved 'avi* could grammatically be taken to mean "an Aramean destroyed my father," it is hardly the sense that immediately comes to mind and it certainly does not fit the context of Deut. 26:5. Very likely, this understanding is also, at least in part, generated by a problem perceived in the biblical text. Given that it is Laban who is elsewhere known as an "Aramean" (Gen. 25:20, 31:20, 31:24)—in fact he is the best-known Aramean in the Bible—the rabbis probably found the designation of Jacob as an Aramean odd and the epithet better suited for Laban. Once "Aramean" was connected to Laban and the phrase understood to mean that an Aramean attempted to destroy Jacob, the rabbis likely found hints to Laban's evil intentions in the story about Jacob's flight from Haran: "So he [Laban] took his kinsmen with him and pursued him a distance of seven days, catching up with him in the hill country of Gilead. But God appeared to Laban the Aramean in a dream by night and said to him, 'Beware of attempting anything with Jacob, good or bad.' Laban overtook Jacob . . ." (Gen. 31:23-25). The words for "catching up" and "overtake" have hostile connotations in biblical Hebrew, and a reading of these verses in conjunction with Deut. 26:5 likely generated the idea that Laban attempted to kill Jacob, and by extension, all of Israel. Such a reading of Deut. 26:5 and Gen. 31:23-25 in light of each other is evidenced in two late midrashim,[20] but seems to underlie the earlier targums and midrashim as well.[21]

Granted that the rabbis found difficulties in the biblical text due to an underlying ideology or assumptions about the biblical text, their understanding of the biblical text very likely also affected their ideology and theology. Thus, rather than regarding rabbinic biblical interpretation as a reflection of an already existing ideology, it should be seen as the outcome of a dialogue between text and reader conditioned by the prevailing assumptions of the rabbinic reader. If this reading seems strange or far-fetched to us, that is because we do not share the exegetical assumptions of the rabbis.

---

20. *Agg. Ber.* ch. 53 [54], p. 108; *Midr. ha-Gadol* to Gen 31:22-23, p. 549.
21. Hedner–Zetterholm, *Portrait*, 47–87.

Midrash, says Boyarin, is the "product of a disturbed exegetical sense" only if we recognize that all exegetical senses are disturbed, including our own.[22] While most rabbinic interpretations clearly evolve around a difficulty in the biblical text, the connection to problems becomes less evident in later midrashic collections where the interpreter sometimes betrays signs of first having thought of an exposition and then having gone looking for a verse to attach it to. Kugel describes the development in the following way: "[T]he text's irregularity is the grain of sand which so irritates the midrashic oyster that he constructs a pearl around it. Soon enough—pearls being prized—midrashists begin looking for irritations and irregularities, and in later midrash there is much material, especially list-making and text-connecting, whose connection with 'problems' is remote indeed; in fact, like many a modern-day homilist, the midrashist sometimes betrays signs of having first thought of a solution and then having gone out in search of a problem to which it might be applied."[23] Nevertheless, the best starting point when reading ancient biblical interpretations is to first attempt to find the problem that bothered the ancient interpreters. Only when that difficulty is identified are we likely to comprehend the interpretation.

At times, rabbinic interpretations appear very strained and one may wonder whether they believed that the biblical text really meant what they asserted it to mean. In order to explain away Jacob's lie in Gen. 27:19, where he claims to be the first-born in order to secure for himself the blessing that rightly belongs to Esau, the rabbis engage in what would seem to be a rather far-fetched and creative exegesis. Exploiting the fact that the biblical text had no punctuation or capital letters, as well as the fact that the verb "to be" is frequently omitted in biblical Hebrew, they reinterpreted Isaac's question and Jacob's response in Gen. 27:18-19: "Who are you, my son?" "I am Esau, your firstborn," to mean: "Who are you? My son? "I am. [But] Esau is your firstborn."[24]

It is obvious that this interpretation is meant to excuse Jacob and improve his image. To a modern reader, this reading appears as an outright manipulation of the biblical text, and one may wonder if the rabbis really believed that the biblical text meant what they claimed it meant. There is often a certain playfulness to midrash, and it is evident that the rabbis

---

22. Boyarin, *Intertextuality*, 18.
23. Kugel, "Two Introductions," 92.
24. *Jub.* 26:13–19; *Tanh.* Toledot 10 (ed. Buber); *Leq. Tov* Gen. 27:19 and Kugel, *Bible as It Was*, 208–14.

were aware that the biblical text on the surface at times meant something else than what they made it out to mean through their interpretations. On a deeper level, though, they believed that the meaning they found in the biblical text was the true one—the one that God had intended. In the view of the rabbis, it would be unthinkable for God to give the blessing to the wrong person, and for Isaac to be unaware to whom he gave his blessing. They believed that the entire story about Jacob's deceit and Isaac's credulity only took place on a superficial level and that God had deliberately designed the story in this way, hinting by means of irregularities in the text that interpretation was in order to disclose the true meaning of the text. The ultimate purpose of biblical interpretation, then, was to reveal the true meaning, hidden under the surface of the biblical text.[25]

PARABLES AS BIBLICAL INTERPRETATION

One tool with which the rabbis discovered hidden meanings in the biblical text was parables: "Do not treat the *mashal* [parable] lightly," they said, "for by means of a *mashal* a person is able to understand the words of Torah."[26] Although there are different kinds of parables, the vast majority of rabbinic parables are preserved in exegetical contexts and serve as tools for scriptural exegesis. Through such fictional narratives the rabbis contemplated the relationship between God and Israel, attempting to make sense of God's actions and Israel's situation. "Beyond all else," says David Stern, a renowned scholar on rabbinic parables, "the mashal [parable] represents the greatest effort to imagine God in all Rabbinic literature."[27] Typically, the parables are ambiguous, suggesting ideas rather than presenting clear-cut answers.

A parable, or *mashal* in Hebrew, usually consists of two parts: a short fictional narrative introduced with the phrase "This may be compared to," followed by a *nimshal*, the situation that the parable attempts to illustrate, typically introduced with the word "thus" or "similarly." The *nimshal* is possibly a secondary feature, a replacement for the real-life situation in

25. Kugel, *Bible as It Was*, 209–10; Stern, "Midrash and Jewish Interpretation," 1871. For general surveys on midrash, see Elman, "Classical Rabbinic Interpretation," 1844–63; Holtz, "Midrash," 177–214; Stern, "Midrash and Jewish Interpretation," 1863–75.
26. *Songs Rab.* 1:8.
27. Stern, *Parables in Midrash*, 93.

which the parable was originally told (the way in which the Gospels generally depict the parables of Jesus), added when the parable was later transmitted orally or committed to writing. In the exegetical settings where most rabbinic parables appear, the *nimshal* gives the audience the information required in order to understand the parable.

The *mashal* and *nimshal* interact and together form a message. Most rabbinic parables contain a point of discontinuity—an unexpected, unexplained, or peculiar element, something that violates the audience's expectations as to human behavior, either in the psychological, social, or religious realm—and in this irregularity the key to the parable's message should be sought. Such points of discontinuity may be a missing link in a series of events, a missing cause or motive for a character's action, a failure to offer reasonable explanations for an occurrence in the story, a contradiction in the text that challenges the audience's understanding of the story, an unexplained departure from accepted norms, or a discrepancy between the *mashal* and the *nimshal*.

In the majority of parables, God is portrayed as a king and Israel as his wife, son or servant. This pertains even though many of these parables have nothing intrinsically royal about them; it is the result of a stereotyping of parables, assimilating them to the literary form of a king-*mashal*. Through this process, an anonymous man or father would be transformed into a king without any change to the parable's plot or meaning. The king in the king-*mashal* is modeled upon the Roman emperor or his procurator or proconsul in the land of Israel, and although the parables are fictional narratives constructed to shed light on a biblical verse, they nevertheless reflect the realities of everyday life of their authors/redactors in the land of Israel.

Since the parables focus on the relationship to God, it is not surprising that the only character in the parable to consistently possess a personality is the king. All other figures are stock characters with little psychological or emotional depth whose behavior is usually predictable or easily explained. The choice of motif for each parable is important for the message, however, since they highlight different aspects of the relationship between God and Israel. For instance, the relationship between a man and his wife is different from that between a man and his son or between a man and his servant, thus making the choice of motif integral to the message of the parable.[28]

---

28. Stern, *Parables in Midrash*, 16–24, 74–79, 93–97.

Below is a parable from *Lamentations Rabbah*, illustrating some of these features. *Lamentations Rabbah*, redacted in the fifth century, is largely preoccupied with the destruction of the temple, applying the complaints and laments over the destruction of the first temple in the book of Lamentations to the destruction of the second temple. The book of Lamentations is still read on the ninth of the Hebrew month of *Av*, in commemoration of the destruction of both the first and the second temples. Understood as a punishment for Israel's sins, it seems way out of proportion to those sins, this parable seems to claim. The people of Israel have tried to the best of their ability to observe the Torah, and God's treatment of them can be compared to an unpredictable king who treats his wife unfairly.

[*When they heard how I was sighing, there was none to comfort me; all my foes heard of my plight and exulted.*] *For You have done it* [Lam. 1:21]. Rabbi Levi said: It is like a consort to whom the king said: Do not lend anything to your neighbors, and do not borrow anything from them. One time the king became angry at her and drove her out of the palace. She went about to all her neighbors, but none of them received her, so she returned to the palace. The king said to her: "You have acted impudently." She said to him: "You are the one who has done it! Because you told me: Do not lend anything to your neighbors, and do not borrow anything from them. If I had lent them an article or borrowed one from them, and if one of them had seen me outside of her home, would she not have received me?" Similarly at the time [following the destruction], the gentile nations went everywhere the Israelites fled and blocked them [from fleeing]: in the east, in the west, in the north, and in the south . . . The Holy One, blessed be He, said to Israel: You have acted impudently! Israel said before the Holy One, blessed be He: "But have You not done it?! For You told us: *You shall not intermarry with them: do not give your daughters to their sons or take their daughters for your sons* [Deut. 7:3]. If we had married our daughters to their sons, or taken their daughters for our sons, and one of them had seen their daughter or their son with us, would they not have received us?" That is [the meaning of], *For You have done it.*[29]

The king, of course, represents God, his wife Israel, and the prohibition of lending to and borrowing from the neighbors stands for the prohibition

---

29. *Lam. Rab.* 1.56. Translation from Stern, *Parables in Midrash*, 79–80, based on the Ashkenazic recension.

for Israel to intermarry with her non-Jewish neighbors. When told in the parable form, however, this prohibition as well as the king's behavior is decidedly odd. For no good reason he prohibits his wife from interacting with their neighbors, thus violating regular accepted norms. Husbands do not usually prohibit their wives from borrowing or lending things from the neighbors; on the contrary, there is a halakhic tradition saying that a wife whose husband does so has the right to ask for a divorce, since such a prohibition will cause her to be disliked by her neighbors:

> If a man places his wife under a vow not to lend or not to borrow a sieve, a
> basket, a millstone, or an oven, he must divorce her and give her ketubah
> to her because he causes her to have a bad name among her neighbors.[30]

The king's unpredictable nature is further emphasized by his sudden anger and decision to drive his wife from the palace. Since no reason is given for these actions either, he appears cruel and despotic. His wife has obviously not defied his prohibition—evident from the fact that the neighbors refuse to take her in—so disobedience on her part cannot be the reason for his anger. The king bans her from the palace, but does not divorce her, thus placing her in a very difficult situation. He seemingly does not want to have anything to do with her, but she is still bound by marriage to him, dependent on him, and cannot remarry. There is a complete breakdown in communication; she does not understand what he wants from her and he makes no attempt to explain or talk to her at all. The parable is told from the wife's perspective, making the audience sympathize with her.

In this parable, the interpreters grapple with God's seemingly unfair and cruel treatment of Israel. In the parable, the wife's predicament is the direct result of her faithful obedience to the king's unreasonable decrees, and similarly, the narrative seems to say, Israel is now exiled and pursued by enemies precisely because she has obeyed the Torah's laws. Indeed, God acts contrary to his own laws when he prohibits Israel to intermarry with her neighbors, condemning her to isolation and persecution. Although the laws in the Torah cannot strictly speaking be against the law since they *are* the law, God nevertheless appears to act against the spirit of his own law, if not against the letter. "For you have done it!" Israel laments, decontextualizing the biblical verse and transforming it

---

30. *b. Ket.* 72a.

into an angry accusation of God's tyrannical actions. Accordingly, the parable's message appears to be clear: God has behaved with obvious injustice toward Israel. He has acted against the spirit of his own law, and all the while Israel has faithfully obeyed his law, and suffered precisely on account of her faithful obedience.[31]

However, a peculiar detail in the parable may hint at a somewhat different understanding or at least a double meaning. The complete lack of understanding and communication between the king and his wife is somewhat odd and surely not the norm in a marriage. If applied to the relationship between God and Israel, it could be taken to indicate a total breakdown in communication between God and Israel and a lack of understanding between them, causing Israel to misinterpret God's actions. The common understanding of the destruction of the temple and the exile is that they are a punishment for Israel's sins, but as such they appear unjust, or at least vastly out of proportion. However, if this is a misinterpretation of God's actions, and if the destruction of the temple and the exile are not a punishment but rather the inevitable outcome of living in a covenantal relationship with the God of Israel, the entire situation changes. By portraying the king and his wife as being bound to one another in such an abnormal relationship, the author of the parable may hint that rather than being understood as a punishment, Israel's misfortunes is a consequence of being singled out as God's people. Her difficulties can be understood as a test that she fails, but not because of any disobedience on her part but simply because she does not understand that being God's people means isolation and occasionally persecution from the non-Jewish peoples around her. If this is the case, God is surely to blame because he has not made any attempt to communicate with Israel and explain to her the reason for her misfortunes, but Israel shares a little of the blame too for accusing God of injustice rather than attempting to understand him and the nature of their relationship.[32]

MIDRASH AND RABBINIC LAW

After having discussed interpretation of non-legal (aggadic) texts, we will now turn to interpretation of legal (halakhic) ones. As with interpretation

---

31. Stern, *Parables in Midrash*, 79–82.
32. Fraenkel, *Darkhe haaggadah*, 329–47.

of aggadic texts, legal exegesis also takes as its point of departure irregularities in the biblical text, such as contradictions, unnecessary words, or repetitions.

In the example below, the well-known Jewish custom not to mix meat and milk is presented as a result of interpretation of Exod. 23:19, "You shall not boil a kid it its mother's milk":

> Abba Hanin said in the name of R. Eliezer: Why is this law stated in three places? [Exod. 23:19, 34:26; Deut. 14:21]. Once to apply to large cattle, once to apply to goats, and once to apply to sheep ... R. Shimon ben Yohai says: Why is this law stated in three places? One is a prohibition against eating it [milk and meat together], one is a prohibition against deriving any benefit from it, and one is a prohibition against the mere cooking of it [milk and meat together].[33]

Based on the multiple occurrences of the injunction to boil a kid in its mother's milk, Abba Hanin extends the prohibition to include cooking other animals' offspring in their mothers' milk too. Based on the same repetition of the verse, R. Shimon ben Yohai extends the prohibition from cooking milk and meat together to eating it and deriving benefit from it, for instance, by selling meat and milk cooked together. According to this text, the custom of not mixing meat and milk originated in a rabbinic attempt to make sense of the repetition of the prohibition to boil a kid in its mother's milk, but one cannot help but wonder whether this exegesis rather serves to anchor an already existing custom in the biblical text.[34]

By contrast, other laws are not presented as being the result of exegesis, but simply seem to rest on rabbinic authority. Such is, for instance, the case with the laws of the Sabbath as stated in the Mishnah where the meaning of the word "work" is defined as encompassing thirty-nine categories of activities with no references to the biblical text (m. Shabb. 7:2). The fact that the Mishnah merely lists the different kinds of work forbidden on the Sabbath with no references to biblical verses suggests that the development of these prohibitions occurred independently of the biblical text. Although the Talmud (b. Shabb. 49b) links them to biblical passages by making a point of the fact that two occurrences of the Sabbath commandment

---

33. Mekh. R. Ishmael Kaspa 5 (Lauterbach, 3:187–90).
34. Stern, "Midrash and Jewish Interpretation," 1867–68.

(Exod. 31:12-17 and 35:1-3) are directly connected to the description of the building of the Tabernacle in the desert, and thus concludes that "work" includes all activities connected to the building of the Tabernacle, this seems to be a later development.[35]

Thus, there are two ways in which rabbinic laws are preserved: independently of biblical verses as in the Mishnah, and in connection with biblical verses as in midrash. In the case of the Mishnah, the laws are based on rabbinic authority rather than on the Bible, whereas in the case of midrash it is the fact that they are derived from the Bible that gives them authority. It also seems that laws originated in these two ways: as extra-textual traditions on the one hand and as a consequence of biblical interpretation on the other. Which one of these is the main source of rabbinic laws is a hotly debated issue among scholars and it recalls the scholarly debate on how much of rabbinic expansions derives from exegesis of the biblical text and how much is generated by outside non-textual concerns, such as ideology and theology, in the case of non-legal texts. In the case of rabbinic law, scholars take similar positions, some arguing that most laws originated as extra-biblical traditions that were only later connected to a biblical verse in order to anchor an already existing custom in the Bible, while others maintain that rabbinic laws were primarily derived through exegesis of the biblical text. Yet others suggest that that the methods coexisted, perhaps represented by different schools.[36]

Given the interaction between the biblical text and ideological assumptions of the rabbinic reader in the production of midrash aggadah, it appears likely that a similar process was at work in the realm of halakhah, so that rabbinic laws developed both as a result of an understanding of the biblical text and independently of it in response to outside concerns. The claim that the two methods were contemporary and existed side by side has received support in the recent scholarship of Azzan Yadin, who has argued that the fact that tannaitic literature contains two distinct approaches to rabbinic law, one giving priority to midrash and the other to traditions

---

35. Safrai, "Halakha," 156–57. Further examples of legal exegesis are found in Harris, "Midrash Halachah," 336–68.
36. In the early twentieth century, the question was debated by two of the most influential rabbinic scholars in Israel, J. N. Epstein and Ch. Albeck. Epstein argued that laws based on midrash were secondary to extra-biblical traditions, while Albeck held that biblical interpretation was the principal source of rabbinic laws. See Harris, "Midrash Halachah," 348–60; Safrai, "Halakha," 146–63. For a brief survey of the debate, see Halivni, *Midrash*, 18–21.

independent of the biblical text, indicates that these two approaches were contemporary and represented by different schools.[37]

Thus, common to all ancient Jewish biblical interpretation, whether applied to legal or non-legal texts, is a set of particular assumptions about the biblical text and a non-contextual approach. Verses are typically interpreted without any regard for the biblical context in which they appear and any verse is considered able to illuminate any other verse. This mode of interpretation continued until the medieval period when it gave way to a more context-oriented approach as a consequence of a shift in assumptions about the biblical text.

COLLECTIONS OF MIDRASH

Rabbinic biblical interpretations were transmitted orally over a long period of time before they were compiled and written down. They were eventually collected into compilations, which include many different, sometimes contradictory interpretations that are placed side by side. The earliest collections of midrash consist of *Mekhilta de-Rabbi Ishmael* and *Mekhilta de-Rabbi Shimon bar Yohai* to Exodus, *Sifra* to Leviticus, *Sifre* to Numbers, and *Sifre* to Deuteronomy. The main bulk of their content dates from the tannaitic period but they were probably redacted at the beginning of the amoraic period.

The tannaitic midrashim fall into two groups based on differences concerning rabbis cited, interpretive terminology and characteristic hermeneutic practices. These two groups have for a long time been associated with the schools of Rabbi Aqiva and Rabbi Ishmael respectively and, as Yadin has recently demonstrated, these differences remain irrespective of whether they can be traced back to the historic figures of Rabbi Aqiva and Rabbi Ishmael. Accordingly, the terms "Rabbi Ishmael midrashim" and "Rabbi Aqiva midrashim" function as a shorthand for a set of distinct and recognizable interpretive practices, assumptions, and terms that appear in the halakhic sections of the tannaitic collections of midrash.

The group of midrashim associated with the school of Rabbi Ishmael is made up of *Mekhilta de-Rabbi Ishmael* (to Exodus) and *Sifre* (to Numbers), while *Sifra* (to Leviticus) and *Sifre* (to Deuteronomy) make up the

---

37. Yadin, "Resistance to Midrash," 35–58.

subgroup associated with Rabbi Aqiva. According to this division, the less known *Mekhilta de-Rabbi Shimon bar Yohai* would be the Rabbi Aqiva school counterpart to the better known *Mekhilta de-Rabbi Ishmael*. The Rabbi Ishmael midrashim generally show a greater interpretive restraint than the Rabbi Aqiva midrashim and seem to consider only particular kinds of textual irregularities to be legitimate targets for interpretation. They also take into consideration the broader biblical context and do not seem to subscribe to the idea that scriptural verses can bear multiple interpretations. Of these, the approach associated with Rabbi Aqiva, according to which every letter of the biblical text can be subject to interpretation, has become the one generally associated with midrash since it is the one that has influenced all subsequent rabbinic literature.[38]

Tannaitic midrashim

School of R. Ishmael		School of R. Aqiva
Mekhilta de-Rabbi Ishmael	*Exodus*	Mekhilta de-Rabbi Shimon bar Yohai
	Leviticus	Sifra
Sifre (to Numbers)	*Numbers*	
	Deuteronomy	Sifre (to Deuteronomy)

The compilations of midrash from the amoraic and post-amoraic periods are numerous, and space permits only the most important ones to be mentioned here.[39] The classic compilations of midrash from the amoraic period include *Genesis, Leviticus,* and *Lamentations Rabbah* and *Pesiqta de-Rav Kahana,* likely compiled during the fifth century, *Genesis Rabbah*

---

38. Yadin, *Scripture as Logos*, xi–xii, 48–79.
39. For detailed information about the compilations of midrash, see Stemberger, *Introduction*, 233–359.

first and the others somewhat later. *Genesis Rabbah* and *Lamentations Rabbah* are verse-by-verse commentaries belonging to the group known as exegetical midrashim. *Leviticus Rabbah* and *Pesiqta de-Rav Kahana* belong to the group known as homiletical midrashim because they are believed to have originated as sermons for the Sabbath or other holy days. They take as their point of departure some of the verses (usually the first) of the weekly portion read in the synagogue and develop a sermon based on them.

Midrash Tanhuma is a homiletic midrash to the Pentateuch that exists in two different textual recensions, one known simply as the printed version and the other as the Buber version since it was published by Salomon Buber. The two versions differ greatly in their commentaries on Genesis and Exodus, but are very similar in their comments on the three remaining parts of the Pentateuch. Buber's version probably represents an Ashkenazi (northern European) tradition. While some scholars date *Midrash Tanhuma* to the first half of the ninth century, others date the main bulk of the contents to the fifth century, with reservation for possible later additions. Some of the material in *Midrash Tanhuma* is also found in the midrashim

Amoraic and Post-Amoraic Midrashim

Genesis Rabbah	early 5th century
Lamentations Rabbah	early 5th century
Leviticus Rabbah	mid 5th century
Pesiqta de-Rav Kahana	5th century
Midrash Tanhuma	5th century with later additions
Deuteronomy Rabbah	5th–9th century
Pirqe de-Rabbi Eliezer	8th–9th century
Numbers Rabbah	9th–11th century
Exodus Rabbah	10th–12th century

The dates given are approximate and refer to the redaction of the main bulk of each work. Thus, the collections include individual traditions that are earlier than the redactional date, as well as additions that are later. Exodus, Numbers and Deuteronomy Rabbah share material with Midrash Tanhuma and thus contain many traditions that are older than the date of their final redactions.

known as *Exodus, Numbers,* and *Deuteronomy Rabbah,* collections consisting of different sources with various origins dating from the mid-fifth
to the twelfth century.

Pirqe de-Rabbi Eliezer is a paraphrase of parts of the Bible, a genre
known as "rewritten Bible." It is the only midrash, with the exception
of some medieval commentaries, that seems to have been written by a
single author and is usually dated to the eighth or ninth century. In the
twelfth and thirteenth centuries, anthologies were published that included
all commentaries known to the compilers, the best known being *Midrash
ha-Gadol* and *Yalqut Shimoni.*

Targums

In its broad sense of biblical interpretation, midrash also includes the Aramaic translations of the Hebrew Bible, known as targums. The Hebrew
word *targum* simply means "translation" in general, but the term is used
exclusively to denote the translation of the Bible into Aramaic. Far from
being literal translations, however, the targums include interpretive traditions, some of which are known from the rabbinic collections of midrash
while others are unique to the targums. The original *Sitz im Leben* of the
targums is most likely the synagogue, where the weekly readings from
the Torah and the Prophets were read first in Hebrew and simultaneously
translated into Aramaic by a translator (*meturgeman*). According to the
Mishnah and Tosefta, the reader would recite a verse from the Torah, after
which the translator would render the same verse in Aramaic, followed
immediately by the reader's recitation of the next verse in Hebrew. In case
of the Prophets, three verses at a time were read and translated in this fashion. The sources emphasize that the reading and translation be conducted
in such a way that the two voices, that of the reader and that of the translator, be clearly distinguishable from each other.[40]

Until recently, it was assumed that the Bible was translated into Aramaic because the Aramaic-speaking masses of Jewish people in the land of
Israel no longer understood biblical Hebrew, but lately a number of arguments against this view have been raised. Contrary to the earlier scholarly consensus that held that Hebrew had ceased to be a spoken language
in the post-Bar Kokhba period, synagogue inscriptions from the Galilee

---

40. See *m. Meg.* 4.4; *t. Meg.* 4:20.

suggest a multilingual milieu where people understood both Hebrew and Aramaic and to a certain extent even Greek. A reexamination of rabbinic sources has likewise led to the conclusion that the targums were intended for an audience that was familiar with both Hebrew and Aramaic and could easily switch between them.

Targums

Pentateuch

Onqelos	3rd century
Neofiti	4th–7th centuries
Pseudo-Jonathan	7th–8th centuries

Prophets

Jonathan ben Uzziel	3rd century

These circumstances, together with the fact that the targums never replaced the reading of the Torah in Hebrew the way that the Greek translation, the Septuagint, did for Greek-speaking Jews, have led Steven Fraade to suggest that the primary function of the targums was to convey to the synagogue audience a correct, that is, a rabbinic, interpretation of the Bible. The simultaneous rendering of the Torah-reading into Aramaic is understood to mediate the content of the Torah-reading and is in some rabbinic sources from the amoraic period compared to what was perceived to have happened at Sinai. Just as God's word was mediated through Moses, the public reading of the Torah in the synagogue is mediated through a translator who is both a bridge and a buffer between the written Torah and its oral reception and interpretation (*y. Meg.* 4:1).

In light of other rabbinic texts, which describe the revelation at Sinai as God speaking in several languages although the Torah was recorded only in Hebrew,[41] the public reading and translation of the Torah in the synagogue may have been perceived as a reenactment of the revelation at Sinai. The rabbis seem to have felt that to comprehend fully the meaning of the Hebrew text of the Torah, the written Torah must be translated into the

---

41. God revealed himself to the Israelites speaking to them in four languages, namely Hebrew, Latin, Aramaic, and Arabic (*Sifre* Deut §343), or in seventy languages (*b. Sanh.* 88b; *Midr. Psalms* 92:3; *Exod. Rab.* 5.9, 28.6).

seventy (that is, the totality) languages in which it was originally heard by Israel. Thus, a translation is in itself a form of explication, also for those who understood the original Hebrew. Although translation/interpretation was considered an integral part of the Torah-reading, the rabbis were also anxious to distinguish between the two. The targum had the advantage of permitting the rabbis to incorporate rabbinic interpretation into the Bible itself, but it also meant that people might confuse the interpretation with the written Torah. In order both to safeguard the written Torah and ensure the flexibility of the interpretation, the rabbis wished to keep the two distinct from one another, and this, argues Fraade, may have been one reason why the interpretation appears in Aramaic. The choice of Aramaic as the voice of interpretive paraphrase clearly distinguishes it from that of the written Torah and allows the two to be heard as distinct voices. In order to illustrate the relationship between the two, Fraade employs a musical metaphor comparing the reader and the translator to a soloist and an accompanist. Just as the musical accompanist enhances the performance of the soloist, so the targum contributes to the understanding of the written Torah, but in both cases the accompanist must not draw attention away from the principal performer. It is for this reason that the accompanist performs on a different instrument, and for the translator of the Torah-reading this different instrument was Aramaic.[42]

The best-known targums are *Onqelos, Pseudo-Jonathan, Neofiti*, and the *Fragmentary Targum* to the Pentateuch along with *Targum Jonathan ben Uzziel* to the Prophets. *Targum Onqelos* and *Targum Jonathan* to the Prophets were likely compiled in Babylonia during the third century, but at least *Onqelos* originally seems to be from the land of Israel. It is believed to have originated during the first half of the second century, and brought to Babylonia after the Bar Kokhba uprising, where it was redacted in the third century.

Neofiti, Pseudo-Jonathan, and the *Fragmentary Targum* were in use in the land of Israel and were collectively known as the Palestinian targum. They do not appear to have become standardized, and accordingly continued to develop during a long period of time, making it very difficult to date them. *Neofiti* is commonly dated to a period between the fourth and seventh centuries while *Pseudo-Jonathan* was probably compiled as late as the seventh or eighth century, even though it contains materials that are much older. The *Fragmentary Targum* consists of comments to scattered

---

42. Fraade, "Rabbinic Views," 253–86.

verses or words and never seems to have been a complete targum. In spite of intense scholarly debate, no consensus about its origin has been reached. Some scholars believe that it originated as an addition to *Onqelos*, while others maintain that it is a variant reading of *Pseudo-Jonathan*.

While *Onqelos* is a relatively literal translation, the Palestinian targumim are considerably more verbose. *Pseudo-Jonathan* has the most extensive additions, being approximately twice as long as the Hebrew text. There are also targums to the Writings (the last part of the Hebrew Bible), of which some are rather literal and others more expansive.[43] In order to illustrate similarities and differences between rabbinic compilations of midrash and the targums, we will presently have a look at the expansion of Gen. 4:8 from *Targum Pseudo-Jonathan*. The biblical text is italicized, and the remaining text consists of interpretation.

> *Cain said to his brother Abel*: "Come, let us both go outside." *When* the two of them had gone *outside* Cain spoke up and said to Abel: "I see that the world was created with mercy, but it is not governed according to the fruit of good deeds, and there is partiality in judgment. Therefore your offering was accepted with favor, but my offering was not accepted from me with favor." Abel answered and said to Cain: "The world was created with mercy, it is governed according to the fruit of good deeds, and there is no partiality in judgment. Because the fruit of my deeds was better than yours and more prompt than yours my offering was accepted with favor." Cain answered and said to Abel: "There is no judgment, there is no judge, there is no other world, there is no gift of good reward for the righteous, and no punishment for the wicked." Abel answered and said to Cain: "There is judgment, there is a judge, there is another world, there is the gift of good reward for the righteous, and there is punishment for the wicked." Concerning these matters they were quarreling in the open country. *And Cain rose up against Abel his brother* and drove a stone into his forehead *and killed him*.

This expansion obviously reflects the same basic problem in Genesis 4 that the midrashim we have encountered attempted to resolve, namely, that God appears arbitrary and even unjust in his acceptance of Abel's sacrifice and rejection of Cain's. The form, however, is different. Instead of quoting

---

43. For a survey of targums, see Alexander, "Jewish Aramaic Translations," 217–54; Grossfeld, *Targum Onqelos*; Klein, *Fragment-Targums*; McNamara, *Targum Neofiti 1*.

the biblical verse and then commenting on it, the targum weaves the biblical verse and its interpretation together so that it is not immediately clear where the one ends and the other starts. The idea that the reason for the murder was a quarrel between the brothers is familiar to us from *Genesis Rabbah* (22.7), and the content of their argument seems to summarize ideas known from other sources. Abel embodies the "correct" rabbinic view of the world and God and argues that his sacrifice was indeed superior to Cain's (cf. *Gen. Rab.* 22.5), while Cain's claims reflect rabbinic doubts as to God's justice, also reflected—albeit less boldly—in other rabbinic sources.[44]

THE BINDING OF ISAAC—THEOLOGY AND BIBLICAL INTERPRETATION

To conclude the discussion of rabbinic biblical interpretation and to illustrate the interwoven nature of rabbinic exegesis and theology, we will now turn to a sample of rabbinic interpretations of the well-known story of God's command to Abraham to sacrifice his beloved son Isaac in Genesis 22, known in Jewish tradition as the *aqedah* ("binding" [of Isaac]).[45]

Isaac—A Willing Sacrifice

As briefly mentioned above, most rabbinic interpretations make Isaac the principle character of the story. According to the aforementioned expansion from *Genesis Rabbah*, it is Isaac himself who, in a dispute with his brother Ishmael, provokes God's command to Abraham to offer him as a sacrifice, providing him with the opportunity to demonstrate his complete obedience and loyalty to God. A similar tradition appears in *Targum Pseudo-Jonathan*, but here the argument concerns not only whom God loves the most, but also who is Abraham's rightful heir:

> *After these words* [Gen. 22:1], after Isaac and Ishmael had quarreled, Ishmael said: "It is right that I should be my father's heir, since I am his

---

44. *Gen. Rab.* 22.9; *Midr. Tanh.* Bereshit 9.
45. For rabbinic interpretations of Genesis 22, see Leibowitz, *Torah Insights*, 21–37; Levenson, *Death and Resurrection*, 173–99; Spiegel, *Last Trial*; Vermes, *Scripture and Tradition*, 193–227; Segal, *Other Judaisms*, 109–30; and Swetnam, *Jesus and Isaac*. For interpretations in the targums, see Hayward, "Present State," 127–50. My presentation below is dependent on these works, in particular on Levenson.

first-born son." But Isaac said: "It is right that I should be my father's heir, because I am the son of Sarah his wife, while you are the son of Hagar, my mother's maidservant." Ishmael answered and said: "I am more worthy than you, because I was circumcised at the age of thirteen, and if I had wished to refuse, I would not have handed myself over to be circumcised. But you were circumcised at the age of eight days. If you had been aware, perhaps you would not have handed yourself over to be circumcised." Isaac answered and said: "Behold, today I am thirty-seven years old, and if the Holy One, blessed be He, were to ask all my members I would not refuse." These words were immediately heard before the Lord of the world, and at once the Memra of the Lord[46] *tested Abraham and said to him, "Abraham!"*

After the emergence of Islam, Ishmael was often identified with the Arabs, and it is possible that *Pseudo-Jonathan*'s version of the argument between Isaac and Ishmael is a later tradition reflecting polemics against Islam. Isaac (the Jews) and Ishmael (the Arabs) are both descendants of Abraham, and Ishmael's descendants could with some justification claim to be God's people as well. Since the kinship with Abraham does not indisputably settle the issue to Isaac's advantage, their dispute will instead be settled by their dedication to God.[47]

More importantly, this expansion clearly articulates the idea, present in practically all rabbinic interpretations, that Isaac was an adult at the time rather than a young boy. The number thirty-seven is arrived at by relating chronologically a number of events, assuming as the rabbis did that there was a significance to the order in which biblical events were told. The beginning of chapter 23 informs us of Sarah's death at the age of 127 years, and from the fact that this piece of information appears directly in connection with the events related in chapter 22, the rabbis deduced that these events were somehow related, and accordingly concluded that Sarah died because she was told that Isaac had actually died. Since we know from Gen. 17:17 that Sarah was ninety years old when Isaac was born, Isaac must have been thirty-seven at the time Abraham received the command to offer him as a sacrifice. Although the exact age varies somewhat, targums and rabbinic sources all agree that Isaac was a grown-up man.[48] Josephus

---

46. The Aramaic word *memra* means "the word" and is typically used by the targums in the place of "the Lord."

47. See *Targ. Ps.-J.* Gen 22:2 note 3 (*Aramaic Bible*, vol. 1B).

48. See, for instance, *Targ. Neof.* Exod 12:42 and *Pirqe R. Eliezer* 31.

sets his age at twenty-five (*A.J.* 1. 227), so the idea that Isaac was an adult obviously predates the rabbinic period.

The implication of the assertion that Isaac was an adult is that he went willingly and knowingly to be offered as a sacrifice. An old man, as Abraham was at the time, could not bind a young man on the altar without his consent. According to the rabbis, Abraham even hinted to Isaac in Gen. 22:7-8, the only conversation taking place between father and son, that he was the lamb intended to be offered as a sacrifice. Genesis 22:8 reads: "And Abraham said, 'God will see to the sheep for His burnt offering, my son,'" and by placing the comma differently the rabbis made Abraham say: "God will see to the sheep, a burnt offering are you, my son," thus revealing to Isaac that he was the intended sacrifice.

Seeing in their own interpretations only an explicit expression of what was implicit in the biblical text, they believed that God had deliberately placed in the text hints to the effect that Isaac was an adult who was knowingly and willingly letting himself be offered on the altar, and all they did was to explicitly express what God had intended. One such hint, they believed, was the repetition of the phrase "the two of them walked

Fig. 6. The *Aqedah* as depicted on the mosaic floor of the Bet Alpha Synagogue in the Galilee. Photograph in the public domain.

together," appearing in both verse 6 and verse 8. Since the Bible, according to rabbinic assumptions, does not contain any repetitions or superfluous information, the second occurrence of the phrase must necessarily add some new information, and since the verse between them relates the conversation between Abraham and Isaac, the rabbis understood this to mean that Abraham in that conversation disclosed to Isaac that he was to be sacrificed. As a sign that Isaac now knows and willingly accepts his fate, the text in verse 8 reiterates that "the two of them walked together." When the phrase occurs the first time, Isaac does not know what lies in wait for him, in verse 7 he is told, and then the phrase is repeated in verse 8 to affirm that in spite of this knowledge, he continues to walk with his father, willingly accepting his fate. *Tg. Pseudo-Jonathan* as well as the other Palestinian targums translate the Hebrew *yahdav* as "together," and then add the explanatory words, "with a perfect heart," to emphasize that Isaac agreed with his father. The targums and rabbinic sources are all anxious to point out that Abraham and Isaac were in perfect agreement concerning the sacrifice and that Isaac was not merely a passive victim.[49]

The idea that Isaac willingly agreed to give up his life in obedience to the divine decree did not originate with the rabbis, as is evident from the fact that the idea appears in a number of pre-rabbinic sources. Josephus, Philo, and 4 Maccabees all maintain that Isaac's near-death was self-conscious and freely chosen, and according to *Biblical Antiquities*, a work erroneously attributed to Philo, preserved in Latin but probably composed in Hebrew sometime in the first century, Abraham reveals to Isaac that he is about to offer him as a burnt offering as soon as they set out on the journey. To this Isaac answers: "Yet have I not been born into the world to be offered as a sacrifice to him who made me?"[50] *First Clement*, one of the earliest Christian writings outside of the New Testament dating from the late first or early second century, likewise states that Isaac, knowing full well what was to happen, was willingly led forth to be sacrificed (*1 Clem.* 31:4).

Thus, the idea of Isaac's voluntary participation in the *aqedah* predates the rabbinic period but was taken up by the rabbis and further developed by them. *Sifre*, the tannaitic midrash to Deuteronomy, says that "Isaac bound himself to the altar,"[51] and according to the targums, Isaac asks his father to tie him carefully to the altar, in case he should become frightened and injure himself while struggling to become free, thus rendering the sacrifice invalid.[52] Isaac's readiness to give up his life is further emphasized in the targumic addition to Gen 22:10, saying: "Come, see two unique ones

49. *Sifre* §32; *Gen. Rab.* 56.4; *Targ. Neof.* Gen. 22:8; *Frg. Targ.* Gen. 22:8; *Targ. Ps.-J.* Gen. 22:10; *Lev. Rab.* 2.10; *Pirqe R. Eliezer* 31; *Exod. Rab.* 1.1, 44.5.
50. *L.A.B.* 32:3. See also Josephus, *A.J.* 1.232 and *4 Macc.* 13:10-12.
51. *Sifre* Deut §32.
52. *Targ Ps.-J.*; *Targ. Neof.*; *Frg. Targ.* Gen. 22:10.

who are in the world; one is slaughtering, and one is being slaughtered; the one who slaughters does not hesitate, and the one who is being slaughtered stretches forth his neck."[53]

Isaac's "Death" Atones for Israel

A number of targumic and rabbinic sources assert that Isaac's death, or near-death, has an atoning effect, and the idea that God will remember the binding of Isaac and on account thereof forgive the sins of Israel is widespread in rabbinic tradition. On the Day of Judgment, according to one tradition, God will show mercy on account of the binding of Isaac: "[W]hen the children of Israel give way to transgressions and evil deeds, remember for their sake the binding of their father Isaac and rise from the throne of Judgment and sit on the throne of Mercy, and being filled with compassion for them have mercy upon them and change for them the Attribute of Justice into the Attribute of Mercy! When? *In the seventh month [on the first day of the month]*" [Lev. 23:24].[54]

A similar targumic tradition says that just as Abraham is about to slaughter Isaac, he prays that God may remember his willingness to sacrifice Isaac and for his sake save Israel's descendants in the future:

And Abraham worshiped and prayed in the name of the Memra of the Lord and said: "I beseech by the mercy that is before you O Lord—everything is manifest and known before you—that there was no division in my heart the first time that you said to me to offer my son Isaac, to make him dust and ashes before you; but I immediately arose early in the morning and diligently put your words into practice with gladness and fulfilled your decree. And now, when his sons are in the hour of distress you shall remember the Binding of their father Isaac, and listen to the voice of their supplications, and answer them and deliver them from all distress, so that the generations to arise after him may say: 'On the mountain of the sanctuary of the Lord Abraham sacrificed his son Isaac, and on this mountain the glory of the Shekhinah[55] of the Lord was revealed to him.'"[56]

---

53. *Targ. Ps.-J.* Gen. 22:10. cf. *Targ. Neof.* Gen. 22:10.
54. *Lev. Rab.* 29.9.
55. The rabbinic name for God's presence.
56. *Targ. Neof.* Gen 22:14. Compare *Targ. Ps.-J.* Gen 22:14.

Here Abraham's obedience to God and his refusal to spare his son has become the cause and condition for future deliverance of his descendants. When God announces his decision to destroy Israel after the sin of the Golden Calf (Exod. 32), Moses asks him to spare them appealing to Isaac's sacrifice: "[R]emember their father Isaac who stretched forth his neck on the altar ready to be slaughtered for your name, and let his death take the place of the death of his children."[57] The idea that a martyr's death has the power to atone for the sins of others and rescue them is a development of a pre-rabbinic theme present already in 4 Maccabees: "Through the blood of these righteous ones and through the propitiation of their death the divine providence rescued Israel, which had been shamefully treated."[58]

In the *Mekhilta*, an early commentary on Exod. 12:13 in which God commands the Israelites to smear blood from the slaughtered paschal lamb on their doorposts so that he will know where they live and spare them when he strikes the Egyptians with the last plague, Isaac takes the place of the paschal lamb and the Israelites are saved on account of the binding of Isaac: "*And the blood on the houses where you are staying shall be a sign for you: when I see the blood I will pass over you, so that no plague will destroy you when I strike the land of Egypt* [Exod. 12:13]. [*W*]*hen I see the blood* [Exod. 12:13], I see the blood of the binding of Isaac."[59] In the blood from the paschal lamb on the Israelites' doorposts, God sees the blood of the sacrifice of Isaac and on his account the Israelites are saved from the last plague and redeemed from slavery. In Genesis 22, Isaac was at the last moment replaced by a ram that was offered in his place, but here we have come full circle and Isaac takes the place of the paschal lamb.

The identification of Isaac with the paschal lamb first appears in *Jubilees*, dated to the middle of the second century B.C.E., albeit it is only implicit there. According to *Jubilees*, God's command to Abraham to offer Isaac as a sacrifice occurred "in the seventh week, in its first year, in the first month, in that jubilee, on the twelfth of that month" (*Jub.* 17:15). The month in which Passover is celebrated is the first month of the year, according to Exod. 12:2, and the twelfth day of the first month is three days before the paschal lamb is to be offered, which occurs at twilight of the fourteenth (Exod. 12:6; Lev. 23:5). Since the journey to the designated

---

57. *Exod. Rab.* 44.5. My translation.
58. *4 Macc.* 17:22.
59. *Mekh. R. Ishmael* Pisha 7 (Lauterbach, 1:57) and the parallel in *Pisha* 11 (Lauterbach, 1:88). Compare also *b. Ber.* 16b, where God sees the ashes of Isaac.

place took Abraham three days (Gen. 22:4; *Jub.* 18:3), the binding of Isaac would coincide with the offering of the paschal lamb on the evening of the fourteenth. This assumption makes the *aqedah* a foundation story for Passover, an interpretation made explicit in the conclusion of *Jubilee*'s retelling of Genesis 22: "And he [Abraham] observed this festival every year for seven days with rejoicing. And he named it 'the feast of the Lord' according to the seven days during which he went and returned in peace" (*Jub.*18:17). The only seven-day festival in the first month is, of course, Passover (Lev. 23:5-8), and *Jubilees* seems to derive its duration, for which the Bible gives no reason, from Abraham's journey—three days to the land of Moriah, three to return, and one day (the Sabbath) without travel. In this interpretation, Passover is celebrated in commemoration of Abraham's refusal to spare his own son when God commanded that he be sacrificed, and by founding the story of Passover upon the *aqedah*, *Jubilees* makes a father's willingness to give up his son a key component of Israel's redemption from Egypt.

It is this line of thought that is further developed in the *Mekhilta* text above, in which the *aqedah* (and the Passover sacrifice) has become the foundation for Israel's rescue from affliction throughout history. This idea is even more clearly expressed in a passage in *Exodus Rabbah* where it is said that Isaac was "born and bound" in the month of Nisan, the month in which "Israel was redeemed from Egypt and in which they will be redeemed in the future," reflecting a view of the *aqedah* as an archetype of redemption and a foreshadowing of the eschatological deliverance, envisioned as a new Exodus.[60]

This is an amazing development in which the original story of a father who is explicitly forbidden to hurt his son (Gen. 22:12) is transformed into one in which he wounds, spills his blood, or even kills the son. "When I see the blood I will pass over you," God tells the Israelites enslaved in Egypt, but the *Mekhilta* interprets this to mean that God saw the blood of Isaac. The idea that some of Isaac's blood was indeed spilled is present in a number of rabbinic sources,[61] and actually appears already in the above mentioned first century work *Biblical Antiquities*: "And he [Abraham] brought him [Isaac] to be placed on the altar, but I gave him back to his father and, because he did not refuse, his offering was acceptable before

---

60. *Exod. Rab.* 15.11; Levenson, *Death and Resurrection*, 176–83.
61. *Mekh. Shimon b. Yohai* Sanya 2 (Nelson p. 6); *Tanh.* Vayera 23; *Midr. ha-Gadol* to Gen. 22:8.

me, and on account of his blood I chose them."[62] According to this source, God made Israel his people on account of Abraham's willingness to offer Isaac and Isaac's readiness to be sacrificed. Thus, the very existence of their descendants is dependent on this act.

Other rabbinic texts speak of Isaac's ashes,[63] rather than his blood, but the atoning effect is the same. These references to the blood and ashes of Isaac could be understood to mean either that God reckoned Abraham's intention to sacrifice him and Isaac's readiness to die as the equivalent of the actual deed,[64] or they could be taken as an allusion that Isaac actually died. Either God views the *aqedah* as if Isaac had been reduced to ashes, although it did not actually happen, or he sees the real ashes as a testimony to the obedience of father and son. In the case of Isaac's blood, an intermediary position is possible, according to which some blood was spilled as a token of the sacrifice Abraham and Isaac were prepared to carry out.

The idea of equating intention with the actual deed is well known in Jewish tradition and may be exemplified by the prayer that a religious Jew says when he dons the prayer shawl (*tallit*), whose fringes (*tzitziot*) serve as a reminder of God's commandments: "May the commandments of *tsitsit* be worthy before the Holy One, Blessed be He, *as if* I had fulfilled it in all its details, implications, and intentions, as well as the six hundred thirteen commandments that are dependent on it."[65] He knows that he has not fulfilled all the 613 commandments but asks God to account him *as if* he had done it. Thus, the allusions to the blood and ashes of Isaac could simply mean that God considers Isaac as having been sacrificed, and according to some sources, he also accounts it to Israel as if they had done it:

> R. Abbahu said: "Why do we blow on a ram's horn [on Rosh Hashanah]? The Holy One, blessed be He, said: 'Sound before me a ram's horn so that I my remember on your behalf the binding of Isaac, the son of Abraham, and account it to you as if you had bound yourselves before me.'"[66]

---

62. *L.A.B.* 18:5.
63. *Gen. Rab.* 49.11, 95.5; *Lev. Rab.* 36.5; *Tanh.* Vayera 23; *Num. Rab.* 17.2; *Midr. ha-Gadol* to Gen. 22:19; *b. Taanit* 16a; *b. Ber.* 62b.
64. *Midr. ha-Gadol* Gen. 22:19.
65. *Artscroll Siddur*, 4–5. Emphasis added. The commandment for Israelites to put fringes on the corners of their garments is found in Num. 15:37-41 where it is also said that the fringes serve as a reminder of all God's commandments: "[L]ook at it [the fringe] and recall all the commandments of the Lord and observe them" (v. 39).
66. *b. Rosh Hash.* 16a.

Some sources, however, go further and hint that Isaac actually died and was subsequently revived:

> R. Judah said: "When the blade touched his neck, the soul of Isaac fled and departed, but when he heard his [God's] voice saying [to Abraham]: 'Do not raise your hand against the boy' [Gen. 22:12], his soul returned to his body, and Abraham set him free, and Isaac stood upon his feet. And Isaac knew that in this manner the dead in the future will be quickened. He opened [his mouth], and said: 'Blessed are you, O Lord, who quickens the dead.'"[67]

Hints to the effect that Isaac really died could actually be found in two passages in Genesis 22 if read with rabbinic eyes. The fact that the angel had to call to Abraham a second time (verse 15) would seem to indicate that Abraham did not listen to the first instruction not to harm Isaac (verse 12), leaving the reader to wonder what Abraham did to Isaac between the angel's two speeches. A second more ominous hint could be found in Gen. 22:19, "Abraham then returned to his servants, and they departed together for Beer-sheba." Only Abraham is mentioned here, and given the emphasis throughout the story that Abraham and Isaac did everything together, this would seem to indicate that Abraham returned alone after having killed Isaac. The fact that the medieval Jewish author Abraham ibn Ezra (1092/93–1167) in his commentary to Gen. 22:19 found it necessary to explicitly refute the idea that Isaac died and was later revived indicates that such a tradition did exist: "Isaac is not mentioned here because he was under the authority of Abraham. The one who says that Abraham slaughtered him and left him and that he was subsequently resurrected contradicts Scripture."[68] Perhaps the need to refute such ideas is also behind the late *Midrash ha-Gadol's* explicit statement that Isaac's willingness to die was considered by God *as if* he had really died, likewise attached to Gen. 22:19. In the end, whether Isaac really died or whether God considers his readiness to die to be the equivalent of his actual death may not be that important to the rabbinic mind, as pointed out by Levenson. Either way,

---

67. This is the second blessing of the *Amidah* prayer, here placed in Isaac's mouth. *Pirqe R. Eliezer* 30 (Friedlander, 31). Compare *Pes. Rav Kahana* suppl. 1.20, where it says that God will in the future resurrect the dead on account of the merit of Isaac who offered himself upon the altar.
68. My translation.

his death—real or symbolic—atones for his descendants and the *aqedah* is the event on account of which God delivered Israel from Egypt and will again deliver them in the future.[69] These expansions illustrate the close relationship between biblical interpretation and rabbinic theology. Irrespective of the precise origin of a particular idea, it is presented as biblical interpretation. Thus, interaction between the biblical text and a rabbinic reader approaching that text with specific assumptions together with theological/ideological concerns gave rise to the idea that Isaac was willing to offer himself as a sacrifice and that on account of his death, whether or not he actually died, God would forgive and redeem his descendants. The general theological problem in Genesis 22 of why a good and omniscient God commands Abraham to sacrifice his beloved son is resolved through the idea that Isaac, rather than being an unknowing passive victim, was an adult willing to be sacrificed. Far from being a pointless, cruel test, as it may at first appear to be, this event has far-reaching theological consequences for Israel.

Isaac and Jesus

It is evident that Isaac in the *aqedah* story, as it was understood in the late Second Temple period and rabbinic interpretations, bears a remarkable resemblance to Jesus as portrayed in the Gospels. Jesus is described as "the beloved son" (Mark 1:11; Matt. 3:17; Luke 3:22), recalling the designation of Isaac in the *aqedah* story where he is repeatedly called *yahid*, "the favored one" (Gen. 22:2, 12, 16), a term that the Septuagint consistently renders as *agapētos*, "beloved."[70] Both Jesus and Isaac are willing to give up their lives, both are identified with the paschal lamb and their deaths, real or symbolic, atone for the sins of their descendants who are redeemed and revived on account of their sacrifice. Noticing these striking similarities, scholars have debated the origin of these traditions, some arguing that the authors of the New Testament designed the story of Jesus' birth, suffering, and death in accordance with the prevalent understanding of Isaac and the *aqedah* story,[71] while others maintain that the ideas originated with the

---

69. Levenson, *Death and Resurrection*, 192–99.
70. Ibid., 200.
71. Le Déaut, *La nuit pascale*; Levenson, *Death and Resurrection*, 176–219; Vermes, *Scripture and Tradition*. See also Spiegel, *Last Trial*, 77–120.

New Testament and argue that the rabbinic interpretation of Genesis 22 came into being in response to the idea of Jesus as an atoning sacrifice.[72]

Although one should not automatically disregard the possibility that rabbinic ideas may have developed in response to Christian claims, it seems much more likely, in this case, to see the Gospel traditions about Jesus as an adaptation and development of the *aqedah* story as it was understood by the late Second Temple period. Jon Levenson has convincingly shown that the key components of the rabbinic interpretation of the *aqedah*, according to which Isaac was a willing participant, choosing to give up his life in obedience to God's decree and that his blood, whether or not it was spilled, was seen as effecting atonement for his descendants, appears already in texts from the first century and even earlier. The idea of a vicarious sacrifice appears already in the ritual of the Day of Atonement, as described in Leviticus 16, and the Gospel traditions about Jesus may be seen as a combination of ideas connected to the Day of Atonement and Passover. From the association of the *aqedah* with Passover in *Jubilees* (and in some rabbinic texts),[73] we may conclude that this connection is likely older than the association of the *aqedah* with the Day of Judgment (Rosh Hashanah). The contemporary custom of reading Genesis 22 on Rosh Hashanah dates from the amoraic period and may reflect a wish to disassociate the *aqedah* from Passover to avoid too close a similarity to the Christian idea of Easter.

It appears very likely, then, that the disciples of Jesus, who were Jews, would interpret the birth, death, and resurrection of their master in the light of contemporary traditions about the binding of Isaac. Jesus's death at the onset of Passover, together with the already ancient association of the *aqedah* with Passover, would naturally lead to the identification of Jesus with the paschal lamb (John 13:1; 18:28; 19:31-37).[74] Perhaps Hebrews (11:17-19) even contains a hint of the tradition of the death and resurrection of Isaac: "By faith Abraham, when put to the test, offered up Isaac. He who had received the promises was ready to offer up his only son, of whom he had been told, 'It is through Isaac that descendants shall be named for you.' He considered the fact that God is able even to raise someone from the dead—and figuratively speaking, he did receive him

---

72. Davies and Chilton, "Aqedah," 514–46.
73. *Mekh. R. Ishmael* Pisha 7 (Lauterbach, 1:57), Beshallah 4 (Lauterbach, 1:222–23), *Targ. Neof.* Exod. 12:42; Exod. *Rab.* 15.11.
74. Levenson, *Death and Resurrection*, 206–8, 218.

back." This is not to say that a complete theology about the atoning power of the binding of Isaac was fully developed at the time of the New Testament. From a common point of departure, the traditions about Isaac and Jesus may have continued to develop in conversation with and in response to one another, especially if, as much recent scholarship suggests, a variety of different versions of Judaism and Christianity with blurred boundaries continued to interact and influence one another for several centuries. It is remarkable that the idea of the atoning power of Isaac's sacrifice is prevalent in so many late rabbinic texts, and it cannot be ruled out that the rabbis adopted these ideas from groups of Jesus-oriented Jews. From these theological ideas, common both to the Jesus movement and rabbinic Judaism, we will now turn to the general Jewish character of the early Jesus movement, and to the role that Jewish hermeneutic tradition played in adapting to a situation in which the end of time was believed to be approaching, precipitating the need to include Gentiles into the covenant between God and the people of Israel.

STUDY QUESTIONS

1. Explain the role that assumptions about the biblical text have for its interpretation.

2. Discuss the roles of textual and extra-textual factors in generating biblical interpretation.

3. Explain the function of parables in rabbinic biblical interpretation.

4. Compare targums and collections of rabbinic midrash. What are the similarities and differences?

5. Discuss the similarities and possible relationships between the binding of Isaac as understood in the late Second Temple period and the Gospel traditions about Jesus.

Suggestions for Further Reading

Early Jewish Biblical Interpretation

Kugel, J. L. *In Potiphar's House: The Interpretive Life of Biblical Texts.* New York: HarperCollins, 1990.

———. *The Bible as It Was.* Cambridge: Belknap, 1997.

Stern, D. "Midrash and Jewish Interpretation." *The Jewish Study Bible: Featuring the Jewish Publication Society Tanakh Translation.* Edited by A. Berlin and M. Z. Brettler, 1863–75. Oxford: Oxford University Press, 2004.

Rabbinic Parables

Stern, D. *Parables in Midrash: Narrative and Exegesis in Rabbinic Literature.* Cambridge: Harvard University Press, 1991.

The Binding of Isaac

Levenson, J. D. *The Death and Resurrection of the Beloved Son: The Transformation of Child Sacrifice in Judaism and Christianity.* New Haven: Yale University Press, 1993.

Segal, Alan, "The Sacrifice of Isaac in Early Judaism and Christianity." In *The Other Judaisms of Late Antiquity*, 109–30, Brown Judaic Studies 127 (Atlanta: Scholars, 1987.

Spiegel, S. *The Last Trial: On the Legends and Lore of the Command to Abraham to Offer Isaac as a Sacrifice: The Akedah.* Translated from the Hebrew with an Introduction by Judah Goldin. Woodstock: Jewish Lights, 1993 (1950).

4

The Jewish Character
of the Early Jesus Movement

Christianity traces its origins to an inner-Jewish movement that grew out of Second Temple Judaism, and should accordingly be placed in that context and understood against the background of ideas, interests, and concerns prevalent in Jewish society at that time. Jesus was a Jewish Torah teacher, Paul a Pharisee, and the Jesus movement began as Jewish prophetic movement rooted in Second Temple Judaism.

The adherents of the Jesus movement believed Jesus to be a prophet and the Messiah, developing an understanding of the Torah with his life, death, and resurrection as an interpretive prism. In so doing, they eventually clashed with nascent rabbinic Judaism, whose adherents were attempting to establish a new leadership based on interpretation of the Torah by a learned non-prophetic group. This process of identity formation in relation to the Jewish leadership in late Second Temple times is reflected already in the Gospels, and polemical claims against contemporary Jewish groups at the time of the redaction of the Gospels has shaped the subsequent understanding of Jesus' teachings within Christian tradition. In the same way, concerns and assumptions of later Christian tradition have, until recently, largely determined the interpretation of Paul.

Placing Jesus and Paul in the context of Second Temple Judaism, this chapter aims at demonstrating how attention to the historical situation of Second Temple times—theological ideas and concerns along with the general approach to biblical interpretation prevalent at the time—impacts our understanding of the New Testament and the early Jesus movement.

JESUS—A FIRST-CENTURY JEWISH TORAH TEACHER

A heightened awareness of the extent to which polemical concerns and theological ideas of a later time have governed our understanding of the beginnings

111

of Christianity, and a greater willingness among scholars to acknowledge that Jesus and most likely also Paul remained committed to a Jewish lifestyle throughout their lives and should be understood within a Jewish context have led to significant breakthroughs in New Testament scholarship. The beginning of this scholarly trend is in large part due to the influential work of E. P. Sanders and has since been developed and continued by others.

Until the middle of the twentieth century, most New Testament scholars assumed that there was a fundamental contradiction between Judaism and Christianity, largely as a result of heavy influence from Protestant theology. While grace and forgiveness were essential tenets of Christianity, Judaism was seen as characterized by empty law observance and the idea of a God distant from humankind. This legalistic religion, with no inner commitment, where humans in vain strive for redemption by performing good deeds, became the standard dark background against which the message of Jesus appeared unique.[1]

Despite several attempts to challenge this image of Judaism, mainly but not exclusively by Jewish scholars,[2] it continued to be the basic assumption of almost all New Testament scholarship up until the end of the 1970s when it was finally reconsidered, mainly as a consequence of the scholarship of E. P. Sanders. In his influential monograph *Paul and Palestinian Judaism* (1977), Sanders showed that the view of Judaism as a legalistic religion, without forgiveness, and the belief in a God far removed from humans, lacks support in Jewish sources and is best understood as a theologically motivated construction by New Testament scholars.

In place of this gloomy picture, Sanders found in Jewish sources ranging from ca. 200 B.C.E.–200 C.E. a basic pattern that he called covenantal nomism. With this term, he attempted to capture the role played by the Torah within the covenant that God had made with the Jewish people. This covenantal relationship was based on God's election of Israel and their subsequent acceptance of the conditions of the covenant—the commandments. The Israelites were expected to keep these commandments to the best of their ability, but it is important to realize that they were given within the framework of the covenant. According to Jewish theology of the time, this meant that although obedience to God's commandments

---

1. For a survey of this distorted picture of Judaism and its influence on New Testament scholarship, see Zetterholm, *Approaches to Paul*, 60–90.
2. For instance, C. G. Montefiore, G. F. Moore, J. Klausner, D. Flusser, W. D. Davies, and G. Vermes.

was assumed to be rewarded and transgressions punished, forgiveness was granted if only there was repentance. As long as a Jewish person shows his or her desire to remain in the covenant by observing the commandments, he or she is granted a share in the world to come. Observance of the commandments, then, is not a way of gaining entrance into the covenant, but a means of staying in.

The inability of humans to fulfill the commandments to perfection was foreseen in the Torah itself and remedy is offered through the sacrificial institution (Lev. 4:1—6:7, 16:1-34), allowing those who have transgressed the law to be forgiven and the broken relationship to be restored. Rather than gaining merits in order to earn redemption, a Jewish person manifests his or her desire to be part of the covenant by performing the commandments while all the same relying on God's grace and forgiveness. In contrast to most previous scholarship, Sanders maintained that God's mercy and forgiving nature was an integral part of ancient Judaism.[3]

Sanders' work essentially changed the view of Second Temple Judaism in New Testament scholarship, and would leave its imprint on nearly all subsequent scholarship on Jesus. At present, virtually all scholars view Jesus as firmly rooted in Judaism, and his message as part of the multifaceted Second Temple Judaism. Jesus' critique of the Pharisees as related in the Gospels is no longer viewed as a condemnation of fundamental tenets of Judaism but rather as disapproval of the religious leadership of the time and its interpretation of the Torah. It is seen in the context of Second Temple Judaism, when various Jewish factions with different views of Torah interpretation and the temple were competing against each other.

The study of parables is an area that clearly illustrates the benefits of understanding Jesus' message in light of ideas and theological concerns of late Second Temple Judaism, a context often obscured by later Christian interpretation. Much of Jesus' teachings appear in the form of parables, a form of instruction that was apparently popular at the time and continued to be used by the rabbis. However, as the adherents of the Jesus movement, at various stages in its development, applied the parables to their present situation, they infused them with new meaning, at times radically different from that which Jesus' original audience is likely to have deduced from them.[4]

The conflict over leadership, for instance—still an inner-Jewish conflict at the time of the redaction of the Gospels—hardened as the number of

---

3. Sanders, *Paul*, 1–426.
4. See Young, *Parables*, 7.

non-Jewish Jesus disciples increased, and eventually the critique that Jesus likely directed at the religious leadership of his time came to be understood as a general critique of Jews and Judaism. The parables of the Wicked Tenants (Matt. 21:33-46; Mark 12:1-12; Luke 20:9-19) and the Wedding Banquet (Matt. 22:1-14; Luke 14:15-24), for instance, were early on read as evidence that God had rejected the Jewish people and that his promises and blessings had been transferred to the Christian church.[5] Unfortunately, these polemical interpretations have shaped the understanding of Jesus' parables in much of subsequent Christian tradition. In order to disentangle the parables from later interpretations, it is fruitful to distinguish between the different layers of the parables: the Jesus level, the Gospel level, and later Christian understanding.

When attempting to reconstruct the parable at the Jesus level (assuming that he actually told the parable in some form), parables preserved in rabbinic literature have proved helpful. Although redacted later than the Gospels, rabbinic parables also have roots in Second Temple Judaism, and having been preserved in an exclusively Jewish context, polemical interpretations have affected and distorted their meaning to a much lesser extent. A comparative study of rabbinic and Gospel parables reveals numerous similarities concerning motifs, message, and shared concerns, lending further support to the assumption that the message of Jesus' parables should be sought in their original Jewish context rather than in later Christian interpretations.[6] One of the first scholars to draw attention to these similarities was David Flusser, who, based on the many common traits of rabbinic and Gospel parables, concluded that they were both part of a common tradition and environment.[7] He found that they reflect the same concerns and points of reference, and that they are very similar with regard to structure, motif, theme, and theological message. Nearly always they concern the relationship between God and humans.[8] The following reading of a few Gospel parables in light of rabbinic parables with similar motifs, themes, and message will illustrate the insights gained by this approach.

---

5. See, for instance, John Chrysostom, *Hom. Matt.* 68.1 (the Wicked Tenants) and 69.1 (the Wedding Banquet) and Irenaeus, *Haer.* 4.36 and Origen, *Cels.* 2.5 (the Wicked Tenants), and the survey in Milavec, "Fresh Analysis," 81–86.
6. For such a comparative study, see Young, *Parables.*
7. Flusser, *Rabbinischen Gleichnisse.*
8. Stern, "Jesus' Parables," 43–44; Young, Parables, 3–38.

Fig.7. The Sea of Galilee. Photograph by Anders Runesson.

THE PARABLES OF JESUS AND THE RABBIS

A *baraita* (a tradition from the tannaitic period) preserved in the Babylonian Talmud (*b. Shabb.* 153a), contains the following parable:

> Rabbi Eliezer said: "Repent and return [*shuv*] to God one day before your death." His disciples said to him: "But a man does not know when he will die!" Rabbi Eliezer replied: "Then all the more reason that he repent today, lest he die tomorrow, and thus his whole life will be spent in repentance [*teshuvah*]. As Solomon said in his wisdom, *Let your clothes always be freshly washed, and your head never lack ointment* [Eccl. 9:8].[9] Rabban Johanan ben Zakkai said: "This may be compared to a king who summoned his servants to a banquet without appointing a time. The wise ones adorned themselves and sat at the door of the palace, for they said: 'Is anything lacking in a royal palace?' The fools, however, went about their work, saying: 'Can there be a banquet without preparations?' Suddenly the king desired [the presence] of his servants. The wise entered adorned, while the fools entered soiled. The king rejoiced at the wise but was angry with the fools and said: 'Those who adorned themselves for the banquet,

9. In Jewish tradition, King Solomon is considered the author of the book of Ecclesiastes, see Eccl. 1:1. My interpretation of this parable is based on Jonah Fraenkel's course on parables in the Babylonian Talmud at the Hebrew University of Jerusalem in the spring semester of 1992.

let them sit, eat and drink, but those who did not adorn themselves for the banquet, let them stand and watch.'"

In this case, the *nimshal* comes before the parable itself, and consists of a call for repentance without delay since the precise time of a person's death is unknown. One should hasten to repair one's relationship to God while there is still time. The Hebrew word for repentance (*teshuvah*) has the same root as the verb "to return" (*lashuv*) and "to answer" (*lehashiv*), indicating that repentance means to answer God's call and return to him. The king in the parable, as always, stands for God and the king's invitation without appointing a time corresponds in the *nimshal* to the fact that death is certain but the precise time unknown.

Not surprisingly, the unexpected element in this parable concerns the king whose behavior is rather odd. An invitation to dinner usually implies a set time, a detail that is highlighted by the fact that the word in rabbinic Hebrew for "to invite" (*lezamen*) contains within it the word for "time" (*zeman*). Thus, the king's invitation of guests without telling them what time to come is surely peculiar. Moreover, a king does not usually invite his servants to a banquet, not a king in antiquity at any rate. Quite understandably, the foolish servants regard such an invitation as absurd, and since no preparations are in sight they go about their usual work. On the contrary, the behavior of the wise servants appears utterly illogical. With no indications whatever that the banquet is actually about to take place, they instantly leave whatever they are doing, dress up and rush to the palace.

The paradox produced by designating as wise those servants whose behavior seems odd, and as foolish those servants who appear to act rationally, suggests that the nature of God is not easily grasped by humans. While the foolish servants assume that God thinks and acts in the same manner as humans do, the wise realize that God is different. In contrast to a banquet arranged by a king of flesh and blood that requires obvious preparations, death may come quietly with no premonition. It is this insight into God's will and character that distinguishes the wise from the foolish.

The wise servants are not otherwise presented as particularly pious or righteous and neither are the foolish particularly wicked. Far from living in opulence, they dutifully go about their tasks, but lack of insight into God's will leads them to make wrong priorities in life. On the contrary, the wise have the ability to see the world through God's eyes and accordingly realize that the king's invitation gives them an opportunity to prepare themselves for the banquet/death by repairing their relationship to God and by spending every day in repentance as if it were the last. Humans tend to focus on the exact moment of death, but for God this is not important, which is suggested by the king's invitation without appointing a time in the parable. He wants humans to live all their lives in constant closeness and fellowship with him; it is the preparations of the banquet rather than the banquet itself that are important to him.

Finally, it turns out that even the servants who did not dress for the banquet are present, although they are not allowed to eat and drink. The king's invitation cannot be refused—death comes to everyone, even to those who are not prepared. God invites everyone to his banquet (the world to come), but he demands preparation (repentance), and there is a time limit (this world) during which humans must make up their minds as to how to relate to that invitation. Giving priority to God calls for decisive action.

It is not only the behavior of the servants that is paradoxical, but also the way the quote from Ecclesiastes is employed. In its biblical context, it seems to mean that one should *enjoy life*, but in the parable it is used to support the idea that humans ought to spend their entire lives in *preparation for death*. The purpose of these paradoxes seems to be to emphasize that God is different from humans and that, as a result, humans cannot easily understand him. What appears odd to humans is wise in God's eyes, and what seems logical and perfectly reasonable from a human perspective may be utterly unwise from God's viewpoint. To be wise, according to this parable, is to see the world with God's eyes.

Shared Motifs and Messages

Although this parable likely represents a later stage in the development of parables, both motif and message are familiar from the New Testament parables such as the Ten Bridesmaids (Matt. 25:1-13; cf. Luke 12:35-48) and the Wedding Banquet (Matt. 22:1-14; Luke 15:16-24). As with the rabbinic parable in *b. Shabb.* 153a, the motif of the parable of the Ten Bridesmaids is an "invitation to a banquet without appointing a time," and both contrast two categories of people—the wise and the foolish. The story about the Bridesmaids portrays five wise and five foolish maidens who go to meet the bridegroom. While the wise maidens bring both lamps and oil, the foolish ones take only their lamps. The bridegroom is delayed, however, and as they wait they all fall asleep. At midnight the groom is coming and the foolish maidens ask the wise ones for oil, but the latter refuse. The foolish maidens then go to buy oil but in the meantime the groom arrives and brings the prepared maidens with him to the wedding banquet. When the foolish maidens return with oil, they find the door shut and when they ask to be let in the groom replies: "Truly I tell you, I do not know you." The parable ends with the call: Keep awake therefore, for you know neither the day nor the hour (Matt. 25:13).

The Gospel parable calls for preparation for the unknown time of the final judgment while the rabbinic one deals with the suddenness of death, but the proper response, whether impending judgment at the unknown time of death or the sudden appearance of the eschatological judge, ought to be the same, namely, a decision to repent, and to give priority to one's relation to God.[10]

The similarities in motif and message between the rabbinic parable in *b. Shabb.* 153a and the parable of the Great Dinner (Luke 15:16-24; *Gos. Thom.* 64), or the Wedding Banquet as it is known in Matthew's version (Matt. 22:1-14), are apparent as well. Below is Matthew's version:

> Once more Jesus spoke to them in parables, saying: "The kingdom of heaven may be compared to a king who gave a wedding banquet for his son. He sent his slaves to call those who had been invited to the wedding banquet, but they would not come. Again he sent other slaves, saying, 'Tell those who have been invited: Look, I have prepared my dinner, my oxen and my fat calves have been slaughtered, and everything is ready; come to the wedding banquet.' But they made light of it and went away, one to his farm, another to his business, while the rest seized his slaves, maltreated them, and killed them. The king was enraged. He sent his troops, destroyed those murderers, and burned their city. Then he said to his slaves, 'The wedding is ready, but those invited were not worthy. Go therefore into the main streets, and invite everyone you find to the wedding banquet.' Those slaves went out into the streets and gathered all whom they found, both good and bad; so the wedding hall was filled with guests. But when the king came in to see the guests, he noticed a man there who was not wearing a wedding robe, and he said to him, 'Friend, how did you get in here without a wedding robe?' And he was speechless. Then the king said to the attendants, 'Bind him hand and foot, and throw him into the outer darkness, where there will be weeping and gnashing of teeth.' For many are called, but few are chosen."

---

10. On the urgent need to always be prepared for the unknown time of death or final judgment in Gospel and rabbinic parables, see Young, *Parables*, 278–83.

An unexpected element in this parable is the reactions of those invited to the wedding banquet. One would imagine that an invitation to a royal wedding is a great honor, but the invited guests are utterly uninterested. Some of them pointedly ignore the invitation and simply go about their every day tasks while others even seize the king's servants and kill them. The seriousness of the distorted priorities of the invited guests soon becomes apparent when the king burns down their city.

Eschatology and the belief in reward and punishment following death or the final judgment are prominent themes in the parables of both Jesus and the rabbis. The fact that rabbinic parables are generally less harsh than those of Jesus, and the consequences of wrong choices less devastating, may be explained by a decline in imminent eschatological expectations in the wake of the destruction of the temple in 70 C.E., and the trampled messianic hopes after the Bar Kokhba revolt of 132–135. Up until these catastrophes, the belief in the imminent judgment of God that would end the present world and its corruption gained greater currency in Jewish thought, but as a result of the devastating consequences of such eschatological fervor, the rabbis were anxious to shy away from apocalyptic hopes and adopted a more this-worldly perspective, emphasizing the importance of the study of the Torah and good deeds.[11]

If we were to assume that this parable in some form goes back to Jesus, it would be reasonable to presume, in light of what we know about the prevalence of eschatological hopes within Second Temple Judaism, that his intention was to emphasize the urgency of time and proper preparation for the impendent judgment. Time is limited, and if one is not ready for the kingdom of God when the eschatological judge appears, one may not get a second chance. On the Jesus level, then, the parable of the Wedding Banquet would seem to have the same message as the one of the Ten Bridesmaids and the rabbinic one about the king who invited his servants to a feast without appointing a time, namely, the urgency of making a decision to attempt to live in accordance with God's will and preparing oneself for God's call.

---

11. Young, *Parables*, 277.

Reinterpretation of Jesus' Parables

However, already in Matthew's rendering it is possible to discern the beginning of a development that in due time would lead to the interpretation of the parable as being about the Jews who rejected the kingdom of God and the Christians who accepted it.

For Matthew, as the representative of a movement of Jewish disciples of Jesus, the invited guests ("many are invited") probably represent Jews not connected to the Jesus movement, while his group—Jewish disciples of Jesus—are the chosen ones ("few are chosen"). It is possible that he, writing his Gospel in the 80s or 90s, considered the parable's servants as representing the prophets, and that he saw in the king's destruction of the city a prediction of Jerusalem's fall in 70 C.E. The destruction of the city is not mentioned in Luke's version of the parable and is part of the Matthean redaction. Matthew appears to direct his focus more on a later audience than on a setting during Jesus' lifetime, and quite possibly he reads into Jesus' parable a later conflict between Jewish disciples of Jesus and other Jews.

Violent attacks against the religious leadership, for which the Pharisees usually stand as representatives, are characteristic of the Gospel of Matthew. The author, like many other Jewish sectarian groups after the year 70 C.E., believed that the religious leaders had corrupted the people and held them responsible for the defeat by the Romans and the destruction of the temple. It appears likely that Matthew's community and nascent rabbinic Judaism were initially very close to one another and likely, to an outsider, indistinguishable from one another. This close relationship may, at least in part, account for the fierceness of the attacks.[12]

In Matthew's time, the conflict over the correct interpretation of the Torah and the legitimate leadership was still an inner-Jewish one, and his critique is directed at the leadership of one of the major groups that he opposed. Later on, however, when the Jesus movement came to be dominated by non-Jews, it turned into a conflict between "the Jews" and the Christian church, with the latter claiming that they had replaced the Jews as the rightful heirs of the biblical blessings and promises. In this historical situation, the two groups of invited guests were understood to represent Jews and Christians respectively. Those who were first invited but ignored

12. Overman, *Matthew's Gospel*; Runesson, "Re-Thinking Early Jewish-Christian Relations," 95–132; Saldarini, *Matthew's Christian-Jewish Community*; Saldarini, "Gospel of Matthew"; Sim, *Gospel of Matthew*; Tomson, *From Heaven*.

the invitation were identified with the Jewish people, while the Christians saw themselves as the few who were chosen, an interpretation that is very far from both the "Jesus level" and Matthew's interpretation.[13]

Another New Testament parable that, along with the parable of the Wedding Banquet, has been understood in Christian tradition as evidence that God had rejected the Jewish people and that his promises and blessings have been transferred to the Christian church is the one about the Wicked Tenants (Matt. 21:33-46; Mark 12:1-12; Luke 20:9-19; *Gos. Thom.* 65–66).[14] Already early on in the history of Christian interpretation, it was read as an allegory where the son was understood to represent Jesus, the servants the prophets, and the wicked tenants the Jewish people. However, if it can be traced back to Jesus himself, his audience can hardly have understood it in this way. Below is Mark's version of the parable:

> Then he began to speak to them in parables. "A man planted a vineyard, put a fence around it, dug a pit for the wine press, and built a watchtower; then he leased it to tenants and went to another country. When the season came, he sent a slave to the tenants to collect from them his share of the produce of the vineyard. But they seized him, and beat him, and sent him away empty-handed. And again he sent another slave to them; this one they beat over the head and insulted. Then he sent another, and that one they killed. And so it was with many others; some they beat, and others they killed. He had still one other, a beloved son. Finally he sent him to them, saying, 'They will respect my son.' But those tenants said to one another, 'This is the heir; come, let us kill him, and the inheritance will be ours.' So they seized him, killed him, and threw him out of the vineyard. What then will the owner of the vineyard do? He will come and destroy the tenants and give the vineyard to others. Have you not read this scripture: 'The stone that the builders rejected has become the cornerstone; this was the Lord's doing, and it is amazing in our eyes'?" When they realized that he had told this parable against them, they wanted to arrest him, but they feared the crowd. So they left him and went away.

---

13. Young, *Parables*, 171–75.
14. For a comprehensive analysis, see Kloppenborg, *Tenants in the Vineyard*, 174–201.

Among those who listened to Jesus, the motif of the vineyard with details such as watchtowers and wine presses were likely to evoke associations to the well-known passage about God's planting a vineyard in Isa. 5:1-7: "My beloved had a vineyard. . . . [He] planted it with choice vines. He built a watchtower inside it, he even hewed a wine press in it. . . . For the vineyard of the Lord of Hosts is the house of Israel." The vineyard motif is common in prophetic literature,[15] and is taken up in rabbinic literature, where the vineyard invariably stands for Israel.

If we for a moment disregard the later Christian interpretation of this parable and on the basis of the Hebrew Bible and Jewish tradition assume that the vineyard represents Israel, who then might the tenants and the son refer to? In all three synoptic Gospels it is clearly stated that the leadership associated with the Jerusalem temple interpreted the parable as directed against them, indicating that Jesus' audience would have identified the tenants with the political and religious leaders. In Mark's version, we have to look back to the passage immediately preceding the parable (Mark 11:27) to ascertain that "they" refers to the "chief priests, the scribes, and the elders," but in the Gospels of Matthew and Luke, their identity is spelled out at the end of the parable. Matthew 21:45 reads: "When the chief priests and the Pharisees heard his parables, they realized that he was speaking about them."[16] Also, in all three synoptic Gospels, the parable is placed in the context of confrontations between Jesus and the religio-political leadership, giving further support to the conclusion that the audience would have understood it as directed against the religious and political leaders.

In these confrontations, the leaders question the authority of Jesus and in response, Jesus challenges them for not recognizing the authority of John the Baptist (Matt. 21:23-27; Mark 11:27-33; Luke 20:1-8). The reference to John the Baptist has led some scholars to identify the son in the parable with John the Baptist. They maintain that the parable was understood by Jesus' audience as a critique of the religious leaders for their mistreatment of John the Baptist, and that as a consequence of the unworthy leadership, the vineyard (Israel) would be entrusted to other leaders.[17] The king's

---

15. See for instance Isa. 2:21 and Hos. 10:1.

16. Luke 20:19 reads: "the scribes and the chief priests." Matthew has added the Pharisees, probably an indication of his conflict with this particular group.

17. Stern, "Jesus' Parables," 65, and Lowe quoted in Fitzmyer, *Gospel according to Luke*, 1278. Stern analyzes the Markan version of the parable and Lowe the Lukan.

somewhat odd decision to eventually send his beloved son, risking his life, is an indication of how precious the vineyard is to him and by implication how precious Israel is to God.

Other scholars argue that the son need not be identified with anyone in particular,[18] but agree that the point of the parable is critique of the religious leadership.[19] This is not to say that the authors of the Gospels did not see a parallel between the mistreatment of John the Baptist by the religious leaders and the latter's role in the death of Jesus, and may have wished their readers to note this resemblance also.[20] Mark's reference to the son in the parable as the king's "beloved son," is an indication that he understood the son to be Jesus, since "beloved son" is elsewhere a common designation for Jesus.

However, one verse in Matthew's version of the parable hints at a different meaning altogether, foreshadowing the traditional Christian understanding of it. Contrary to the motif as commonly understood, Matt. 21:43 takes the vineyard to represent the kingdom of God: "Therefore I tell you, the kingdom of God will be taken away from you and given to a people that produces the fruits of the kingdom." Whereas Mark and Luke, in line with Jewish tradition, understand the vineyard to be Israel, Matthew identifies the vineyard with the kingdom of God and seems to imply that rather than Israel being given to other leaders, the kingdom of God will be given to another people.

Interestingly, the phrase "the kingdom of God will be taken away from you" does not appear in either Mark or Luke (cf. Mark 12:9 and Luke 20:16). A majority of scholars believe that Matthew knew the Gospel of Mark and reworked it, and so it would appear that verse 43 is a revision of Mark's text, giving the parable a completely new meaning. It is very unlikely that Jesus' audience understood the vineyard to be anything other than Israel, since this is what the well-known motif implies, and the fact that the text states that the religious leadership understood the parable to be directed against them suggests that this was the understanding at some stage of the Matthew level as well.

The somewhat unusual wording in verse 43 may in fact suggest that it is a revision of the original form of the Gospel of Matthew. While Matthew usually uses the expression "the kingdom of heaven" (*hē basileia tōn ouranōn*) in accordance with the Jewish practice to avoid speaking directly

---

18. Milavec, "Fresh Analysis," 99–104.
19. Ibid., 81–117; Stern, "Jesus' Parables," 42–80.
20. Stern, "Jesus' Parables," 65–66.

about God, verse 43 says "the kingdom of God" (*hē basileia tou theou*), raising the possibility that another hand is behind this verse.[21] Based on these observations, some scholars indeed claim that verse 43 is a later addition to the Gospel of Matthew, reflecting a development where the split between Matthew's community and Judaism had become irreversible.[22]

As was noted above, there is much to suggest that the Gospel of Matthew originated in a community of Jewish disciples of Jesus, to which non-Jews could belong only if they converted to Judaism and accordingly also became Jewish disciples of Jesus. Many portions of the Gospel of Matthew seem to have a completely inner-Jewish perspective, evident in passages such as: "I was sent only to the lost sheep of the house of Israel" (Matt. 15:24), and "These twelve Jesus sent out with the following instructions: Go nowhere among the Gentiles, and enter no town of the Samaritans, but go rather to the lost sheep of the house of Israel" (Matt. 10:5-6).[23]

However, some scholars speculate that the Gospel of Matthew was taken over by a group of Gentile Christians in the process of separation between Judaism and Christianity. For these Christians who were trying to find a place for themselves in a movement dominated by Jews, texts suggesting that Jesus turned primarily, or even only, to Jews were likely disturbing, and in order to legitimate their own place in the community, they may have made certain additions that modify the inner-Jewish perspective of the original Gospel of Matthew. A greater openness toward non-Jews was achieved through the addition of statements such as: "Go therefore and make disciples of all nations" (Matt. 28:19).[24]

---

21. "The kingdom of heaven" appears 31 times in Matthew, while "the kingdom of God" only appears 4 times.
22. See Davies and Allison, *Matthew*, 3:186; Zetterholm, *Formation of Christianity*, 211–16. For a different view, see Runesson, "Matthew's Gospel," 133–51, who argues that Matthew uses the word "*ethnos*" (people) in the sense of "group" rather than "people" and the kingdom of God as referring to Israel. Thus, in his view, the Matthean version also reflects an entirely inner-Jewish debate and Matthew, like Mark, is simply saying that Israel will be given a new leadership. See also Kloppenborg, *Tenants in the Vineyard*, 191–97.
23. See also Matt. 5:47, 6:32, 18:17.
24. See also Matt. 10:18, 24:14. There seems to be an emerging consensus that the Gospel of Matthew reflects the development of at least one group of Jesus disciples from being a part of Judaism to becoming a non-Jewish church; see for instance Saldarini, "Gospel of Matthew," 23–38; Sim, *Gospel of Matthew*, 2–9; Zetterholm, *Formation of Christianity*, 211–16.

Thus, three different levels may be discerned in the parable of the Wicked Tenants: the Jesus level, the Gospel level, and later Christian interpretation. At the Jesus level, the vineyard stands for Israel and the point seems to be critique of the religious leadership, possibly occasioned by the particular instance of their mistreatment of John the Baptist. At the Gospel level, the point is still critique of the religious leaders, although in a broader sense, since the context is one of conflict over leadership and authority between the Jesus movement and other Jewish groups. The authors of the Gospels likely understood "the son" as referring to Jesus— as indicated by their designation of him as the "beloved son," a term that elsewhere is used for Jesus—and the vineyard may have been understood as a particular group within Israel, namely the community of Jesus disciples. Finally, in later Christian tradition, foreshadowed by the reworking of the original Gospel of Matthew (Matt. 21:43), the parable was read as a prophecy about the death of Jesus and the destruction of Jerusalem, where the tenants were identified with the Jewish people, the son with Jesus, and the vineyard taken to mean the kingdom of God, which would be given to another people—the Gentile Christians.

The parable of the Wicked Tenants, then, illustrates how attention to biblical literature and rabbinic parables can help us get behind later Christian interpretations and reconstruct the way in which Jesus' Jewish audience is likely to have understood this parable. The fact that "vineyard" is a symbol for Israel in both biblical and rabbinic literature strongly suggests that this is how "vineyard" was understood by Jesus' audience and the authors of the Gospels too. Any other understanding of "vineyard" likely reflects polemical concerns. To be sure, polemical concerns are sometimes reflected in rabbinic parables too, although most of them have been used to convey theological messages in exclusively Jewish contexts. Some, however, seem to reflect a situation where Jesus-oriented groups laid claims to be the true heirs of the Bible's promises and blessings and to be designed particularly to refute these claims. One such parable appearing in *Sifre*, a tannaitic midrash to Deuteronomy, employs motifs so similar to the parable of the Wicked Tenants that it raises the possibility that it came into being in direct response to the Matthean version of it.

PARABLES AND POLEMICS

In commenting upon Deut. 32:9, "For the Lord's portion is His people, Jacob his own allotment," *Sifre* employs a motif similar to that of the Gospel parable of the Wicked Tenants:

> *For the Lord's portion is His people, Jacob his own allotment* [Deut. 32:9]. It is like [*mashal le*] a king who owned a field, which he leased to tenants. When the tenants began to steal from it, he took it away from them and leased it to their children. When the children began to act worse than their father, he took it away from them and gave it to [the original tenants'] grandchildren. When these too became worse than their predecessors, a son was born to him. He then said to the grandchildren: "Leave my property. You may not remain therein. Give me back my portion, so that I may acknowledge it." Likewise [*kakh*] when our father Abraham came into the world, unworthy [descendants] issued from him, Ishmael and all Keturah's children.[25] When Isaac came into the world, unworthy [descendants] issued from him, Esau and all the princes of Edom, and they were worse than their predecessors. When Jacob came into the world, he did not produce unworthy [descendants], rather all his children were worthy, as it is said, *Jacob was a perfect man, dwelling in tents* [Gen. 25:27]. Now, from what point does God acknowledge his portion? From Jacob, as it is said, *For the Lord's portion is His people, Jacob his own allotment* [Deut. 32:9].[26]

The motif bears a striking resemblance to the parable of the Wicked Tenants: a king, a son, and unworthy tenants, and in both the king persists in entrusting his property to misbehaving servants before finally entrusting it to his son. Only the property is different, being a field rather than a vineyard, and somewhat surprisingly the field is considered important enough to be given to the king's son.

According to the *nimshal*, the son is Jacob, who in Jewish tradition is identified with the people of Israel. This, together with the fact that Ishmael and Esau are rabbinic code names for the non-Jewish nations, suggests that the point of the parable is to justify God's election of Israel, which, one might argue, took place at the expense of the other nations. The point here is that the election begins with Jacob, not with Abraham,

---

25. Keturah was one of Abraham's wives according to Gen. 25:1.
26. *Sifre* Deut §312.

and therefore does not include all of Abraham's offspring. The election belongs exclusively to the descendants of Jacob, namely to the people of Israel, an argument that may have been designed to refute the claim made by Gentile Christians that God's blessings and promises had been transferred to a "new people."

The elevation of Jacob at the expense of Abraham may also imply a polemic argument directed at Paul's claim that true faith had been achieved already by Abraham, and his contention that, based on God's covenant with Abraham, non-Jewish disciples of Jesus could be included into the covenant with Israel's God (Rom. 4; Gal. 3). Such a conclusion may be implied by the parable's startling assertion that Jacob alone is God's child; all the others, Abraham, Isaac and their respective descendants, are merely said to be tenants on the land.[27]

Although it is not entirely obvious what the field stands for, it clearly has great value in the eyes of the king, since he entrusts it to his son as soon as he has one. From his persistence in passing it on, first to the children of the unworthy tenants and then to their grandchildren instead of finding better tenants, also indicates that he was really anxious for these tenants to have the field, hoping all the while that they would change and appreciate it. A reasonable guess is that the field stands for the Torah, especially given the tradition, widespread in tannaitic literature, that God first offered the Torah to the nations of the world (Esau, Ammon, Moab, and Ishmael) and gave it to Israel only after they had rejected it.[28] A passage in *Sifre* Deut. §343 in particular emphasizes the efforts that God made in trying to offer the Torah to the non-Jewish nations: "There was not a single nation among the nations with whom he did not speak, knocking on each one's door to ask if they wanted to receive the Torah." Thus, in addition to its claim that Israel, as Jacob's descendants, was the only nation worthy of God's election, the parable may hint at the tradition of God's insistent efforts at offering the Torah to the non-Jewish nations before giving it to Israel, as an additional justification of the election of Israel.

The need to legitimize their status as God's people was an urgent concern for both Jews and Christians, as is evident from biblical interpretations of both groups. Affirmation of the continued status of Israel as God's people,

---

27. Stern, "Jesus' Parables," 60–63.
28. *Sifre* Deut §343; *Mekh. R. Ishmael* Bahodesh 5 (Lauterbach, 2:234–37. For later versions of this narrative, see *b. Avod. Zar.* 2a–2b; *Exod. Rab.* 27.9; *Lev. Rab.* 13.2; *Num. Rab.* 14.10; *Pirqe R. Eliezer* 40 (Friedlander 41); *Targ. Ps.-J.* and *Targ. Neof.* on Deut. 33:2.

as well as awareness of the Christians' claim of being the "true Israel" (*verus Israel*),[29] is reflected in *Song of Songs Rabbah*, a midrash on the book of Song of Songs. It was compiled in the middle of the sixth century but also contains earlier traditions. There we find the following parable:

> The straw, chaff, and the stubble were arguing with each other, each claiming that for its sake the ground had been sown. Said the wheat to them: "Wait till the threshing time comes, and we shall see for whose sake the field has been sown." When the time came and they were all brought into the threshing-floor, the farmer went out to winnow it. The chaff was scattered to the winds; the straw he took and threw on the ground; the stubble he cast into the fire; the wheat he took and piled in a heap, and all the passers-by when they saw it kissed it, as it says, *Kiss ye the corn* [Ps. 11:12].[30] So of the nations some say: "We are Israel, and for our sake was the world created," and others say: "We are Israel, and for our sake the world was created." Says Israel to them: "Wait till the day of the Holy One, blessed be He, comes, and we shall see for whose sake the world was created," and so it is written, *For lo! That day is at hand, burning like an oven. [All the arrogant and all the doers of evil shall be straw, and the day that is coming— said the Lord of Hosts—shall burn them to ashes and leave of them nor stock not boughs]* [Mal. 3:19]; and it is written, *You shall winnow them and the wind shall carry them off* [Isa. 41:16]. But of Israel it is said, *But you shall rejoice in the Lord, and glory in the Holy One of Israel* [ibid.].[31]

It is not explicitly stated that the other nations are the Christians, but it is evident from other sources relating similar disputes, such as the following passage from *Midrash Tanhuma*, where Moses asks God to write down the Mishnah:

> Rabbi Judah bar Shalom said: "When the Lord said to Moses, '*Write down [these commandments]*' [Exod. 34:27], Moses asked him to write down the Mishnah too. But the Holy One, blessed be He, foresaw that a time would come when the nations of the world would translate the Torah, read it in Greek and say: 'We are Israel . . .' The Holy One, blessed be He, will then say to the nations of the world: 'You say that you are my children.

---

29. On this claim, see Simon, *Verus Israel*, 65–97.
30. This is the understanding of the midrash. The meaning of the Hebrew is uncertain.
31. *Songs Rab.* 7.3. An older version is found in *Gen. Rab.* 83.5.

That may be, but those who have my mystery, they are [certainly] my children.' And what is the mystery? It is the Mishnah that was given orally."[32]

The fact that the "nations of the world" are said to read the Torah in Greek identifies them as Christians. The Christians took over the Hebrew Bible from the Jews, read it in its Greek translation (the Septuagint), and argued that the biblical promises and blessings had been transferred to them. Since the Bible was no longer Israel's exclusive property, the distinguishing trait of the true children of Israel was now considered oral tradition, here referred to as the Mishnah. In contrast to the Bible, oral tradition distinguished Jews from Christians, and, accordingly, this is what defines the identity of the true heirs of the biblical promises and blessings in the view of the rabbis. In this account, God's refusal to commit rabbinic interpretive tradition to writing was meant to ensure that the Christians would not take over this too and claim it to be theirs.

The struggle between Jews and Christians in antiquity was to a large extent a struggle over the interpretation of the Bible, in which each side claimed to possess the correct interpretation. The various versions of the early Jesus movement interpreted the Torah with the life and death of Jesus as the hermeneutical key, maintaining that they possessed the correct interpretation of Judaism and were therefore the rightful heirs of biblical tradition. Non-Jesus-oriented Jews, some of these groups maintained, did not understand their own scriptures and as a result the biblical promises had been passed on to the new people of God, namely the Christians. By contrast, the rabbis held that the rabbinic oral tradition was the key to understanding the Torah, and the sign that confirmed their continued status as the true children of God.

It is evident, then, that a comparison of Gospel parables to rabbinic ones reveals close similarities concerning motifs, concerns, and theological messages that likely go back to first-century Judaism. As paradoxical as it may at first seem, the use of similar motifs in rabbinic parables may actually help us get behind later interpretation conditioned by the Christian identity-formation process and concomitant rivalry with Judaism. Interpretation of a parable is determined largely by the context in which it is told or read, and since rabbinic parables have been preserved in an exclusively Jewish context and used mainly to convey ideas about

---

32. *Tanh.* Ki Tissa 34. My translation. See also *Tanh.* Vayyera 6 (ed. Buber); *Exod. Rab.* 47.1; *Pes. Rabb.* 5.

Israel's or humanity's relationship with God, their interpretations have not been affected by the polemical debate between Jews and Christians in the way the Gospel parables have. However, a few rabbinic parables seem to have come into being in direct response to claims made by Jesus-oriented groups, and in these cases they have a clear polemical purpose. Thus, while most rabbinic parables can serve as a help to reconstruct the meaning of the Gospel parables at the Jesus-level, some are polemical responses to Gospel parables as they were later understood, reflecting a later stage of Jewish-Christian relations.

PAUL—A FIRST-CENTURY JEWISH THEOLOGIAN

The scholarly debate on the Jewish character of the Jesus movement that began with Jesus' place within Judaism is increasingly focusing on Paul's relation to Judaism, with a growing number of scholars seeing Paul as a Torah-observant Jew who never left Judaism. The idea that Paul was concerned primarily with non-Jews, whom he wanted to include in the covenant with the God of Israel without first turning them into Jews, is becoming more common, and his negative statements about the law are being explained, at least in part, by his desire to prevent non-Jews from keeping commandments that were given to the Jewish people.[33]

This stands in stark contrast to earlier Pauline scholarship that basically understood Paul to be in opposition to Judaism. During the nineteenth century, that view was reinforced as a consequence of the general cultural climate and especially through the writings of the German biblical scholar F. C. Baur (1792–1860), who was heavily influenced by the philosopher G. F. Hegel. According to Hegel, the development of the world takes place in dialectic triads toward higher and higher stages. Every thesis generates its antithesis, and the two are then resolved in a synthesis. Applying this system to the development of Judaism and Christianity, Baur saw in the Jesus movement's separation from its Jewish heritage a process by which Christianity transcended Judaism reaching a higher stage of development. The superiority of Christianity thereby received a legitimacy that almost appeared scientific.[34]

---

33. See Zetterholm, *Approaches to Paul*, 127–63; Gager, *Reinventing Paul*, 43–75.
34. Zetterholm, *Approaches to Paul*, 35–40.

As noted above, the view of Judaism as a dark background to Christianity influenced scholarship on the historical Jesus, and this is all the more true concerning Pauline scholarship. If Judaism was characterized as a legalistic system in which people struggled in vain to fulfill obsolete commandments, it was no wonder that Paul turned away from it, establishing a new religion based on grace and forgiveness. Several modern scholars, among them Krister Stendahl and David Flusser, made attempts to modify the prevailing view of Paul and Judaism, but as was the case with Jesus and Judaism, it was only with the scholarship of E. P. Sanders that the traditional view of the relationship between Paul and Judaism was seriously challenged.

Sanders's writings not only undermined the traditional idea of an opposition between Jesus and Judaism, but also challenged the assumption that Paul opposed the Jewish law. According to Sanders, Paul saw nothing wrong with the Torah. Rather, it was his belief that God had chosen to save humankind through Christ that led him to the conclusion that the Torah did not lead to salvation.[35] If, as Sanders showed, Second Temple Judaism was not characterized by legalism and self-righteousness, and if the Jews did not believe that they earned salvation by observing the commandments of the Torah, this could hardly have been the reason for Paul's attacks on the law. This insight paved the way for a completely new approach to the study of Paul that in many ways is much more radical than Sanders's.[36]

A growing number of scholars now consider Paul to have remained within Judaism throughout his life, and rather than arguing over whether or not Paul opposed parts of the Jewish law, the issue under discussion is what it meant to be a Torah-observant Jew in the Diaspora during the first century. In Acts, Paul is indeed portrayed as being Torah-observant, sacrificing in the temple (Acts 21:26) and asserting that he has never "committed an offense against the law of the Jews, or against the temple, or against the emperor" (Acts 25:8). The author of Acts was apparently aware that already during Paul's lifetime there were rumors that he taught Jews to "forsake Moses" and not to "circumcise their children or observe the customs" (Acts 21:21), but dismisses them as false. Paul, according to Acts, "observe[s] and guard[s] the law" (Acts 21:24).

---

35. Sanders, *Paul*, 431–552.
36. For a survey of the new perspective on Paul, see Zetterholm, *Approaches to Paul*, 95–126.

Greater emphasis is also attributed to Paul's own statement that his mission is directed to the Gentiles (Rom. 11:13, 15:16; Gal. 2:2), that is, that he saw his mission as directed predominantly to the non-Jewish disciples of Jesus within the Jesus movement. Accordingly, his negative statements about the law should not be understood as an attack on the Torah itself, it is argued, but more likely served the purpose of dissuading the non-Jewish members of the Jesus movement from considering themselves righteous and saved based on their observance of the Torah.

The great attraction that Judaism seems to have held for non-Jews in antiquity is well documented, and there is much to suggest that these non-Jewish adherents to the Jesus movement wanted to and even insisted on observing the Torah.[37] The Jewish historian Josephus writes: "The masses have long since shown a keen desire to adopt our religious observances; and there is not one city, Greek or barbarian, nor a single nation, to which our custom of abstaining from work on the seventh day has not spread, and where the fasts and the lighting of lamps and many of our prohibitions in the matter of food are not observed" (C. Ap. 2.282). With respect to the Jews in the city Antioch, he writes: "they were constantly attracting to their religious ceremonies multitudes of Greeks, and these they had in some measure incorporated with themselves" (B.J. 7.45). Although Josephus likely exaggerates, the attraction that Judaism held for non-Jews is well attested in Roman sources also. Many adherents to Greco-Roman religion simply seem to have incorporated the God of Israel into their pantheon together with other gods and goddesses.[38] Thus, it is very likely that many of the non-Jews who joined the Jesus movement had long been in close contact with Jews and had already adopted Jewish traditions and customs.[39]

For Paul, however, it appears to have been extremely important to uphold the distinction between Jews and non-Jews within the Jesus movement.[40] In part, this may have been a consequence of his belief in the one true God. If the non-Jews had to become Jews in order to be saved, God would not be the God of the entire world but merely the God of the Jews

---

37. Murray, *Jewish Game*, 11–41, and Kimelman, "Identifying Jews, " 301–33.
38. For a survey of a variety of ways of relating to Judaism by non-Jews, see Cohen, *Beginnings*, 141–62.
39. Zetterholm, "Missing Messiah," 43–46.
40. See, for example, Tucker, *Remain in Your Calling.*

(Rom. 3:29).[41] Paul may also have believed that the Torah was reserved exclusively for the Jewish people, but to this we will return later.

In contrast to the later Christian assumption, Paul was bothered not by continued Torah observance on the part of Jewish Jesus disciples but by the desire of the non-Jewish members of the Jesus movement to keep the commandments of the Torah and by their claim to righteousness based on such observance. Like any other first-century Jew, Paul most likely considered the Torah as God's gift to the Jewish people and as a sign of the covenant, taking continued Torah observance for granted among the Jews in the Jesus movement as well as among non-Jews who had converted to Judaism: "Once again I testify to every man who lets himself be circumcised that he is obliged to obey the entire law" (Gal. 5:3). In line with some other first-century Jews with a pessimistic view of the fate of non-Jews, Paul may have believed that for non-Jews who had not accepted the Torah, attempts to observe its commandments without the framework of the covenant and the means of atonement it provides would lead to destruction. According to this way of reasoning, the Torah is a blessing for those within the covenant but its commandments a curse for those outside of it.[42] The idea that the Torah could function in different ways for different groups is fully compatible with the lines of thought of Second Temple Judaism.

It seems that Paul envisioned two separate groups within the covenant; the Jewish disciples of Jesus who were expected to observe the Torah on the one hand, and the non-Jewish disciples of Jesus, included into the covenant through Jesus, but who were not to observe the Torah the same way Jews did, on the other: "This is my rule in all the churches. Was anyone at the time of his call already circumcised? Let him not seek to remove the marks of circumcision. Was anyone at the time of his call uncircumcised? Let him not seek circumcision" (1 Cor. 7:17-18). It may well have been the case that Paul considered belief in Jesus, the Messiah, as a necessary condition for remaining in the covenant also for Jews. Such eschatological exclusiveness was not unique to Paul, as seen, for instance, in the Qumran community, which also perceived itself as the only true remnant of Israel. Toward the end of his life, however, Paul had to contend with the fact that many of his fellow Jews had not embraced Jesus as the Messiah as he had hoped. In Romans 9–11, he develops the idea that this is the result of the

---

41. Nanos, *Mystery of Romans*, 184.
42. Gaston, *Paul and the Torah*, 100–106; Stowers, *Rereading of Romans*, 176–93; Zetterholm, *Approaches to Paul*, 127–63.

divine plan and that God has temporarily rejected the Jewish people as part of his strategy to include the non-Jews into the covenant. In the end though, he affirms, all Israel will be saved (Rom. 11:26).[43]

If the scholars of this new approach to Paul are at all correct, one may conclude that Paul came to be misunderstood very early. In a way similar to Jesus' parables, a later Christian theology was read into his letters according to which God has rejected the Jews and replaced them with the church.

Fig. 8. Ruins of the Acropolis of ancient Corinth. Photograph by Dieter Mitternacht.

PAUL AND JEWISH BIBLICAL INTERPRETATION

Paul, it seems, believed that through the life and death of Jesus, non-Jews could be incorporated into the covenant with Israel's God without first becoming Jews. While the idea that non-Jews would in some way also be saved at the end of time (Isa. 2:2-4) was widespread in Second Temple Judaism, the idea of including non-Jewish disciples of Jesus into the covenant,

---

43. Zetterholm, "Abraham Believed," 115. For a survey of the so-called radical new perspective on Paul, see Zetterholm, *Approaches to Paul*, 127–63. Among the representatives of this approach are Eisenbaum, *Paul Was Not a Christian*; Nanos, *Irony of Galatians*; Nanos, *Mystery of Romans*; Runesson, "Re-Thinking Early Jewish-Christian Relations," 59–92; Tomson, *Paul and the Jewish Law*.

giving them a status equal to that of the Jews, was not self-evident. From a Jewish point of view, the basic assumption was that one had to belong to the people of Israel in order to be part of the covenant, and accordingly the natural thing to do, if non-Jews were to be included, would have been to make them Jews. Thus, Paul faced a dilemma, since he believed that the rules had changed with Jesus (as they had previously been changed at Sinai), and that the non-Jews had a place in the covenant precisely as non-Jews. From the way he solves this predicament, it is evident that he shared the approach to the biblical text prevalent among Jewish interpreters of his time. In Rom. 4:1-12, he writes:

> What then are we to say was gained by Abraham, our ancestor according to the flesh? For if Abraham was justified by works, he has something to boast about, but not before God. For what does the scripture say? *Abraham trusted in God, and it was reckoned to him as righteousness* [Gen. 15:6] . . . Is this blessedness, then, pronounced only on the circumcised, or also on the uncircumcised? We say: "Trust [*pistis*] was reckoned to Abraham as righteousness." How then was it reckoned to him? Was it before or after he had been circumcised? It was not after, but before he was circumcised. He received the sign of circumcision as a seal of the righteousness that he had by trust [*pistis*] while he was still uncircumcised. The purpose was to make him the ancestor of all who are faithful [*patera pantōn tōn pisteuontōn*] without being circumcised and who thus have righteousness reckoned to them, and likewise the ancestor of the circumcised who are not only circumcised but who also follow the example of the trust of our father Abraham before he was circumcised [*tēs en akrobystia pisteōs tou patros hēmōn Abraam*].[44]

In order to find a theological solution that made it possible to include non-Jews in the covenant without making them Jews, Paul appeals to Gen. 15:6 and argues that Abraham, on account of his trust in God, was called righteous *before* he was circumcised (Gen. 17:9-27) and *before* the Torah was given at Sinai (Exod. 19–24).[45] The rendering of *pistis* as "faithfulness" rather than the common translation "faith" is a consequence of the realization that the word in antiquity seems to refer less to an abstract, interior belief and more to specific character traits and resulting behavior.

---

44. Translation modified based on Johnson Hodge, *If Sons*, 82–83.
45. Zetterholm, "Abraham Believed," 112–15.

Accordingly, translations such as "faithfulness" or "trustworthiness" for *pistis* are more appropriate, as is "to trust" or "to be loyal" for the verb *pisteuō*. In this case, the "faithfulness of our father Abraham" likely stands for his trusting acceptance of and response to God's promise of a son. Abraham's trust thus brings about God's gracious act of granting him descendants who will be blessed thanks to Abraham's faithfulness.[46]

Since trust in God is not dependent on circumcision or the Torah, the model of Abraham provides Paul with a solution to his problem. As descendants of Abraham, who was called righteous before he was circumcised and without observing the Torah because it was not yet given, the non-Jewish disciples of Jesus can enter into the covenant with Israel's God on basis of their trust in God. In the fashion of the exegetes of his time, Paul attributes significance to the order of events in the biblical text, and we must assume that he considered his interpretation to be entirely justified and in accordance with the deeper meaning of the Torah. In Rom. 3:31, he says: "Do we then overthrow the law by this faith? By no means! On the contrary, we uphold the law." Like any other ancient interpreter, he surely had an ulterior motive, but his assumptions about the biblical text also played an important part in the formation of his theology.

In Paul's thinking, Abraham's trust and God's faithfulness are intertwined, an idea for which he may have found inspiration or support in the ambiguous formulation of Gen. 15:6: "He put his trust in God and he reckoned it to him as righteousness." This could be understood to mean that God considered Abraham righteous on account of his trust, but since it is not clear from the Hebrew text who the subject of the second phrase is, it could also be taken to mean that Abraham trusted in God and considered him, God, righteous or faithful. The Septuagint reflects this ambiguity of the Hebrew and could likewise be read either way. The fact that Paul, as he quotes the verse in Rom. 4:3, obviously understands it to mean that God reckoned Abraham's trust as righteousness does not mean that he was not also aware of the other possible understanding. Irrespective of which understanding is more plausible, a "rabbinic" mode of reading could easily exploit the textual ambiguity, reading it both ways in order to make a theological point.

Indeed, in Gal. 3:6-9, Paul seems to understand *pistis* with regard to both Abraham and God, saying that Abraham put his trust in God and out of faithfulness God has found a way to make the non-Jews righteous

---

46. Johnson Hodge, *If Sons*, 82–84.

also: "Just as Abraham *trusted in God* [*episteusen tō theō*] *and it was reckoned to him as righteousness* [Gen 15:6; Rom 4:3] so you know that those who descend from faithfulness [*hoi ek pisteōs*], these are the sons of Abraham. The scripture, having foreseen that God would justify the gentiles out of faithfulness [*ek pisteōs*], proclaimed the good news beforehand to Abraham that, *All the peoples of the earth will be blessed in you* [Gen. 12:3, 18:18]. For this reason, those who descend from faithfulness [*hoi ek pisteōs*] are blessed with the faithful Abraham [*syn tō pistō Abraam*]."[47] The translation of *hoi ek pisteōs* in (Gal. 3:7) as "those who come out of faithfulness," rather than the common "those who believe," reflects the understanding of *pistis* as "faithfulness" and takes into account the preposition *ek*, which often means "come out of" or "spring from."[48]

In Paul's reading, Scripture foretold that non-Jews would be justified "out of faithfulness"—Abraham's and God's. Johnson Hodge, however, argues that this faithfulness refers also, and even specifically, to Christ's faithfulness, which Paul tells us elsewhere is responsible for the justification of the non-Jews (Gal. 2:16; Rom. 3:22, 26). Paul understands Christ's faithfulness (*pistis Christou*) as his willingness and ability to carry out God's plan for his death and resurrection. According to this understanding, it is not the believer's faith in Christ that makes him or her righteous, but rather Christ's faithful obedience to God's plan. Through his death and resurrection, Christ brings about God's righteousness.[49] However, one might add that although the faithfulness of Christ is surely the main point, faith in the sense of trust is required from humans also. Echoing the double meaning of *pistis* in the Abraham story, the faithfulness of Christ is a replica of God's faithfulness, and just as Abraham trusted God's promises, the Jesus disciples must put their trust in Christ. In Paul's thinking, for non-Jewish disciples of Jesus to trust Christ likely means to have confidence that their inclusion into the covenant on the basis of Jesus' death and resurrection really works and that accordingly, there is no need for them to imitate Jewish Torah observance.

In Gal. 3:16-17, Paul again interprets scripture in a way akin to what we find in rabbinic literature. Exploiting the fact that the promises were made to Abraham's offspring in the singular (Gen. 12:7), he argues that "offspring" refers to Christ: "Now the promises were made to Abraham

---

47. Translation modified based on Johnson Hodge, *If Sons*, 84.
48. Ibid., 79–82, 84–86.
49. Ibid., 85–90. See also Hays, *Faith*, 161–62.

and to his offspring. It does not say, 'And to offsprings,' as of many; but it says, 'And to your offspring,' that is, to one person, who is Christ. My point is this: the law, which came four hundred thirty years later, does not annul a covenant previously ratified by God, so as to nullify the promise." The covenant between God and Israel at Sinai, of which the Torah is the sign cannot annul God's previous promise made to Abraham, Paul argues, and therefore the non-Jews must not become Jews. The promise made to Abraham is good for all his descendants, "not only the one who comes out of the Law [ek tou nomou] but also for the one who comes out of the faithfulness of Abraham [ek pisteōs Abraam]" (Rom. 4:16).

Non-Jews and the Torah—Different Approaches

As within other Jewish groups, there seem to have been various different views on how Jews were to relate to non-Jews within the Jesus movement and how the latter were to relate to the Torah. One was the Pauline view, according to which non-Jewish disciples of Jesus had a place in the covenant as non-Jews, on a par with the Jews, but without being obliged to observe all of the Torah's commandments as were Jews. This must be understood in a context in which it was probably taken for granted that the non-Jews would adapt, or more likely, had already adapted, to Jewish food regulations and were expected to keep the more general ethic commandments of the Torah. What exactly Paul had in mind when he warned non-Jewish disciples of Jesus against law observance is not altogether clear, but apparently the Torah, in his view, was not the sign of the covenant for non-Jews the way it was for Jews.

As is evident from Acts 15, others, however, considered it necessary for non-Jewish disciples of Jesus to become Torah-observant Jews in order to be included in the covenant with Israel's God: "Then certain individuals came down from Judea and were teaching the brothers, 'Unless you are circumcised according to the custom of Moses, you cannot be saved,'" and further in verse 5: "But some believers who belonged to the sect of the Pharisees stood up and said, 'It is necessary for them to be circumcised and ordered to keep the law of Moses.'" Possibly, the original community of Matthew was made up of a group holding similar views.

There may also have been a third view, whose proponents wanted to include the non-Jews in the covenant without requiring them to convert to Judaism, but expected them to keep as many of the Torah's commandments as possible. Such a position may be reflected in the *Didache*, a text that was probably redacted around the turn of the first century C.E.[50] It is considered one of the most important literary witnesses of the Jesus movement outside of the New Testament, but it appears to originally have been a Jewish text designed to give instructions to non-Jewish disciples of Jesus, as indicated by its full title: "The teaching of the Lord through the twelve apostles to the Gentiles [*tois ethnesin*]." *Didache* 6:2–3 reads: "For you can bear the entire yoke of the Lord [*holon ton zygon tou kyriou*], you will be perfect; but if you cannot, do as much as you can. And concerning food, bear what you can. But especially abstain from food sacrificed to idols; for this is a ministry to dead gods."

This passage seems to represent an adjustment to the perspective of non-Jewish disciples of Jesus, who were perhaps not capable of bearing the entire "yoke of the Lord" and may have had difficulties in observing all of the Jewish dietary laws. While it has been suggested that the phrase "the Lord's yoke" refers to Jesus' teachings in the Sermon on the Mount, it seems more likely to understand it as referring to the Torah as interpreted by Jesus (cf. Matt. 11:28-30). The Torah in rabbinic literature is quite often referred to as a "yoke,"[51] so it is natural to understand it in this sense here also. If this saying originated or was adopted in a milieu where the Torah was still faithfully observed by Jewish adherents to the Jesus movement, it would be an appeal to non-Jewish Jesus disciples to observe the Torah as far as they can.[52] As we will presently see, Paul and the *Didache*'s respective views of how non-Jews are to relate to the Torah roughly correspond to rabbinic views as known to us from tannaitic literature.

---

50. Sandt and Flusser, *Didache*, 48.

51. See for instance *m. Avot* 3:5; *b. Sanh.* 94b (the yoke of the Torah); *m. Ber.* 2:2 (the yoke of the kingdom of heaven and the yoke of the commandments).

52. Draper, "Troublesome Apostles," 360–65; Sandt and Flusser, *Didache*, 240–43. On the various approaches within the early Jesus movement, see also Flusser, "Jewish-Christian Opponents," 195–211; Zetterholm, "Didache," 73–90.

THE NON-JEW IN EARLY RABBINIC JUDAISM

In recent years, attention has been drawn to the fact that tannaitic literature seems to reflect two different approaches to how non-Jews are to relate to the Torah, associated with the schools of Rabbi Ishmael and Rabbi Aqiva, respectively. According to the position attributed to Rabbi Aqiva, the Torah is God's exclusive gift to the Jewish people and reserved for them only, while the approach associated with Rabbi Ishmael held that God had intended the Torah for all peoples. The Aqivan position would ultimately dominate, but in tannaitic times the two views apparently coexisted. The fact that the Torah was not revealed in the land of Israel, but rather in the desert, a public place, is taken by the *Mekhilta* as evidence that it was intended for all nations: "*[Israel] encamped in the wilderness* [Exod. 19:2]. The Torah was given in public, openly in a free place. For had the Torah been given in the land of Israel, the Israelites could have said to the nations of the world: 'You have no share in it.' But now that it was given in the wilderness publicly and openly in a place that is free to all, everyone wishing to accept it could come and accept it."[53]

The proponents of this view probably welcomed proselytes, but they also seem to have encouraged non-Jews to keep the commandments without assuming their conversion. In *Mekhilta de-Arayot*, preserved in *Sifra* but generally considered to be an independent literary unit from the school of Rabbi Ishmael, a non-Jew who observes the Torah is compared to the high priest:

> *You shall keep my laws and my rules, and by doing them man [*'adam*]*
> *shall live* [Lev. 18:5]. Rabbi Yirmia used to say: "How do we know that
> even a non-Jew who 'does Torah' [*'oseh torah*] is like the high priest?
> Scripture says, *by doing [this] man shall live* [Lev. 18:5]. Priests, Lev-
> ites, and Israelites it does not say here [rather Scripture says 'man']. And
> likewise it says, *this is the Torah of man [ve-zot torat ha-'adam]* [2 Sam
> 7:19]. Priests, Levites, and Israelites it does not say here. And likewise it
> says, *Open the gates, and let . . .* [Isa. 26:2]. Priests, Levites, and Israel-
> ites it does not say here, rather, *Open the gates, and let a righteous nation*
> [*goy tsaddiq*] *enter, [a nation] that keeps faith* [Isa. 26:2].[54]

---

53. *Mekhilta R. Ishmael* Bahodesh 1 (Lauterbach, 2:198).
54. *Sifra* on Lev. 18:1–5. My translation.

The midrash emphasizes that none of the quoted verses mentions priests, Levites, or Israelites, the three groups that make up the people of Israel. Rather, it simply says "a person" [*'adam*], thereby asserting that the Torah is not for Israel only but for all humanity, and to highlight this point a non-Jew who "does Torah" is compared to the high priest, who enjoys the highest status possible. While the expression "do Torah" [*'oseh torah*] can mean either "study Torah" or "fulfill the commandments," it is used in tannaitic literature in the latter sense.[55] Thus, according to this approach, attributed to Rabbi Ishmael, non-Jews may observe the Torah and it is considered meritorious for them to do so.[56] In direct contrast to this idea, we find in *Sifre* Deut §345 the view that the Torah is betrothed to Israel and is like a married woman in relation to non-Jews:

> [*Moses gave us the Torah*] *as the heritage of the congregation of Jacob* [Deut. 33:4]. Read not "heritage" [*morashah*] but "betrothed" [*me'orashah*], showing that the Torah is betrothed to Israel and has therefore the status of a married woman in relation to the nations of the world, as it is said, *Can a man rake embers into his bosom without burning his clothes? Can a man walk on live coals without scorching his feet? It is the same with one who sleeps with his fellow's wife; none who touches her will go unpunished* [Prov. 6:27-29].

Instead of reading "heritage" (*morashah*), the *Sifre* turns it into the similar-sounding Hebrew word for "betrothed" (*me'orashah*), asserting that the Torah is reserved for Israel only. At Sinai the Torah was given as a sign of the monogamous relationship into which God and Israel had entered, and as a result, non-Jewish involvement with the Torah outside of a legally defined commitment to it is comparable to adultery. The "nations" referred to are non-Jews, quite possibly disciples of Jesus, some of whom studied the Torah and observed the commandments but did not submit to the rabbinic interpretation of it.[57]

Thus, interpretations asserting that the Torah was intended for all nations seem to have originated in the school of Rabbi Ishmael (*Mekhilta de-Rabbi Ishmael* and *Sifre* to Numbers), while those claiming that the

---

55. Hirshman, "Rabbinic Universalism," 108.
56. Hirshman, "Rabbinic Universalism," 101–15. See also Flusser, "Jewish-Christian Opponents," 204–5; Sandt and Flusser, *Didache*, 266–67.
57. Fraade, *Tradition*, 57–58.

Torah is for Israel only derive from the school of Rabbi Aqiva (*Sifra* and *Sifre* to Deuteronomy). As we noted in chapter three, this division into two schools has received renewed support in recent scholarship on midrash.[58] Rabbi Ishmael was a priest according to rabbinic sources, and even if one should be careful not to draw too far-reaching conclusions from this information, it is not unlikely that such universalistic ideas flourished in priestly circles. The priestly sources of the Torah are among the most hospitable to the stranger (*ger*) and consistent with the universalism of Isaiah (40–66), who envisioned a Judaism open to all. Interestingly, this universalism is not at all messianic or eschatological.[59]

Although too brief to allow any firm conclusions, the *Didache*'s appeal to non-Jews to keep as many commandments as they can possibly reveals an approach similar to that of the school of Rabbi Ishmael. By contrast, Paul seems to combine an interest in the salvation of non-Jews with the view of the Torah as belonging exclusively to Israel, similar to the position of the school of Rabbi Aqiva.[60] Paul was a Pharisee, and although the suggestion is admittedly speculative, it would not be unreasonable to imagine that the view of the Torah as the exclusive property of the Jewish people was prevalent in Pharisaic circles.[61]

Not surprisingly, the Noachide laws—commandments that were considered binding for non-Jews who were not full members of the Jewish community—figure quite prominently in the Rabbi Aqiva midrashim, while the term is never explicitly mentioned in the Rabbi Ishmael midrashim.[62] The exact content of these laws varies, but an early list appears in *t. Avod. Zar.* 8:4: "Seven commandments were given to the children of Noah: to establish courts of law, [they are forbidden to engage in] idolatry, blasphemy, fornication, bloodshed, theft . . . and the eating of flesh cut from a living beast" (8:6). Quite possibly the Apostolic Decree, which commands non-Jewish disciples of Jesus to abstain from "things polluted by idols and from fornication and from whatever has been strangled and from blood" (Acts 15:20), is an early version of the Noachide commandments.[63] These rules were apparently

---

58. See Yadin, *Scripture as Logos*, x–xii.
59. Hirshman, "Rabbinic Universalism," 108; Yadin, *Scripture as Logos*, 165–67.
60. Zetterholm, "Missing Messiah," 55; Zetterholm, "Jews, Christians, and Gentiles," 250.
61. Sandt and Flusser, *Didache*, 269.
62. Hirshman, "Rabbinic Universalism," 112.
63. In addition to 15:20, the Apostolic Decree is quoted in Acts 15:28-29 and 21:25. The earliest extant text that connects the figure of Noah to a universal ethic that is binding upon the children of Noah is *Jub.* 7:20-21 (second century B.C.E.).

a minimum requirement that the non-Jewish disciples of Jesus had to keep in order to coexist with Jews in the same community of Jesus disciples.

Thus, Paul and the *Didache* may represent two different understandings of or reactions to the Apostolic Decree. For the author of *Did.* 6:2-3, for whom full Torah observance on the part of non-Jews was apparently desirable, the Apostolic Decree might have defined the minimum standard for non-Jewish Jesus disciples, while for Paul, who was anxious to dissuade them from Torah observance, it may actually have constituted both a maximum and a minimum—a minimum requirement of what non-Jews had to do, and a maximum of what they were allowed to do. Paul's vision of two separate categories within the covenant presumes that the difference between Jews and non-Jews is upheld, not unlike the school of Rabbi Aqiva, but if the non-Jews observe the commandments like the Jews, this difference would be blurred. In any case, he seems to have shared their view of the Torah as reserved for Israel only.[64]

Thus, if Jesus and Paul are placed in the context of the diversity within Second Temple Judaism, and seen in the light of subsequent schools of thought in early rabbinic Judaism, new perspectives emerge. During the first century, the dividing line was between Jews and non-Jews rather than between Jews and Christians, since Christianity did not yet exist independently of Judaism. For the Jewish disciples of Jesus, the major question seems to have been how Jews were to relate to non-Jews within the Jesus movement and how the latter were to relate to the Torah. Some of these approaches, it seems, are represented by Paul, Matthew, and the *Didache*.

However, none of these early visions was implemented by the Christian church. When, after some time, non-Jewish Christians became the majority, the problem became reversed and a completely new model developed, in which non-Jews were the norm and Jewishness and Torah observance were perceived as the problem. It is this later situation that has long been the starting point for Pauline scholarship, but the fresh insights that emerge from recent scholarship are slowly changing the picture. Some ideas that originated as polemical claims, or even misconceptions, unfortunately came to be understood as timeless theological truths and thus significantly shaped subsequent Christian tradition. If their polemical origin is recognized, we will be in a better position to liberate Christianity from its anti-Jewish elements and recognize that they need not be an integral part of Christian tradition.

---

64. Flusser, "Jewish-Christian Opponents," 195–211; Sandt and Flusser, *Didache*, 238–70; Zetterholm, "Didache," 73–90, and Zetterholm, "Missing Messiah," 33–35.

Study Questions

1. What is the significance of recognizing the similarities between rabbinic and Gospel parables?

2. Which important insights have paved the way for a different understanding of Jesus and Paul?

3. How do the views of non-Jews and their relationship to the Torah evidenced in the New Testament and early Christian writings fit into Jewish theological ideas about non-Jews and the Torah as evidenced in early rabbinic literature?

4. What are the major differences between the new perspectives on Paul and the traditional one?

Suggestions for Further Reading

Becker, E. M., and Runesson, A., eds. *Mark and Matthew: Comparative Readings I: Understanding the Earliest Gospels in Their First-Century Settings*. Tübingen: Mohr Siebeck, 2011.

Overman, A. J. *Matthew's Gospel and Formative Judaism: The Social World of the Matthean Community*. Minneapolis: Fortress Press, 1990.

Sanders, E. P. *Paul and Palestinian Judaism: A Comparison of Patterns of Religion*. Philadelphia: Fortress Press, 1977.

Thoma, C., and M. Wyschogrod, eds. *Parable and Story in Judaism and Christianity*. New York: Paulist, 1989.

Tomson, P. J. *"If This Be from Heaven": Jesus and the New Testament Authors in Their Relationship to Judaism*. Sheffield: Sheffield Academic, 2001.

Young, B. H. *The Parables: Jewish Tradition and Christian Interpretation*. Peabody: Hendrickson, 1998.

Zetterholm, M. *Approaches to Paul: A Student's Guide to Recent Scholarship*. Minneapolis: Fortress Press, 2009.

5

Continuity and Change in Contemporary Judaism

After the diversion to the Jesus movement in the previous chapter, we now return to rabbinic Judaism and direct our attention to its development in modern times, in particular to the ways in which the various denominations of contemporary Judaism handle the tension between continuity with the past and adaptation to the present. In light of the strong statements.

In light of the strong statements affirming the human role in adapting and reshaping the word of God found in some rabbinic aggadic texts, contemporary Judaism, at least in some of its forms, seems surprisingly restrained in this regard. In part this may be explained by the fact that the permission to innovate in these aggadic texts is so general that it is not easily translated into practice, and in part because Jewish tradition has always attributed a greater significance to legal texts. It should also be remembered that the rabbinic texts permitting and endorsing innovation and change likely served to justify changes that had already taken place and should accordingly not be taken as evidence of a radical inclination toward change on the part of the rabbis of ancient times.

In an effort to preserve continuity with past generations of legal authorities and in order as much as possible to avoid arbitrariness, Jewish tradition developed a model whereby law is determined through a system based on a combination of legal precedent and moral values. This legislative process requires attention to a number of different considerations: textual factors, such as legal precedents in the Bible and traditional halakhic literature; general moral and theological principles emanating from the Bible and tradition; as well as non-textual factors, such as the present social reality, developments in science and technology, and contemporary moral sensibilities. Interpreters take all these factors into account when legislating on new issues, but they differ over which of these are more important. The amount of weight attributed to textual factors is determined by the interpreter's view of the Bible (Written Torah) and tradition (Oral Torah). A legislator who sees the Bible as God's unmediated word and rabbinic tradition as divinely revealed is likely to attribute a greater significance to them than one who considers them a human record of an encounter with God.

Jewish law is constantly changing because of the need to address new issues and reexamine old ones in light of new knowledge and changing moral sensibilities. To illustrate this, I have chosen two examples that pose different problems for the modern interpreter. The first concerns the issue of same-sex relations, where a change of the traditional Jewish legislation involves the uprooting of a biblical prohibition and reinterpretation of a longstanding tradition. The second involves questions of medical ethics, which raises the problem of legislating on issues for which Jewish traditional sources offer no explicit advice. The revised legislation within the Conservative movement regarding same-sex relations and the debate preceding it illustrate the problem that arises when moral values conflict with a biblical prohibition and its subsequent interpretation in halakhic literature, while issues of medical ethics demonstrate the difficulties involved in drawing conclusions about modern phenomena not even remotely addressed by the Bible or traditional halakhic literature. Legislation on such issues is preceded by a complex interaction between textual and extra-textual factors and between legal precedents and moral and theological concerns. Before discussing particular issues, however, a brief survey of the most important denominations of contemporary Judaism and their respective approaches to the Bible and tradition is called for.

MOVEMENTS WITHIN CONTEMPORARY JUDAISM

As a consequence of the Enlightenment with its ideas of tolerance and its emphasis on rational thought and equal rights for all citizens, the Jews of western and central Europe were, by the end of the nineteenth and the beginning of the twentieth century, increasingly accepted as full citizens in the countries where they resided. They were no longer required to live in ghettos, or *shtetls*, and were allowed to participate as full members in society. As individuals, Jews were granted equal rights, but as a community they lost their juridical autonomy, in accordance with the classic statement by the French count Clermont Tonnerre: "We must refuse everything to the Jews as a nation and accord everything to Jews as individuals."[1]

Inspired by events and thoughts prevalent in the society surrounding them, a Jewish Enlightenment movement known as *haskalah* developed. It flourished in Germany at the end of the eighteenth century and somewhat later in Eastern Europe. Its leaders—among them Moses Mendelssohn (1729–1786)—called for a modernization of Jewish culture and religion that would strive to harmonize Judaism with contemporary intellectual currents of thought. Influenced by the Enlightenment's emphasis on rationality and morality, they wanted to refashion Jewish tradition while maintaining a Jewish identity and faith in God. They resisted Jewish insularity and opposed distinctive traits such as traditional Jewish garb and hairstyle, promoting universal and moral teaching rather than uniquely Jewish commandments and customs. They encouraged the Jews to speak the vernacular of the country of their residence rather than Yiddish, while also endorsing Hebrew and promoting the development of a Hebraic culture. They introduced new subjects, such as math, languages, arts and sciences into the traditional curriculum, preparing Jews for involvement in the non-Jewish world. A new German translation of the Bible, written with Hebrew characters, was published. The leaders of the *haskalah* attempted to strike a balance, avoiding narrow provincialism on the one hand and the abandonment of Judaism on the other. Combining modernization, rationalism, and conciliation with the non-Jewish world, the *haskalah* offered a new identity that would allow Jews to be both Jews and members of modern society.

With emancipation, the Jewish communities became a religious denomination that was largely voluntary. When given the opportunity of full participation in society, many Jews wished to downplay the national features of Judaism, and for some the step to assimilation was short. If the nationality of a Jew living in Germany was German and if being Jewish was understood only as a matter of religious association, conversion to Christianity would be a natural step once the person was no longer religiously Jewish. Conversion also facilitated the admission into society, and as many as two hundred thousand German Jews may have converted to Christianity during the nineteenth century.

---

1. The quote is taken from Clermont-Tonnerre's (1757–1792) speech on the status of non-Catholics in France given on December 23, 1789.

In response to the new ideas and the social circumstances to which they gave rise, Judaism underwent a radical change. Various Jewish denominations developed, mainly as a result of different views as to the extent and pace by which Jewish tradition ought to adapt to a new reality. Various positions also revolved around questions of religious authority, the status of tradition, and the nature of Jewish peoplehood. Whereas previously, the only option had been traditional Judaism, it was now possible to express one's Jewish identity in a variety of ways.[2]

The Reform Movement

The continued efforts to modernize Jewish tradition, making it compatible with contemporary intellectual currents and concerns, eventually gave rise to what would become known as Reform Judaism. The intention of the reformers was not to found a new movement but rather to adapt and make Jewish tradition relevant to contemporary society and thus to prevent further conversions to Christianity. However, resistance from those who rejected the innovations and the pace with which they were implemented eventually led to a split.

In continuity with the *haskalah*, the Reform Movement emphasized the moral and universal aspects of Judaism, privileging them over the details of traditional Jewish law and practice. The essence of Judaism was not careful observance of halakhah, they argued, but rather the teachings of ethical universalism as expressed by the biblical prophets. Ethical monotheism, the belief in a God who guides humanity by ethical principles, became a central tenet within the Reform movement.

The reformers' focus on combining a Jewish identity with full participation in the non-Jewish society initially led them to downplay and even deny the national character of Judaism. Prayers for the return to Jerusalem and the establishment of a Jewish state were removed from religious services, and Hebrew as the language of the liturgy was replaced by the vernacular. Services were shortened, and choirs and organ music were introduced.

Many of the early reformers were laymen whose rationale for change was essentially pragmatic, but as an increasing number of rabbis joined, they justified the reforms with reference to a historical understanding of Judaism. Jewish tradition had always been subject to evolutionary processes, they

---

2. A brief survey of Jewish Enlightenment and emancipation is found in Dubin, "Enlightenment and Emancipation," 29–41.

argued, and accordingly the changes that were now being introduced did not constitute a violation of Jewish tradition. Rather, they were an expression of a development that had always characterized Judaism. Although new reforms were being implemented at a faster rate than before, change itself was not foreign to Jewish tradition, they maintained, and the changes were necessary to preserve the essence of Judaism.

Halakhah was not considered binding in its entirety but was to be evaluated from the perspective of contemporary beliefs and moral values. The commandments that were consistent with the ideals of ethical monotheism ought to be observed, but those that were not, or were perceived to be in conflict with these ideals, should be abandoned. Among the commandments considered outdated were the dietary laws and the Sabbath regulations. The principle of individual autonomy was adopted, according to which every Jewish individual has the right to choose the degree to which he or she wants to observe Jewish law.

During its early stage, in the latter half of the nineteenth century and the beginning of the twentieth century, the Reform Movement was very radical. To be a good Jew was virtually synonymous with being a good person, and everything typically Jewish such as the Hebrew language, Jewish nationality, and Jewish customs and traditions were downplayed in favor of an ethical message. In the 1930s, however, increased anti-Semitism undermined the idea that Judaism was a mere religious community and led to a revaluation of Zionism by the leadership of the Reform Movement.

Beginning in the mid-twentieth century, the ideological development within Reform Judaism has taken a traditionalistic direction, reclaiming particularistic practices, the Hebrew language and Jewish tradition, placing more weight on the importance of being part of the Jewish people. The principle of individual autonomy is still embraced, but members are increasingly encouraged to study Jewish tradition and observe Jewish practices. It is no longer unusual for Reform Jews to keep some of the dietary laws (*kashrut*), and some Sabbath regulations.

In the second half of the nineteenth century, Reform Judaism was brought by immigrants from Europe to the United States, where its three central organizations were subsequently founded: the Union of American Hebrew Congregations (UAHC), now called the Union of Reform Judaism (URJ)—an umbrella organization for all American Reform Jewish congregations, the Hebrew Union College (HUC)—a theological seminary for training rabbis, and the Central Conference of American Rabbis (CCAR)—the association of Reform rabbis. Today, Reform Judaism is one of the largest Jewish movements with its stronghold in the United States. It is present also in some European countries and naturally in Israel, but many still consider it primarily an American movement.

Since the early 1970s, the Reform movement ordains women to the rabbinate,[3] and in a controversial departure from Jewish tradition, it recognizes a child born to one Jewish parent, whether the mother or the father, as Jewish if given a Jewish upbringing. This decision, taken in 1983, sparked a bitter controversy with other Jewish denominations that continue to embrace the traditional definition of a Jew as someone born to a Jewish mother.[4]

Orthodox Judaism

The numerous innovations that the reformers introduced in the beginning of the nineteenth century gave rise to two slightly different responses that eventually developed into two separate denominations, namely the Orthodox and the Conservative movements. They both rejected the radical changes of the reformers, but the latter were more open to change than the former, thus representing an intermediary position between Reform and Orthodox Judaism.

Orthodox Judaism lacks a central organization, and is the most diverse and multifaceted movement within contemporary Judaism. Although there is agreement on basic issues of religious observance, there is no universally accepted body issuing halakhic rulings. Orthodox Judaism consists of two main groups: the Modern Orthodox, who accept some innovation and adaptation of traditional Judaism and believe that a strict observance of Jewish practices can be reconciled with involvement in modern society, and the *Haredim* (or ultra-Orthodox, as they are sometimes called), who adhere to traditional Judaism as they think it was before the emancipation and live in isolation from modern society.

The spiritual father of the Modern Orthodox was Samson Raphael Hirsch (1808–1888), who played an important role in the struggle against

---

3. The first woman to become a rabbi was Regina Jonas, who was ordained in Germany in 1935. She perished during the Holocaust, and only in the early 1970s did the Reform Movement begin ordaining women on a regular basis.
4. For more comprehensive presentations of Reform Judaism, see Borowitz, *Meaning of Judaism*, 415–33; Cohn-Sherbok, *Modern Judaism*, 73–100; and Washofsky, *Jewish Living*.

the radical innovations of the reformers in the nineteenth century. He insisted that Jewish teachings and practices had to take precedence, but did not preclude the possibility of adapting these to contemporary circumstances, and unlike the more traditionalist strand among the Orthodox, he believed that traditional Judaism was possible to reconcile with interaction and involvement in the non-Jewish society.

In his view, acquisition of secular knowledge did not constitute a threat to religion, and he himself had a solid education in classical languages, history, and philosophy. He coined the motto, *Torah im derekh eretz* (Torah together with the way of the land), by which he meant that knowledge of and faithfulness to the Torah could be fruitfully combined with involvement in the surrounding society. His idea developed as an educational program, in which an understanding of Jewish tradition and sources constituted the core, but where a secular education also had a place and was considered capable of contributing to an understanding of Judaism. Provided Judaism was placed first and its values placed above the values of modern society, ways could be found to accommodate Jewish tradition to modern society.

The Modern Orthodox today follow Hirsch's model and interact intellectually and physically with the surrounding society. They dress in modern fashion, although men typically wear a *kippah* even on weekdays and not only in the synagogue. They engage in science and secular education, usually with the exception of modern biblical scholarship. Its thesis that the Pentateuch is composed of different sources from different time periods threatens the traditional view that Moses received the entire Torah on Mount Sinai and is therefore rejected by many. Others, however, find no difficulties at all with critical biblical scholarship and do not hesitate to engage in it. In sum, there is great diversity within Modern Orthodoxy, and in particular concerning theological matters.

Orthodox Jews account for about twenty percent of Israel's Jewish population and make up the largest religiously affiliated group there, whereas in the United States Orthodox Judaism is the smallest among the Jewish denominations. In Europe most Jewish congregations are formally Orthodox, but since they often include Jews of a wide range of religious convictions and praxis, they tend to be rather diverse.[5]

---

5. A brief survey of the emergence of Modern Orthodoxy is found in Freud-Kandel, "Modernist Movements," 81–86. For a more comprehensive survey, see Cohn-Sherbok, *Modern Judaism*, 25–49.

Haredim ("those who fear [God])," is a collective name for the group within Orthodoxy who, at least in principle, reject all changes in tradition since the emancipation and adopt an isolationist attitude to secular society and modern culture. During the nineteenth and early twentieth centuries, the term *Haredim* was used as a Hebrew translation of "Orthodox," but after the establishment of the Zionist movement, it was limited to denote non-Zionist separatist Orthodox. The *Haredim* make up only a small part of world Jewry, but they often attract attention because of their distinct way of dressing in accordance with nineteenth-century Eastern European fashion. The men wear long black coats and hats and have beards and sidelocks, and the women have long dresses or skirts and cover their hair with a wig or kerchief.

The *Haredi* world is distinguishable from pre-emancipation traditional Judaism by its conscious ideological commitment to protect Jewish tradition from the processes of modernization and secularization. While before the Enlightenment observance of Jewish law and customs was perceived as a natural part of life in a Jewish society, the threat to the traditional way of life following emancipation made those who remained faithful to traditional Jewish life feel the need to actively protect it from influences from the modern world. Yet, as a counter-reaction to modernization, ultra-Orthodoxy is itself a modern phenomenon, and in spite of its rejection of modernity, it adopts many of its means and techniques in order to protect itself against the threats of modernization and secularism. For example, *Haredim* refrain from watching television or reading newspapers in order to avoid exposure to the secular world, but they may well make use of computers for their own educational purposes.

Their rejection of innovation is in part motivated by their fear that any change might be the beginning of a development that will eventually lead to disintegration of traditional Jewish society. Thus, rejection of modernity is part of a general strategy of segregation and self-insulation. Their insistence to continue to dress in the traditional manner of Jews in Eastern Europe is a manifestation both of their rejection of change and wish to keep apart from their surroundings. In addition, the distinct dress is a symbol of their identity.

The *Haredi* school of thought traces its origins to the writings of Rabbi Moses Sofer (1762–1839), known as Hatam Sofer, after the title of his most famous book. He led the struggle against modernism, secularism, and the Reform Movement and resisted any innovation, not only in halakhah, but in all other areas as well. Unlike the Modern Orthodox, the *Haredim* are

opposed to secular studies and have established their own educational institutions. The *Haredi* world consists of a variety of rather diverse movements
that sometimes strongly oppose each other. The issue of Zionism and the
modern State of Israel was a matter of contention, some groups rejecting it
for theological reasons and others because the Zionist movement was dominated by secular Jews. While most groups have now accepted the state's
existence and participate in Israeli political life, some are still anti-Zionist.

An important dividing line within the *Haredi* world is the one between
Hasidim, adherents to an originally charismatic movement that emerged
in the eighteenth century under the leadership of Baal Shem Tov (1700–
1760), and the non-Hasidic *mitnagdim* (Hebrew for "opponent"), opponents of Hasidism. An important leader of the opponents to Hasidism was
Rabbi Elijah ben Shlomo Zalman, the Gaon of Vilna (1720–1797), and
his followers are known as *litvaks* (Lithuanians) after their spiritual center
in Lithuania.

As a reaction to the immense importance attributed to Torah study,
the Hasidim emphasized prayer as the central part of religious life, and
joyfulness and ecstasy were distinguishing traits of early Hasidism. The
Hasidim maintained that closeness to God could be experienced not only in
prayer or study but in any area of everyday life, such as eating and drink-
ing. Unlike other modern Jewish denominations that employ a rabbi, the
Hasidic groups have charismatic leaders known as rebbes. A rebbe inherits
his position as leader of the group and is not trained for it the way a rabbi is.

The Hasidim belong to different groups that are often named after the
European cities or villages in which the group originated, and each group
has a set of distinguishing features in their dress, making it possible to
identify the particular group to which they belong. Among the largest and
best-known groups are the Satmar Hasidim, originally from Hungary and
Romania, and the Belz Hasidim from the Ukraine and Poland. A Hasidic
movement that is somewhat more open to modern society is *Habad*,[6]
also known as the Lubavitch Hasidim, who attempt to combine Hasidic
charismatic fervor with the traditional ideal of Torah study. They do not
oppose secular studies to the same extent as other Hasidic movements,
and they are known for their missionary efforts attempting to encourage
secular Jews to become more religious. They are also known for their claim
that their rebbe, Menachem Mendel Schneersohn (1902–1994), was the

---

6. *Habad* is an abbreviation of the Hebrew words for wisdom (*hokhmah*), understanding (*binah*), and knowledge (*da'at*).

Messiah. After the death of Schneersohn, there was a split in the movement between those who wanted to deemphasize the messianic identity of the rebbe, and those who continued to insist that he was the Messiah and who await his return.

Most *Haredim* have large families and are often quite poor. In order to provide for their families, the women sometimes go to work outside of the *Haredi* areas. Through this exposure, and in many other ways as well, modern secular society penetrates *Haredi* society. Areas with a large *Haredi* population in Israel include Jerusalem and Bnei Brak outside of Tel Aviv. In the United States, many live in neighborhoods of New York City, such as Williamsburg, Borough Park, and Crown Heights, and in suburbs of New York, such as Muncey and Kiryas Joel. There are also some *Haredi* centers in Europe, in the vicinities of Antwerp, London, and Paris.[7]

Conservative Judaism

The Conservative Movement is mainly an American phenomenon, but like the other denominations it has German roots. The beginnings of the movement can be traced back to Zacharias Frankel (1801–1875), who headed the Jewish Theological Seminary in Breslau. He believed in the necessity of innovation but considered Reform Judaism as too radical. He formulated his notion of Judaism as positive historical, "positive" indicating his wish, unlike the Reform Movement, to retain the prescriptive practices of Jewish tradition, and "historical" signifying the ability to adapt in response to changing historical circumstances. Thus, Conservative Judaism represents an intermediary position between Reform and Orthodox Judaism and is conservative in relation to the Reform Movement. Frankel believed that rabbinic tradition was shaped by humans rather than revealed to Moses at Mount Sinai, but argued that it ought to be observed in spite of its human nature. It should, however, be continually interpreted and adapted rather than seen as eternal and unchanging.

The Conservative Movement was formally established in America with the founding of the Jewish Theological Seminary of America in 1886, designed to train rabbis embracing a more Americanized form of Judaism than that practiced by immigrants from eastern Europe. Adherents to the

---

7. A brief survey of *Haredi* society is found in Don-Yehiya, "Traditionalist Strands," 93–105. For more comprehensive presentations of Hasidism, see for instance Cohn-Sherbok, *Modern Judaism*, 50–72; Heilman, *Defenders of the Faith*.

Conservative Movement consider innovation to be necessary and supported by tradition, and argue that they are more true to tradition by carefully adapting it than by holding on to its letter.

The size of the Conservative Movement in the United States is approximately equal to that of Reform Judaism. It has three central parts: its five rabbinical schools (Jewish Theological Seminary of America in New York, Ziegler School of Rabbinic Studies at the American Jewish University in Los Angeles, Seminario Rabbinico Latin Americano in Buenos Aires, the Schechter Institute of Jewish Studies in Jerusalem, and the Jewish Theological Seminary in Budapest); the Rabbinical Assembly of America (an international organization of Conservative rabbis); and the United Synagogue of Conservative Judaism, an association of Conservative synagogues in the United States and Canada, and its affiliate, Masorti Olami (the World Council of Conservative Synagogues), representing Conservative/Masorti synagogues all over the world. In Israel there is extensive collaboration between the Conservative and the Reform Movement who join forces against the Orthodox.

Within Conservative Judaism, halakhah is considered binding, but not unchanging. Jewish law has always been re-interpreted and adapted, it is argued, but unlike in Reform Judaism, the individual has no right to determine which innovations are legitimate. That authority is reserved for the Jewish people—*kelal Israel,* meaning "the congregation of Israel." In practice, this means that the religious leaders, that is, the rabbis, make halakhic decisions, but they are also to take into consideration the views of the members of Conservative congregations. While Orthodoxy in general emphasizes halakhah and Reform Judaism champions the biblical prophetic texts, Conservative Judaism has adopted a broader, less clearly defined focus on "tradition."[8]

On the individual level, identification with a specific movement may be somewhat fluid, especially in Israel, where both Conservative and Reform Judaism are perceived by many as American phenomena. Thus, an Israeli Jew who sympathizes with the ideology of the Conservative Movement may define him or herself as "liberal Orthodox" rather than "masorti" and belong to an Orthodox synagogue. The determining factor for membership to a specific denomination is commonly the degree of halakhic observance rather than theological beliefs. Within Reform Judaism and the

---

8. Cohn-Sherbok, *Modern Judaism,* 101–21; Dorff, *Conservative Judaism,* 20–46; Freud-Kandel, "Modernist Movements," 86–87.

Conservative Movement, there is usually a correspondence between the two, but this is not necessarily the case within Orthodox Judaism, among whose adherents one may find people who combine a strict observance of halakhah with very liberal theological ideas.

Denominations of Contemporary Judaism

Reform Judaism

Orthodox Judaism
Modern Orthodox
Haredi
    Hasidim
    Mitnagdim (Litvaks)
Conservative Judaism
Reconstructionist Judaism

Reconstructionist Judaism

Reconstructionist Judaism emerged out of Conservative Judaism and has retained a close association with the Conservative Movement. Reconstructionism is associated with Mordecai Kaplan (1881–1983), and its ideas were meant to influence all Jewish movements, and in particular those who were unaffiliated. The Reconstructionist Movement is not very large, but Kaplan's ideas have had a considerable impact on other Jewish denominations as well.

Kaplan championed a Judaism that would attract Jews who were no longer able to accept belief in the miraculous, and notions such as divine revelation, Israel as God's chosen people, and the Messiah. He found the ethical message of Reform Judaism appealing, but argued for the importance of preserving rituals, once they were relieved of their references to supernatural elements.

In his well-known book *Judaism as a Civilization* (1934), Kaplan describes Judaism as an evolving religious civilization. It is religious because the belief in God has always been at the center of Judaism, and it is a civilization because it also includes Jewish culture, history, language, literature, and customs. He stressed the centrality of Jewish peoplehood and Jewish cultural identity. From this perspective, a non-religious Jew is a manifestation of Jewish civilization just as much as a religious Talmud student.

Halakhah is not considered binding but is seen as a valuable cultural remnant that should be sustained unless it clashes with modern ethical sen-

Fig. 9. The Synagogue in Malmö, Sweden, built in 1903. Photograph by Stefan Hedner.

sibilities. Most Reconstructionist Jews do not believe in divine revelation or intervention, or in a personal God, but there is a considerable theological diversity within the movement. A summary of current beliefs is found in the "Platform on Reconstructionism" from 1986, which states: "Judaism is the result of natural human development. There is no such thing as divine intervention; Judaism is an evolving religious civilization. . . . Reconstructionist Judaism is based on a democratic community where the laity can make decisions, not just rabbis; the Torah was not inspired by God; it only comes from the social and historical development of the Jewish people."[9]

REVELATION AND RELIGIOUS AUTHORITY IN CONTEMPORARY JUDAISM

Orthodox Judaism—The Twofold Revelation

Many Orthodox Jews embrace the traditional rabbinic view according to which God revealed to Moses at Sinai not only the Written Torah but also its authentic interpretations. Over time, these divinely revealed interpretations were disclosed and given explicit formulation by the rabbis, and in the process of the transmission of this twofold Torah from generation to genera-

9. "Platform on Reconstructionism"; Cohn-Sherbok, *Modern Judaism*, 130–54; Dorff, *Conservative Judaism*, 149–53; Freud-Kandel, "Modernist Movements," 87–88.

tion, additional legislation and interpretation have been incorporated. As a result, the Bible is read through the prism of tradition, that is, the interpretation given to it by previous generations of rabbis, and accordingly the Bible means whatever rabbinic literature and later commentaries say that it means. This notion of revelation serves as the basis for the legal system.

Thus, having a divine origin, rabbinic regulations are binding for all times and cannot be subject to external criteria of contemporary relevance. This applies to all of rabbinic law, and thus rational commandments have no precedence over those that seemingly lack a rational basis. On the contrary, it is commandments that appear arbitrary—such as the dietary laws, or the biblical prohibition against wearing cloth made of a mixture of linen and wool—that offer the best opportunity to serve God. Halakhah, accordingly, occupies a very central place in the life of a Jew.

To be sure, Orthodox Judaism also adapts to new circumstances, but the emphasis on the divine origin of rabbinic tradition (the Oral Torah) makes them more reluctant to change and innovate. Above all, the traditional view of revelation affects the way they view the result of the act of interpretation. The doctrine of the twofold revelation leads to an inclination to view the halakhic decisions they arrive at as having been revealed already at Sinai and merely newly discovered, rather than perceiving them as the product of human reasoning. They essentially embrace the view that emerged during the amoraic period, according to which the oral law in its entirety, or at least all interpretative possibilities, were given to Moses at Sinai. According to this view, the interpretation by the rabbis is only an explicit expression of what is implicit in the Bible (Written Torah).[10]

Total commitment to all rabbinically interpreted biblical laws, even those which are unintelligible to human reason, and the idea that humans must submit to God's will even when that will conflicts with contemporary accepted notions of morality, is typically associated with Joseph B. Soloveitchik (1903–1993), one of the most influential rabbis within Orthodoxy. In his well-known essay, "The Lonely Man of Faith," published in 1965, Soloveitchik emphasizes obedience to God's will as the hallmark of the Orthodox Jew, in contrast to the assertive and creative, not particularly submissive ideal that he puts forth in his earlier work *Halakhic Man* from 1944. Soloveitchik captures the tension articulated in rabbinic literature between the freedom and responsibility of humans as God's partners in

---

10. Cohn-Sherbok, *Modern Judaism*, 43; Dorff, *Conservative Judaism*, 116–17; Gillman, *Sacred Fragments*, 13–16.

creation on the one hand, and submission to God on the other. In his later work, he favors submission, and although he portrays the negation of the human intellect as an active heroic gesture rather than submission to authority, some argue that his position may serve as support for the claim that Judaism must create obedient personalities who submit to authority at the expense of independent moral or rational considerations.[11]

David Hartman (b. 1931), a student of Soloveitchik but a representative of the more liberal wing of Orthodoxy, has strongly criticized the notion of surrender of human rationality and sacrifice of humans' ethical sense, arguing that this is not required by Jewish tradition. According to Hartman, the full unfolding of the rational and ethical capacities of humans is implicit in the covenantal relationship with God. If the mutuality implied in the covenant is to be taken seriously, the ethical and rational capacities of humans must never be crushed: "In asking the Judaic community to interpret and expand the norms of Judaism to cover all aspects of life, the God of the covenant invites that community to trust its own ability to make rational and moral judgments."[12] Our appreciation of what is considered just and fair should never be undermined through appeals to the absolute authority of halakhah, Hartman argues. History has shown the dangers that ensue when people claim that religious traditions transcend human understanding and embody absolute universal truth. Since human minds are limited, they are vulnerable to misunderstanding God's plainest words, and all the more so when it comes to the manifold implications that halakhic tradition has inferred from Scripture. Having no infallible assurance that we are acting according to a divine command, our conviction of what is just and fair must never be compromised, Hartman insists.[13]

Inherent in the covenantal relationship with God is not submission but rather mutuality, where God trusts humans to use their intellect and moral sense to interpret the Torah and apply it to new situations. Referring to the stories of the Oven of Akhnai (*b. B. Metzia* 59b), Moses' visit to Rabbi Aqiva's study house (*b. Menah.* 29b), and the parable of the wheat and the flax (*S. Eliahu Zuta* 2), Hartman maintains that God has made humans his covenantal partners responsible for intellectually developing the Torah. Humans are entrusted with the task of developing a viable legal system by reasoning and the application of hermeneutic principles rather than blindly

---

11. See Hartman, *Living Covenant*, 60–89, for a summary.
12. Ibid, 97–98.
13. Ibid, 89–108.

accepting decisions and interpretations of the past: "With the development of the oral tradition, Israel became a partner in the development of revelation; revelation ceased being the divine Word completely given at Sinai and became an open-ended Word creatively elaborated by countless generations of students."[14] While many Orthodox Jews place emphasis on the divine aspect of oral tradition, Hartman stresses the human component, embracing the rabbinic view of revelation as expressed in the early rabbinic texts that portray human interpretation as a part of revelation itself.

Various attempts have been made to promote unity and to overcome the divisions within the Orthodox fold. The Union of Orthodox Jewish Congregations is a federation of Orthodox synagogues in the United States and Canada that fosters Orthodox beliefs and practices, sponsoring elementary and secondary day schools oriented toward Orthodoxy as well as *yeshivahs* (institutes for higher religious learning). Affiliated with the Union of Orthodox Jewish Congregations is the Rabbinical Council of America (RCA), a federation of rabbis most of whom are Modern Orthodox. Modern Orthodoxy is very diverse, having no single leader or official committee, but its rabbis tend to follow the views authorized by the Rabbinical Council of America. The non-hasidic *Haredi* community generally follows halakhic decisions issued by rabbis belonging to the Union of Orthodox Rabbis of the United States and Canada, and each Hasidic group has their own rebbe, who is their halakhic authority.

The Rabbinical Council of America gives advice on halakhic matters by issuing *responsa*, rulings given by rabbis in response to questions addressed to them. *Responsa* (sing. *responsum*) literally means "answers," and the tradition of writing *responsa* on halakhic issues goes back to the time of the rabbinic academies in Babylonia. In contemporary Orthodox Judaism, *responsa* are usually authored by individual rabbis, some of whom have acquired an expertise in specific complex areas such as, for instance, medical ethics.

Conservative Judaism—The Bible as Midrash

The theology of revelation is not uniform within the Conservative Movement but most Conservative Jews agree that the Bible (Written Torah) was written down by human beings and can accordingly be studied in the same way as any other text. Some believe that the authors were divinely inspired and that it contains God's will in the form of a specific message, while others

14. Ibid, 35–36. See also 32–41.

see the Torah as the human record of the encounter between God and the people of Israel at Sinai. Both positions share the view of the Bible as the product of the human experience of God, and as such marked by the practices, values, and attitudes of the time in which it was produced. If these are no longer adequate expressions of the present day understanding of God's will, they must be responsibly adapted and changed.

The Conservative theologies of revelation are to a large extent influenced by Abraham Joshua Heschel (1907–1972), who described revelation as God making his presence known. God is beyond human understanding and description, and accordingly one cannot establish the exact content of revelation, Heschel argues. Humans can only sense his presence, and the Bible is an interpretation of the human encounter with the divine: "As a report about revelation the Bible itself is a midrash."[15] Midrash is a later interpretation of a biblical text, and Heschel sees the Bible itself as a human interpretation of some prior revelation that is beyond human comprehension.

According to Heschel, two events occurred at Sinai: God's giving of the Torah and Israel's receiving it. Both parties were active in the encounter, and as a result the outcome (the Bible) is marked both by its divine origin and its human appropriation. Here we may recall Heschel's apt summary of Judaism as "a minimum of revelation and a maximum of interpretation."[16] Thus, the Bible contains God's will, but it is a human understanding of the divine will. Heschel's understanding of revelation as embodying both a divine and a human component bears great resemblance to the view of revelation in early rabbinic texts that describe Israel's interpretation as part of divine revelation itself.

Conservative Judaism considers halakhah binding because it is based on God's will, as it was understood by previous generations of Jews, but being shaped by humans, it can and must change in order to remain relevant. Jews continue to have encounters with God and the law must be adapted to reflect the new understanding of God's will that results from those encounters. All agree that innovation and adaptation are necessary, but those who see revelation as an encounter with God, rather than as an articulation of a specific message, are more inclined to adapt Jewish law in accordance with changing circumstances. It is the responsibility of the rabbis, representing the Jewish community (*kelal Israel*), to determine the content of halakhah

---

15. Heschel, *God in Search*,185.
16. Ibid., 274.

for each generation. Jewish law needs not only to be renewed and adapted but also safeguarded, since it is an expression of previous generations' understanding of God's will, and serves to preserve the Jewish people.

Others claim that Jewish law is binding because the Jewish people have accepted it as such. Whether or not the giving of the Torah at Sinai is perceived as a revelation of God is dependent on whether the Jewish people understand it as such. In the same way, the decision of a particular rabbi about a matter of Jewish law may be just his opinion, or it may be a revelation from God; which of the two it is is determined by how the Jewish community perceives it. According to this view, Jewish law is the product of human reasoning—a reaction to an event that the Jewish people *perceive* as revelation.[17]

Conservative Judaism holds that the development and adaptation of Jewish law are determined through the halakhic process, a system based on a combination of legal precedent and moral values. In this system, reinterpretations and adaptations are implemented through reasoned arguments. The idea that halakhic decisions should be made by the sages in each generation, while taking into consideration the views prevalent in Conservative congregations, is translated into practice through the Committee on Jewish Law and Standards (CJLS), the central authority on halakhah within the Conservative Movement. Whenever a new issue is addressed by the law committee, a number of rabbis are appointed to study the matter in depth, either together or individually, comparing it to related or similar cases in rabbinic sources, the law codes and *responsa* literature, explaining potential difficulties, proposing solutions, and eventually arguing for a halakhic decision that he or she considers most compelling. Based on the *responsa* thus produced, the CJLS makes a decision by means of a vote by its members.

The CJLS consists of twenty-five rabbis who have the right to vote, and five laypeople, who participate in deliberations but do not have a vote. Six (or more) votes are necessary in order for a position to be recognized as an official position of the committee. Accordingly, the Conservative Movement can issue several, sometimes contradicting, official positions. When more than one position is authorized, the rabbi of each congregation adopts the position he or she finds most compelling. The official positions of the CJLS are seen as important guidance, but each individual Conservative rabbi has the authority to make decisions on halakhah. In the case of issues not dis-

---

17. Cohn-Sherbok, *Modern Judaism*, 112–21; Dorff, *Conservative Judaism*, 96–150; Dorff, *Love of God*, 29–37; Gillman, *Sacred Fragments*, 24–25.

cussed by the CJLS, each congregational rabbi makes halakhic decisions based on legal sources and his or her own judgment. Conservative Judaism insists that a rabbi must always use his or her own judgment when making decisions and may not simply appeal to tradition or authoritative texts.

While *responsa* cannot be enforced on rabbis, there are a few standards of rabbinic practice which are enforced by the Rabbinical Assembly, such as prohibitions to officiate at intermarriages, to officiate at the remarriage of a Jew whose previous marriage has not been terminated according to halakhah, or to take any action that would imply that Jewishness can be confirmed in any other way but matrilineal descent or halakhic conversion.[18]

True to its legacy from the rabbinic period, Conservative Judaism preserves minority views leading to diversity within the movement. Unlike the principle of individual autonomy of the Reform Movement, Conservative Judaism, in common with Orthodoxy, insists that halakhic decisions should be made by the religious authority in each generation. However, Orthodox Judaism has a significantly different understanding of how halakhah is determined, and, accordingly, Orthodox rabbis generally do not consider the decisions of the Conservative law committee as normative. Thus, in spite of their common commitment to halakhah, their interpretations and decisions often differ considerably.

Reform Judaism—Revelation as a Personal Encounter with God

The theologies of revelation within the Reform Movement are in part influenced by the existential theology of Franz Rosenzweig (1886–1929) and to some extent also by Martin Buber's classical philosophical work, *I and Thou*. Revelation is perceived as the creation of such an I-Thou relationship between the personal God of the Bible and the human being, a mutual relationship with each partner affecting the other. Not revealed—neither at Sinai nor in any authentic I-Thou relationship—is any form of a behavioral code. For Rosenzweig, revelation means God's entering into a unique relationship with Israel, and the Torah is Israel's response to this revelatory encounter, spelling out how Israel understood its relationship with God. Buber and Rosenzweig agree that laws are not part of the content of revelation, but the latter maintains that a sense of "being commanded" is. What was revealed, then, was not specific commandments but the sense of being commanded.[19]

---

18. Dorff, *Conservative Judaism*, 158–61.
19. Gillman, *Sacred Fragments*, 22–24.

Many Reform Jews embrace a view of "progressive revelation," by which is meant that God reveals his will to humanity through the use of human reason and moral striving. Revelation is seen as a continuous process and as humanity gains more experience on this earth, the scope and accuracy of revelation also progresses as time goes on. Both the Bible and rabbinic tradition are seen as an outcome of the human effort to understand God's will and as such are marked by human values informed by historical events and circumstances. The view of the Bible and Jewish tradition as products of the human mind explains how the Reform Movement at times can let contemporary sensibilities supersede traditional Jewish values and why some commandments are seen as irrelevant and are abandoned. Having been formulated by humans, they were predicated on specific historical circumstances and when the circumstances change, the meaning and relevance of the commandments may also change. The notion that humankind's understanding of revelation increases over time also contributes to the view that the legislation of earlier generations is no longer binding.[20]

Thus, halakhah in its entirety is not binding, and unlike the Conservative Movement, Reform Judaism insists that the individual has the right to decide the extent to which he or she wishes to observe the Jewish law. However, an increasing interest in traditional Judaism among Reform Jews has led to a greater concern for Jewish law, illustrated by a statement made in 1960 by Reform Rabbi Solomon Freehof, then chairman of the responsa committee of the Central Conference of American Rabbis: "[T]he law is authoritative enough to influence us, but not so completely as to control us. The rabbinic law is our guidance not governance."[21] Jewish law serves as a guide but it is not binding. Accordingly, the Reform Movement does not make any halakhic decisions on behalf of its members, but the Central Conference of American Rabbis and its Israeli counterpart, *Moetzet rabbanim mitqadmim* (MARAM), nonetheless publish responsa intended as guidance. With the increased interest in traditional Judaism, greater significance is attributed both to the CCAR and its *responsa* committee. Within the Reform Movement, responsa are seen as a way to promote a certain viewpoint by means of argumentation, as articulated by Mark Washofsky, the current chairman of the responsa committee:

---

20. Dorff, *Conservative Judaism*, 153–57.
21. Freehof, quoted in Borowitz, *Meaning of Judaism*, 420.

[A] responsum is essentially an argument, a reasoned attempt to justify one particular course of action . . . it seeks to win its point through persuasion. . . . We see *halakhah* as a discourse, an ongoing conversation through which we arrive at an understanding, however tentative, of what God and Torah require of us. . . . Torah, if it is to serve us as a sure source of religious truth, cannot exist in the absence of certain essential moral and ethical commitments . . . while our responsa seek to uphold traditional halakhic approaches whenever fitting, we reserve to ourselves the right to decide when they do not fit . . . [and] modify or reject those interpretations in favor of others that better reflect our religious mind and heart.[22]

Halakhah, then, is seen as an ongoing discussion, an attempt to find out what God expects from the Jewish people. It is valuable as a voice of Jewish tradition and as a tool to argue and justify a view or course of action, but the right to ultimately make decisions lies with the individual Jew.

Having surveyed the theologies of revelation within the denominations of modern Judaism and their respective commitment to halakhah, we will now turn to their treatment of problems related to recent halakhic issues, exemplified by same-sex relations and medical ethics.

A BIBLICAL PROHIBITION IN CONFLICT WITH MODERN KNOWLEDGE AND MORAL SENSIBILITIES

Conservative Judaism

In 2006 the Conservative Movement's Committee on Jewish Law and Standards voted on the issue of homosexual relations and subsequently issued two contradicting majority positions: one confirming the earlier prohibition against same-sex relationships, and one sanctioning same-sex unions albeit with certain restrictions.[23] The deliberations within the Conservative Movement preceding these official positions illustrate how a movement committed to halakhah dealt with the dilemma posed by the fact that both the Bible and a longstanding unanimous Jewish tradition seem to support a prohibition that many within the movement wished to modify. They also demonstrate

---

22. Mark Washofsky, quoted in Borowitz, *Meaning of Judaism*, 427.
23. A minority view arguing that homosexuality is an illness that can be cured was also approved with six votes.

the significance that the respective views of the Bible and tradition have for the decision-making process, making it a good starting point for a discussion about the balance between continuity and change in contemporary Judaism.

Until recently, Jewish law as understood by all modern denominations prohibited homosexual relations based on Lev. 18:22 and 20:13 and their interpretation by the rabbis. Lev. 18:22 reads: "Do not lie with a male as one lies with a woman; it is an abhorrence," and Lev. 20:13 specifies that the punishment for transgression of this prohibition is death. This seems rather straightforward, but the recent acknowledgement that homosexuality is an integral component of individual identity, rather than a matter of choice, made some Conservative rabbis want to reconsider Jewish legislation on the issue. If homosexuality is an inborn orientation that cannot be changed, homosexual acts can no longer be regarded as a rebellion against Jewish law, they argued. The misery that the traditional stance imposed on gays and lesbians and their families was an additional factor leading to a wish to modify Jewish law on this issue.

Those in favor of change were faced with two major obstacles: the biblical prohibition and a longstanding unanimous tradition forbidding homosexual relations. While the biblical prohibition in Lev. 18:22 could be reinterpreted by placing it in its historical context, the longstanding unanimous rabbinic tradition prohibiting same-sex relations was not easily overcome. In the case of the biblical prohibition, some argued that the original intent behind it was to ban idolatrous cults and practices, or alternatively that it concerned the often unequal, violent, and exploitative nature of same-sex relations in the ancient world and accordingly did not apply to present-day homosexual relationships of equality and mutual respect. Others argued that homosexuality as an orientation (as opposed to oppressive same-sex acts) was not known or addressed, let alone prohibited, either by the Torah or halakhah, and that accordingly, one was not dealing with a previously considered and previously outlawed phenomenon, but with an entirely new situation.[24] However, these reinterpretations could not change the fact that the rabbis of ancient times understood it as forbidding all intercourse between men and added a ban of homosexual activity among women. Because Jewish tradition is based on the rabbis' understanding of the Bible, their interpretation is what counts, no matter what the biblical verse may originally have meant. Moreover,

---

24. See for instance Artson, "Gay and Lesbian Jews." For a survey of similar arguments, see Solomon, "Sexuality," 407–8.

the tradition was unanimous. If there had been a long legislative history on the issue in which rabbis of the past had differed, it would have been different, since those desiring a modification could then have appealed to a different line of precedent for support. In the absence of such precedents, those who wished to modify the halakhah were faced with the difficulty of overturning strong precedent.[25]

After extensive deliberations, the CJLS issued two majority positions in December 2006, one reaffirming the prior position, which denied ordination as clergy to active homosexuals and prohibited same-sex commitment ceremonies, and one allowing ordination as clergy of gay and lesbian Jews while at the same time retaining the biblical ban on male homosexual intercourse. According to the first position, homosexual relations cannot be halakhically condoned. Even though homosexual orientation may be inherent, homosexual actions are biblically prohibited, and accordingly homosexuals should remain celibate. To allow same-sex relations would mean crossing the boundary of legitimate halakhic decision-making, thus nullifying the entire halakhic system. However, it affirms that gays and lesbians are welcome in Conservative congregations and should not be denied any honors within worship and lay leadership positions.[26]

The second official position restricts the prohibition on homosexual relations to what the rabbis understood Lev. 18:22 and 20:13 to mean, namely anal intercourse, and while upholding this prohibition, it removed the rabbinic extensions of the prohibition to women and other forms of male-male sexual activity, permitting the latter. This ruling allows ordination of gays and lesbians as rabbis or cantors and sanctions acknowledgement of such relationships through commitment ceremonies, although they are to be distinguished from the ceremonies for "marriage" (*kiddushin*) for two reasons: first, the liturgy for Jewish weddings speaks of a bride and a groom and thus does not fit the context of a homosexual couple, and, second, because the authors wanted to avoid the concept underlying *kiddushin* that either party acquires the other (*kinyan*), a feature of traditional Jewish marriage that many Conservative rabbis find difficult and do not want to import to these new ceremonies for gay men and lesbians.[27] This distinction between biblical law and rabbinic extensions of it is what allowed a reinterpretation toward greater leniency, since rabbinic

---

25. Dorff, *Love of God*, 232–34.
26. Roth, "Homosexuality Revisited."
27. Dorff, Nevins, and Reisner, "Homosexuality," 1–36.

laws, having a lower degree of authority than biblical prohibitions, can be uprooted in certain circumstances.

Human Dignity

Appealing to a principle known as human dignity (*kevod haberiot*),[28] according to which a rabbinic law may be overturned in order to preserve the dignity of an individual, Rabbis Dorff, Nevins, and Reisner argued that the prohibition against homosexual relations was degrading for gay and lesbian Jews, causing them physical and psychological harm, and advocated a change citing previous cases where rabbinic prohibitions had been set aside for the sake of human dignity. Based on a discussion of legal precedents in rabbinic sources, the law codes, and responsa literature, they concluded that the biblical prohibition against intercourse between men remains but the rabbinic prohibition against other forms of homosexuality ought to be removed for the sake of human dignity.[29]

The various responsa that Conservative rabbis have written on this issue—both those that are recognized as official positions of the Conservative Movement and those that are not—display a certain tension between the importance attributed to the biblical text and its rabbinic interpretations on the one hand and to non-textual factors on the other. While all agree that extra-textual factors, such as historical context, science, morality, and theology are a part of the halakhic process, some tend to favor a legal reasoning based mainly on legal precedent while others believe that moral, social, and historical factors should have a stronger impact on the legislation. Those in favor of the latter position argue that the ultimate meaning of a text depends on the interpreter; on his or her choice of which sources should be emphasized and which should be ignored; and on how they ought to be applied. Accordingly, proper legal reasoning is not simply a matter of deductive reasoning from previous texts, but requires attention to the historical realities behind the relevant texts and an evaluation of traditional texts in light of our present-day knowledge and beliefs. In other words, the judge in every generation must judge "according to what he sees with his own eyes" (*b. Bava Batra* 131a).[30]

---

28. "So great is human dignity that it supersedes a negative commandment of the Torah," see *b. Ber.* 19b; *b. Shabb.* 81b, 94b; *b. Eruv.* 41b; *b. Meg.* 3b; *b. B. Kama* 79b; *b. Menah.* 37b–38a.
29. Dorff, Nevins, and Reisner, "Homosexuality," 1–36.
30. Dorff, "Jewish Norms."

The responsa behind the two majority positions within the Conservative Movement can be said to emphasize differing strands of Jewish tradition that have always been in competitive tension. The one upholding the prohibition on homosexual relations emphasizes the legal precedents and obedience to God, treating the non-textual factors as secondary in importance, while the other one puts moral considerations first, stressing the extra-textual factors.[31]

The Balance between Halakhah and Aggadah
In a responsum that is also a general essay on the approaches to law, in particular on the methods that have been used to analyze and develop halakhah, Rabbi Gordon Tucker discusses the interrelationship between law and narrative (halakhah and aggadah) in the decision-making process. He argues that the methods used in the Conservative Movement have been conceived in an overly narrow way, privileging halakhic precedent while setting aside aggadic texts, leading to a situation where legislation does not reflect theological convictions and moral sensitivities. He analyzes the two main arguments against normalization of homosexual partnerships, namely the biblical prohibition (the argument from Scripture) and its interpretation in Jewish law (the argument from tradition), dismissing the first and suggesting a modification in method concerning the second.

He points out that the argument from Scripture assumes infallibility of the Torah, reflecting the belief that it expresses directly and completely the will of God, a notion that is not accepted by most Conservative Jews. Citing Heschel's statement that "as a report about revelation, the Bible itself is a midrash," he points out that the argument from Scripture loses much of its force for people who believe that it is the result of a human interpretation of God's word. He concludes by observing that if one believes that the Torah as we have it reflects both its divine origin and its human interpretation, one cannot rule out that Lev. 18:22 and 20:13 reflect a human understanding in a particular context. Furthermore, even if the verses were an unambiguous, infallible expression of God's will, other equally clear verses have been subjected to modification and contextualization, and the rabbis of the Talmud did not, for example, hesitate to interpret away the commandment to kill a rebellious son (Deut. 21:18) despite the fact that they surely did not

---

31. Dorff, *Love of God*, 236.

share the contemporary Conservative Movement's theology of revelation, argues Tucker.

After having relativized the argument from Scripture, Tucker goes on to discuss the argument from tradition, which, assuming the canonicity of early legal material, is the more weighty one. While developing halakhah on the basis of precedent in earlier legal texts has the benefits of ensuring stability, mitigating against randomness and caprice and safeguarding continuity with tradition, it ought to be balanced by an increased attention to values expressed in aggadic texts, he argues. Therefore, in addition to the conventional halakhic methods based on precedent, aggadic texts that reflect theological and moral underpinnings ought to be allowed a more significant role in the halakhic process.

This is perfectly legitimate, he points out, and was done in normalizing the status and role of women in the Conservative Movement. Egalitarian communities were not born of a straight derivation from halakhic precedents; they were rather a result of a combination between halakhic tradition and aggadic texts. An interaction between a halakhic tradition to which these communities felt bound and their understanding of principles from aggadic texts led them to the conviction that the tradition was wrong in excluding women from public roles. Egalitarianism, says Tucker, was subsequently legitimized in the traditional way through appeal to legal precedent, but the stimulus for change was a result of a sense that halakhah cannot be restricted only to legal precedent. Passages such as Gen. 1:27 and 5:2, stating that humans were created male and female and that "adam"—human—was the name given to both sexes, were read in conjunction with a passage from *Sifre* to Numbers saying that God's compassion extends to both males and females, citing as proof text, "The Lord is good to all, and His mercy is upon all His works" (Ps. 145:9).

Through such a merging of halakhah and aggadah, solutions were found also for women whose husbands have left them but refuse or are unable to grant them a bill of divorce, making it impossible for them to remarry (*agunot*), and Tucker advocated that this be done in the case of gays and lesbians also. Citing another version of the aggadic passage according to which God's compassion extends to everyone, he argues that the main point of this narrative is to teach us that we are not entitled to claim that the discriminations we make are necessarily God's will. Rather, it teaches that, "God is more accepting, more emphatic, more compassionate than we are."[32]

> God's mercy is not like the mercy of human beings. For human beings have more compassion for males than for females. But the Holy and Blessed One is not like that; God's compassion extends to both males and females. God's compassion extends to everyone, as it is written: *who gives food [lehem] to all flesh* [Ps. 136:25], and *who gives the beasts their food [lahmah]* [Ps. 147:9]. And it is also written, *the Lord is good to all, and His mercy is upon all His works* [Ps. 145:9].[33]

Pointing out that the word *lehem* (bread or food) is sometimes used as a euphemism for sexual satisfaction,[34] Tucker argues that this midrash reminds us that God seeks to provide *lehem*, that is, all needs, including sustenance and sexual fulfillment, to all creatures. If this applies even to the beasts of the field, it must apply all the more to humans and could be applied to *agunot* and gays and lesbians. If the legal precedents cannot accommodate the basic theological axiom to which this midrash appeals, they need to be read in conjunction with all the narrative texts that say that humans were meant to live in loving partnership and those that forbid us to stigmatize people for conditions that they did not choose or control, concludes Tucker. Such a combination of legal precedents and aggadic texts would, in his view, enable the Conservative Movement to demonstrate both its commitment to halakhah *and* compassion, enabling its rabbis to declare the relationships of gays and lesbians to be condoned by Jewish law without imposing any restrictions.[35]

Tucker's analysis explains why the Jewish movements committed to halakhah are so cautious in their interpretations and adaptation of biblical and rabbinic commandments in spite of the very radical rabbinic texts permitting innovation. The latter are all aggadic, and such texts have traditionally

32. Tucker, "Halakhic and Metahalakhic Arguments," 28.
33. *Yalq. Shimoni* Pinhas 773. Full or partial parallels are found in *Sifre* to Numbers Pinhas 133; *Tanh.* Nitsavim 5 (ed. Buber).
34. Genesis 39:6 says that Potiphar had such confidence in Joseph that he entrusted everything to him "save the *lehem* that he ate," and *Genesis Rabbah* explains *lehem* as a euphemism for sexual relations.
35. Tucker, "Halakhic and Metahalakhic Arguments," 1–31.

played a very minor role in the halakhic process. Since legislation based solely on aggadic texts would inevitably lead to anarchy and arbitrariness, most halakhic authorities would insist that legal precedents cannot be dismissed, but in the view of some rabbis, aggadah ought to be allowed a more significant role in the halakhic process than it has traditionally had.

Orthodox Views

In reaction to the Conservative Movement's decision to allow ordination of gays and lesbians, and the permission of its rabbis to officiate at same-sex commitment ceremonies, the Orthodox Rabbinical Council of America (RCA) issued a statement reaffirming the joint position of the RCA and the (*Haredi*) Orthodox Union from 2004 that "homosexual behavior is, and has always been, absolutely forbidden by Jewish law and tradition, and that any attempt to characterize Jewish law and tradition to the contrary must be rejected." It continues: "At the same time we reaffirm that those who, in spite of their acceptance of these principles, have difficulty in living up to these standards, should be treated with compassion, sensitivity, and understanding, in our synagogues, and in society at large."[36]

As usual within Orthodoxy, one finds a broad spectrum of different views, ranging from the influential *Haredi* Rabbi Moshe Feinstein (1895–1986), who in a responsum from 1976 maintains that homosexuality is unnatural and constitutes a rebellion against God,[37] to modern Orthodox Rabbi Steven Greenberg, who argues that homosexual relationships may be condoned by halakhah.[38] Contextualizing the verses from Leviticus, Greenberg asserts that it is likely that the original intent of the prohibition against homosexual relations was to prohibit exploitation and humiliation of another human being. In light of the view of sexuality in antiquity, it is likely, he maintains, that it was forbidden for a man to sexually penetrate another man because this was considered humiliating for the latter. Thus he concludes that the prohibition emerged in a culture where women were inferior to men, and by sexual penetration a man was cast into the realm of women and thus humiliated.[39]

Acknowledging that identifying the rationale for the biblical prohibition has little significance for halakhah, he reasons in much the same way

---

36. Rabbinical Council of America, "Response."
37. Feinstein, *Iggerot Moshe, Orah Hayyim*, vol. 4, no.115, quoted in Cohen, "Bibliography."
38. Greenberg, *Wrestling with God*.
39. Ibid., 192–214.

as Conservative Rabbis Dorff, Nevins, and Reisner, proposing a compromise position, according to which the biblical prohibition of intercourse between men should be retained, but like the family purity laws relegated to the private sphere. Just as heterosexual couples in an Orthodox community are presumed to keep the family purity laws, gay men would likewise be expected to refrain from intercourse, but just as rabbis do not check to see which couples do or do not observe the laws of family purity (especially if they have reason to believe that the couple does not observe them), they would not interfere in the private sphere of a gay couple. In this way, it would no longer be a public issue but a matter of personal piety. Like the rabbis behind the more lenient Conservative responsum, he considers the prohibition against all other forms of homosexual relations to be of rabbinic rather than biblical origin and as such possible to abrogate if considered harmful to the human dignity of an individual. While recognizing its imperfections, Greenberg suggests this as a possible first step for gay persons in search of a pragmatic halakhic solution and for rabbis who feel caught between their desire to help and their responsibility to the canons of sacred tradition.[40]

More representative of Modern Orthodoxy is probably Rabbi Norman Lamm (b. 1927), a disciple of Soloveitchik and former president of Yeshiva University, who in 1974 wrote an article for the *Encyclopaedia Judaica Yearbook* entitled "Judaism and the Modern Attitude to Homosexuality," where he states that homosexual relations can never be condoned by halakhah. However, he continues by arguing for an understanding attitude toward gay people based on a view of homosexuality as sickness, which diminishes the culpability of the practitioner. He considers homosexual acts as an expression of an internal compulsion that gays cannot be held accountable for, and while insisting on the abhorrence of the sin, he advocates compassion for the sinner. Engaging in homosexual relationships is a violation of Jewish norms in the same category as Sabbath desecration or disregarding the laws of kashrut.[41]

Lamm's position has gained foothold in Modern Orthodox Judaism but is, with a few exceptions, largely rejected by *Haredi* Judaism. However, Rabbi Shmuley Boteach (b. 1966), a disciple of the Lubavitch Rebbe Menachem Mendel Schneerson, has expressed a view that echoes Lamm's, maintaining that homosexual acts are not a more serious violation of Jewish law

40. Ibid., 245–50.
41. Lamm, "Judaism and the Modern Attitude."

than smoking a cigarette on the Sabbath or eating a cheeseburger: "Like Shabbat and Kashrut, homosexual sex is prohibited not because it violates any ethical norms but because there's a biblical injunction,"[42] he argues. In a similar vein, Chaim Rapoport, a Lubavitcher Hasid, breaks new ground in recognizing the struggle of many Jewish gays and lesbians in trying to remain faithful to Judaism while not denying their sexual identity. While recognizing the challenge they face, he asserts that all same-sex relations are forbidden and recommends that gays and lesbians remain celibate.[43]

Reform Judaism

Since the Reform Movement does not consider halakhah binding, its adherents are not obliged to take legal precedents into consideration when formulating their standpoint on new issues or when reinterpreting old ones, but they nevertheless anchor their decisions in Jewish tradition and often take classical texts as a point of departure as though they did consider them authoritative. In the case of same-sex relations, they argue that the contemporary understanding of homosexuality as an inborn orientation rather than a matter of choice requires a new interpretation of the law if the Jewish values of human dignity and justice are to be upheld.

In the late 1980s, the Hebrew Union College changed its admission rules to allow gay and lesbian students, and this decision was affirmed in 1990 by the Central Conference of American Rabbis, arguing that "all rabbis, regardless of sexual orientation, be accorded the opportunity to fulfill the sacred vocation that they have chosen."[44] Rabbis are encouraged to officiate at same-sex commitment ceremonies, but a majority maintains that such ceremonies may not be defined as "Jewish marriage" (*kiddushin*): "[H]omosexual relationships, however exclusive and committed they may be, do not fit within this legal category: they cannot be called *kiddushin*."[45]

---

42. Boteach, "Dr. Laura Misguided." This position, however, drew criticism from within the Orthodox camp. See, for instance, Adlerstein, "Dawn of the Orthodox."
43. Rapoport, *Judaism and Homosexuality*. See also Greenberg, *Wrestling with God*, 224–27, for a range of views within Orthodoxy.
44. "Report" (CCAR).
45. "Homosexual Marriage" (CCAR Responsum), "Resolution" (CCAR). See also Solomon, "Sexuality," 409–10.

Fig. 10. Interior of the Hurva Synagogue, the Jewish Quarter of the Old City, Jerusalem. Photograph by Anders Runesson.

WHEN BIBLE AND TRADITION OFFER NO GUIDANCE

The progress made by medical science over the last half century creating previously unimaginable possibilities to predict, prevent, and cure diseases and improve the quality of life for many people has raised a different set of problems for halakhic authorities. While these developments are surely something to be grateful for, they raise new and difficult moral questions that nobody could have predicted a century ago and have introduced choices and possibilities for which Jewish legal tradition offers very little or no guidance.

Mining Talmudic texts for advice on how to relate to brain death, stem cell research, gene therapy, or cloning, for instance, is perhaps to some extent a modern equivalent of the endeavor by the rabbis of the rabbinic period to establish the exact meaning of the vague biblical term "work," but the fact that the classical Jewish sources do not at all address the questions of medical ethics that contemporary rabbis pose to them makes it extremely difficult to draw conclusions from them on these issues. The attempts to construct guidelines and answers from the authoritative texts based on analogy become especially challenging in view of the fact that the authors of those texts could not even have imagined the problems that contemporary rabbis ask them to solve. For instance, is it reasonable to draw conclusions concerning euthanasia based on traditional sources, which permit people to pray for the speedy death of a dying person in great pain when it is evident that they do not directly concern questions of euthanasia at all? Halakhic authorities differ over these questions, but most Jewish ethicists assume that Jewish tradition has something to contribute to questions of medical ethics even though they may differ over the relevance of a given text to a specific case.

The Legal Approach

As we have seen above, moral decisions in Jewish tradition are made primarily within the framework of Jewish law, and the most common procedure among Jewish ethicists, regardless of denomination, is to seek to identify precedents from Jewish legal tradition (rabbinic literature and responsa), extrapolate from these texts principles and norms, and apply them to a new set of facts. In spite of a common method, however, different authorities reach very diverse conclusions, illustrating the difficulties with this method, especially when applied to issues of medical ethics. Because these issues are often so far removed from the reality in which the traditional texts were produced, identifying precedents is nearly always a matter of controversy. Even when contemporary halakhic authorities agree on a number of valid precedents, they frequently disagree as to which general legal or moral principles can be derived from them, how they are to be applied to contemporary situations, and on the significance attributed to factors outside of the text.

Two different positions among Orthodox halakhic authorities on whether brain death is a sufficient criterion for establishing the death of an individual according to Jewish tradition may serve to illustrate these problems. Virtually all contemporary halakhic authoritites cite a text from the Babylonian Talmud (*b. Yoma* 85a), in which the cessation of breathing is regarded as the critical determinant of death, as the *locus classicus* for the Jewish definition of death. This understanding is confirmed by medieval sources, including *Shulhan Arukh*, and, more recently, by rabbinic authorities of the nineteenth and twentieth centuries who expand the talmudic definition of death to include the cessation of cardiac activity. Thus, the classic Jewish understanding of death involves the cessation of both cardiac and respiratory activities.

Adhering to a literal understanding of the precedent, one halakhic authority rules that brain death and irreversible coma are not sufficient to establish a person as dead according to Jewish law, since the sources on the topic, in his opinion, clearly define death as the complete cessation of cardiac and respiratory activities. No advance in modern medical technology can alter these criteria.

Others, however, argue that the sources must be understood in light of their general intent rather than literally. While not disputing the reading of the talmudic passage, they maintain that advances in technology and knowledge must also be taken into account, and that in light of these, more sophisticated standards for determining whether respiratory and cardiac activities have ceased are called for. Jewish law naturally employs the criteria of its day, which means that just because in talmudic times death was defined by the cessation of breathing should not automatically be the criterion by which we determine death at present. In their view scientific, evidence and progress have the right to guide and inform Jewish legal interpretation, and they argue that the sources are best understood by also taking contemporary medical advances into consideration.

Accordingly, the modern knowledge that the brain and the brain stem control all bodily functions, including respiration and heart activity, leads to the conclusion that a person whose brain does not show any signs of activity may be considered dead even though the heart may still be beating. Appealing to an earlier responsum, they contend that if it can be medically determined that there is no circulation to the brain, the patient is equivalent to a decapitated person whose heart may still momentarily be beating but such a person, according to Jewish law, is dead. In other words, not all organs need to cease functioning for death to be said to occur, and in their view, the classic respiratory and circulatory death in earlier sources is, in reality, brain death.[46] Thus, although based on the same precedent, these rulings are nevertheless different, one of them resting solely on the traditional texts while the other also takes the reality of recent medical progress into account.

---

46. Ellenson, "Guidance from a Heritage," 131–33.

Clearly then, the same basic approach can be applied in different ways rendering different conclusions. In general, Reform and Conservative halakhic authorities are more inclined than Orthodox ones to take non-textual factors into account (although as the example above shows, some Orthodox legislators do too), and they also typically show a greater awareness of the fact that interpreting a text is a dialectical process determined as much by the reader as by the text. Accordingly, Reform and Conservative ethicists more often emphasize the role of the interpreter, showing awareness that legal precedents are also the outcome of an interpretive act.

Further, non-Orthodox rabbis regard contemporary moral sensitivities as a valid source of authority, while Orthodox authorities, with some exceptions, generally do not. On this matter, Reform and Conservative legal authorities differ somewhat in that Reform rabbis tend to consider contemporary moral values to be decisive and mainly appeal to classical texts for support of a decision already made on other grounds, while Conservative rabbis are more careful to root their decisions in tradition, seeing ethical concerns as important although not the only part of the legal process. Uniting the proponents of the legal approach in spite of their differences, however, is their assumption that traditional sources, and legal precedents in particular, have a bearing on contemporary problems of medical ethics.[47]

Interestingly, the somewhat narrow focus on the text characteristic of many Orthodox rabbis leads to very different outcomes when applied to the issue of same-sex relations on the one hand and to medical ethics on the other. In the case of homosexual relations, for which there is a more or less explicit biblical prohibition, such text-centeredness results in a stringent position. By contrast, concerning issues of medical ethics, about which the Bible and halakhic literature contain few explicit statements, the same text-centeredness frequently leads to quite permissive attitudes. In the absence of explicit prohibitions, the commandment to save life and the mandate to heal[48] are allowed to dominate the decision-making process.

For instance, along with representatives of the Reform and Conservative movements, the Union of Orthodox Jewish Congregations of America

47. Newman, "Woodchoppers and Respirators," 140–60, and Dorff, "Methodology," 161–76.
48. See *m. Yoma* 8:6; *b. Yoma* 85a; *b. Sanh.* 73a; *b. B. Kama* 81b, 85a; *Shulhan Arukh* Yoreh Deah 336:1.

and the Rabbinical Council of America in 2001 expressed their support for embryonic stem cell research, citing the responsibility to save human life and the mandate to heal.[49] Orthodox rabbis also at times refer to *Tiferet Israel*, a commentary on the Mishnah by Israel Lipschitz (1782–1860), which states that if the Torah does not specifically prohibit something, it is permissible.[50] Thus, text-centeredness along with this guideline occasionally make Orthodox rabbis more open to new technology than Conservative and Reform rabbis, who attribute more importance to contemporary moral considerations.[51]

The Non-Legal Approach

Because of the disparity between contemporary medical conditions and those described in halakhic literature and because of the concomitant difficulties in identifying precedents and drawing conclusions from them, a number of rabbis from all three of the major Jewish denominations have suggested abandoning legal methodology altogether. These rabbis maintain that the narrow search for precedents in Jewish legal literature leads to unwarranted extrapolations of principles and norms from earlier sources and does not do justice to the modern issues. Instead they propose an alternative, non-legal approach, which they call "covenantal." This approach rests on the dialectical relationship between God and humanity found in the Bible and affirms the notion that "humankind is created so as to be God's partner in completing creation."[52] God's covenant with Israel does not restrict human freedom, but presupposes it, as articulated by the Reform Rabbi Eugene Borowitz: "Though God's sovereign rule of the universe is utterly unimpeachable, people under the covenant need not surrender their selfhood to God. If anything, to participate properly in the alliance they must affirm their freedom, for they are called to acceptance and resolve, not servility."[53]

---

49. Wahrman, *Brave New Judaism*, 60–61.
50. *Tiferet Israel* on *m. Yad.* 4:3.
51. See for instance the issue of cloning, Dorff, *Matters of Life*, 313–24.
52. Ellenson, "Guidance from a Heritage," 136, quoting Rabbi Irving Greenberg (Orthodox), who has coined the term "covenantal approach," and is one of its major proponents. Other representatives are Rabbi David Hartman (Orthodox), Rabbi Daniel Gordis (Conservative) and Rabbi Eugene Borowitz (Reform).
53. Borowitz quoted in Ellenson, "Guidance from a Heritage," 136–37.

Since human beings are created in the image of God, they share in God's power, giving them the ability to make their own ethical decisions. The dialectical interaction between power and partnership that characterizes the relationship between God and humanity in the Bible provides the proper model for Jewish medical ethics as well, the proponents of the non-legal model argue. Rather than relying on analogies and principles drawn from traditional halakhic literature, human beings are entrusted with the responsibility to make their own moral decisions. This idea is in line with the covenantal theology described above, which allows and requires human beings to make their own moral decisions.

According to the non-legal model, one would still look to traditional Jewish literature for guidance but rather than searching for particular cases bearing outer (and sometimes superficial) resemblance to the contemporary issue at hand, one should look for precedents relevant to the making of an ethical decision. This approach leads to a much freer use of the entire classical Jewish literature, including aggadic texts. In contrast to the legal model, where the authority to make decisions lies with the rabbis, proponents of the covenantal approach see the individual, the patient in the case of medical ethics, as the one who is empowered to make decisions. He or she may well seek advice from a rabbi or a doctor, but in the end each individual has the right to make decisions about treatment and life-prolonging measures.[54] The non-legal model clearly rests on the assumption that human interpretation is a legitimate part of divine revelation from its very beginning.

However, inherent in the non-legal model is the risk of anarchy and arbitrariness, and it has been criticized for failing to provide guidance to the individual. Emphasizing the advantages of the legal approach, Rabbi Elliot Dorff proposes a modified legal model, arguing that if properly applied it is possible to benefit from the wisdom of the past without being enslaved by it. Contrary to the non-legal model, the legal approach has the advantage of continuity with the past. Unlike an individual, a halakhic authority must justify innovations in terms of the tradition and provide a thorough rationale if he or she deviates from it, thus ensuring that it will be taken seriously into account. The legal model also establishes a minimum moral standard, telling people what is expected of them and helping to translate lofty moral aspiration into concrete modes of behavior.

---

54. Ellenson, "Guidance from a Heritage," 129–39.

Properly applied, the legal model at times involves stretching both halakhic and aggadic sources beyond their original meaning, Dorff argues. Rather than mindlessly applying the specifics of particular legal precedents, more general theological and legal concepts emerging out of Jewish tradition should be applied to the matter at hand, taking into consideration the historical context of past medical decisions and the differences between medical conditions then and now. Only when Jewish legal sources are placed in their historical context can one identify the relevant similarities and differences between conditions of the past and our time, and only then can they be applied wisely to contemporary situations. Thus, in order for the legal method to work, halakhic authorities need to give careful attention not only to detailed legal precedents and their historical context but also to contemporary scientific and technological developments and moral values. Finally, but not least, there must be a constant interaction of the law with theology and morality.

An important point for Dorff is that morality is not extrinsic to the process of determining Jewish law, but rather a vital factor within the system. In his view, morality ought to be an integral part of the process of determining Jewish law, along with theology, anthropology, history, eschatology, economics, science, and politics. The ultimate goals of Jewish law being moral and theological, it must be affected both by moral and theological principles from within the tradition (aggadah) and moral sensibilities in the environment in which it functions.

Many rabbis, particularly within the Conservative movement, emphasize that Jewish law (halakhah) ought to reflect Jewish ethical values (aggadah) and if a given law no longer does so, it should be modified. Dorff points out that it is evident from those rabbinic sources that reinterpret biblical commandments, such as those about the rebellious son and an eye for an eye, that the rabbis of the rabbinic period felt that they had the authority to reinterpret laws that did not concur with their moral values and that precedent for that can be found within the Bible itself, for instance in the sections that portray Moses and Aaron as arguing with God for a just or merciful revision of the law (Lev. 10:19-20; Num. 9:6-14, 27:1-11). Accordingly, to preserve laws that do not reflect moral values would actually be a violation of tradition, and it is the responsibility of contemporary halakhic authorities to continue the tradition of ensuring that Jewish law accords with Jewish theology and morality.[55]

Thus, a tension between legal and non-legal texts permeates the decision-making processes within contemporary Judaism. While most halakhic authorities privilege halakhah over aggadah (proponents of the legal model), some argue for the abandonment of the legal model altogether in favor of a non-legal approach (advocates of the covenantal model), and yet others strive to strike a balance between the two (proponents of a modified legal approach). As the examples of the deliberations about same-sex relations and issues of medical ethics both demonstrate, halakhic sources have typically been given precedence over aggadic texts, which explains why Jewish tradition, in spite of the existence of many radical texts affirming the authority of humans to innovate and adapt, is nevertheless relatively cautious and restrained in its interpretation and adaptation of the Bible and of the legislation of previous generations.

The emphasis on the interaction between legal and non-legal texts, expressed by many contemporary rabbis, recalls Bialik's classic characterization of halakhah and aggadah as two sides of the same coin. Just like water and ice are two different forms of the same substance, halakhic and aggadic texts are two equally important parts of divine revelation. Bialik's comparison of halakhah and aggadah to ice and water can serve as a reminder of the importance of keeping both forms together. As pointed out by many, a one-sided reliance on halakhah leads to a legalistic system in which the laws do not reflect the theological beliefs, while too much of an emphasis on aggadah runs the risk of anarchy and a loss of continuity with the past. Ideally, there ought to be a balance between the two so that the laws constitute a concrete formulation of the theology and ideals inherent in the aggadic texts.

THE LEGACY OF CLASSICAL RABBINIC JUDAISM

Underlying the focus on the text among many Orthodox rabbis—at times to the exclusion of other factors—is likely their view of the Bible as wholly divine and all rabbinic laws and customs as divinely sanctioned and somehow included in the revelation at Sinai. This position echoes the view expressed in some rabbinic texts from the amoraic period, which claim

---

55. Dorff, "Methodology," 161–67; Dorff, *Love of God*, 211–43.

that rabbinic tradition was given in its entirety as a body of set teachings to Moses at Sinai alongside the Written Torah (*b. Ber.* 5a; *b. Meg.* 19b). As a consequence of this view, Orthodox rabbis, with some important exceptions, tend to perceive the result of their legislative and interpretive activity as divinely revealed.

To be sure there are exceptions to this generalization of the Orthodox position, once again highlighting the diversity within Orthodoxy. In addition to the exceptions already cited, it is worth mentioning Blu Greenberg, the well-known advocate of feminism as applied to Orthodox Judaism, who clearly acknowledges the human component in the shaping of Jewish tradition. She argues that the inequity of women in traditional Judaism is a consequence of sociological factors of ancient times rather than theologically sanctioned, and accordingly maintains that one is not obliged to "make an eternal principle out of an accident of history." She points out that rabbinic tradition stresses humanity's role as "a partner in the task of perfecting an imperfect world," emphasizing that halakhah is a system that is being perfected continually.

Unlike the assumption that rabbinic tradition is divinely revealed, common within Orthodox Judaism, non-Orthodox rabbis in general seem to have adopted the tannaitic view of human interpretation as an integral part of divine revelation (*Sifre* Deut. §313; *Mekh. R. Ishmael* Bahodesh 9) and acknowledge that their conclusions are the outcome of human interpretation of God's word based on a selection of texts. They claim that their conclusions are neither necessarily the intended original meanings nor the only possible ones. They admit that innovations and adaptations are the outcome of human interpretation, and maintain that such interpretive activity, governed by the decisions of previous halakhic authorities and a sense of what is morally right, accords with God's will as expressed, for instance, in the parable of the wheat and the flax (*S. Eliahu Zuta* 2), and in the story about Moses and Rabbi Aqiva (*b. Menah.* 29b). Since they acknowledge the human role in the shaping of tradition, they are generally more inclined to accept innovations and adaptations than those who regard rabbinic tradition as divinely revealed. These different theologies of revelation are seldom openly stated but seem to underlie and inform the decision-making process in the respective movements of contemporary Judaism.

The impact from the rabbinic period can also be discerned in the various strategies adopted by contemporary rabbis in order to bring about change. Drawing on *m. Eduy.* 1:5, which states that minority opinions should be preserved so that a future court can rely on them and rule in accordance with them, some contemporary rabbis consider it legitimate to rely on a minority opinion from Jewish legal tradition and, based on that, rule against the prevailing custom and tradition if the contemporary situation is different from the one in which the majority opinion was shaped. This was not an option for the issue of same-sex relations, since there was no minority opinion available, and in most cases of issues of medical ethics it is not an option either, since Jewish legal tradition seldom offers any explicit opinion, either a majority or minority one, on these matters. The strategy was used, however, by some rabbis in the Conservative Movement in arguing for the ordination of women to the rabbinate.

Others, however, regard the rabbinate as the ultimate authority and argue that a halakhic authority can overturn precedent if there is sufficient cause and if the original reasons for the ruling or norm no longer exist— even if there is no specific source from tradition to support the change. According to this reasoning, minority opinions cannot overturn the prevailing precedent, only rabbinic authority can. In the particular case of the ordination of women, the proponents of the first approach seemed more liberal, since they were able to free themselves from precedent and tradition by invoking a minority opinion from rabbinic literature permitting the ordination of women, while proponents of the latter had to work with the prevailing precedent. Ultimately, however, the ordination of women was justified according to both approaches.[56]

Halakhic authorities claiming that one may not rely on minority opinion to introduce changes find support in *m. Eduy.* 1:6, which states that minority views are preserved as evidence that they have already been considered and rejected and accordingly cannot be invoked by religious authorities of a later time. Documented as a minority view, the dissenting opinion is considered rejected forever. The Mishnah presents the second opinion as a minority opinion in the name of Rabbi Yehudah, whereas the view that codifying minority views preserves them as future options is presented as a majority opinion.

Interestingly, the editor of the Tosefta has inversed the sayings, stating the view that minority opinions are mentioned only to be rejected as the majority view and the view that minority views should be preserved for future courts to rely on as a minority view (*t. Eduy.* 1:4). While the redac-

---

56. See Fine, "Women and the Minyan."

tor of the Mishnah seems to have envisioned a flexible code, the redactor of the Tosefta seems to have wanted to strengthen the tradition that had evolved based on majority opinions.[57] Another area in which the legacy of the rabbinic period is clearly sensed is the style and character of modern responsa literature. The talmudic style of examining positions, explaining the details and arguing for or against them by means of other available sources, is a characteristic of contemporary legal reasoning also.

When contemporary Judaism as a whole is compared with rabbinic Judaism, one might get the impression that the rabbis of ancient times were considerably more radical and innovative than many contemporary halakhic authorities. There may be some truth to this, and possibly the destruction of the Second Temple changed Jewish reality to such an extent that radical innovations were necessary to ensure the survival of Judaism, but the innovative nature of classical rabbinic Judaism may nonetheless be less radical than what it appears to be. One must bear in mind that some of the radical rabbinic texts permitting and encouraging reinterpretation and change likely served to legitimize innovations that had already taken place, and are accordingly not so much evidence of the rabbis' inclination toward radical change as of their need to justify traditions and customs that had already developed. By necessity, the idea of an authoritative tradition also makes innovations more difficult in a later period since one has to contend with the interpretations and legislations of earlier generations. Either way, the ability to adapt to new circumstances—whether particular adaptations were introduced deliberately by the rabbis or justified only long after the event—is surely one of the key factors in the survival of Judaism.

The early rabbinic view of human interpretation as part of divine revelation probably responded to the need to refashion Jewish tradition after the destruction of the temple. The later rabbinic notion that rabbinic tradition in its entirety was given to Moses at Sinai alongside the written Torah likely developed in a polemical situation in which the rabbis had to defend their tradition and their authority to interpret and legislate against groups who championed other authorities. Ironically, this view, which probably evolved as a means to justify changes that had taken place, largely serves as an argument *against* innovation and change in contemporary Judaism.

To preserve continuity with the past by anchoring new decisions in traditional literature and to continuously wrestle with biblical and rabbinic

---

57. See Halbertal, *People*, 51–52.

texts is a way for modern-day Jews to attempt to find out what God asks of them, and most of them seem to sense that as long as the Bible and rabbinic tradition are studied and taken seriously, change may be justified. For most people within a tradition that imagines that God himself studies with the rabbis and listens to their views, the role of humans in shaping the content of Judaism is acknowledged as being immensely important. Since what matters is not what the texts say but how they are understood and have been understood by the religious authorities in every generation, this religious leadership—those to whom God's word is entrusted—is endowed with enormous power. An awareness of this power is evidenced in a passage where God himself comforts those who have become the victims of religious leaders who oppress others armed with words of the Torah:

> *I further observed all the oppression that goes on under the sun* [Eccl. 4:1]. Daniel the Tailor interpreted the verses as applying to *mamzerim*.[58] *Behold the tears of the oppressed* (ibid.)—If the parents of these *mamzerim* sinned, what does it have to do with these poor sufferers? If this man's father cohabited with a forbidden woman, what sin has he himself committed and what concern is it of his? *And there is no one to comfort them, but in the hands of their opporessors there is power* [ibid]). This refers to the Sanhedrin who comes to them with the power derived from the Torah and removes them from the community because it is written, *No mamzer shall be admitted into the congregation of the Lord* [Deut. 23:3]. *And there is no one to comfort them* [Eccl. 4:1]. The Holy One, blessed be He, said: "It is my task to comfort them."[59]

This is an amazing acknowledgement of rabbinic power and self-criticism. The text is authored by a religious elite, and yet members of this same elite do not refrain from acknowledging that power and criticizing the misuse of it. It also evidences a remarkable awareness of the role of the interpreter. God is blameless—and so is the law—because the decisive power is not in the text, but in the hands of its appointed interpreters. In this story, the religious leaders are at fault because they have failed to balance the law about *mamzerim* in Deuteronomy against the general biblical concern for justice and fairness.[60] Again, we may recall the parable of the

---

58. A *mamzer* is a child born from a relationship that is forbidden according to Jewish law.
59. *Lev. Rab.* 32.8.
60. Greenberg, *Wrestling with God*, 211–12.

king who was pleased with the servant who, through his own abilities, had transformed beyond recognition the wheat and the flax entrusted to him but was displeased with the one who had preserved the original form of that which he had been given.

In much of Jewish literature, there is a general awareness of the tension between continuity with the past and the necessity of adaptation and change. The creative ability to handle this tension is no doubt one of the most important factors behind the survival of Judaism. The notion that human interpretation is part of divine revelation allows for adaptation and change, and that notion, shared by the rabbis of the rabbinic period and most contemporary Jews, is itself evidence of the continuity with the past. In various ways and with different emphases, the movements of contemporary Judaism have sustained the legacy of the rabbinic period by continuing to develop and apply the interpretive principles that the ancient rabbis initiated. It does not seem unreasonable to suggest that such awareness of the tension between the wish to preserve continuity with the past and the need to adapt to the present—and the ways in which to handle this balancing act—could serve as a source of inspiration for other religious traditions. Perhaps for Christianity in particular, which shares the view of the Hebrew Bible as authoritative and which developed in a milieu steeped in Jewish notions of revelation and interpretation.

STUDY QUESTIONS

1. Explain the various views on the nature of the Bible and rabbinic tradition within the different denominations of contemporary Judaism. How do these views impact the legislative process in the respective denominations?

2. What needs to be taken into account when making decisions on Jewish law? What happens when different factors conflict with one another?

3. In which ways is the legacy of classical rabbinic Judaism discerned in the various denominations of contemporary Judaism?

SUGGESTIONS FOR FURTHER READING

On Theology and Authority in Contemporary Judaism

Borowitz, E. B. *Studies in the Meaning of Judaism*. Philadelphia: Jewish Publication Society, 2002.

Cohn-Sherbok, D. *Modern Judaism*. London: Macmillan, 1996.

Dorff, E. N. *Conservative Judaism: Our Ancestors to Our Descendants*. New York: United Synagogue of America, 1983.

———. *For the Love of God and People: A Philosophy of Jewish Law*. Philadelphia: Jewish Publication Society, 2007.

Gillman, N. *Sacred Fragments: Recovering Theology for the Modern Jew*. Philadelphia: Jewish Publication Society, 1990.

Hartman, David. *The God Who Hates Lies: Confronting and Rethinking Jewish Tradition*. Woodstock: Jewish Lights, 2011.

Roth, Joel. *The Halakhic Process: A Systemic Analysis*. New York: Jewish Theological Seminary of America, 1986.

On Homosexuality

Dorff, E. N. *For the Love of God and People: A Philosophy of Jewish Law*. Philadelphia: Jewish Publication Society, 2007 (chapter 6).

Greenberg, S. *Wrestling with God and Man: Homosexuality in the Jewish Tradition*. Madison: University of Madison Press, 2004.

Rapoport, C. *Judaism and Homosexuality: An Authentic Orthodox View*. London: Valentine Mitchell, 2004.

On Medical Ethics

Dorff, E. N. *Matters of Life and Death: A Jewish Approach to Modern Medical Ethics*. Philadelphia: Jewish Publication Society, 1998.

Dorff, E. N., and L. E. Newman, eds., *Contemporary Jewish Ethics and Morality: A Reader*. New York: Oxford University Press, 1995.

Wahrman, M. Z. *Brave New Judaism: When Science and Scripture Collide*. Hanover: Brandeis University Press, 2002.

Washofsky, M. *Jewish Living: A Guide to Contemporary Reform Practice*. New York: UAHC, 2001.

Glossary

aggadah • the non-legal portions of rabbinic literature. Aggadah includes legends, folklore, anecdotes, homilies, ethical teachings, and reflections on theology. While halakhah will determine how and when a commandment should be observed, aggadah provides the rationale behind it.

amora (pl. amoraim) • Aramaic term for sages who flourished during the amoraic period, approximately 225–550 C.E.

baraita • traditions from the tannaitic period that were not included in the Mishnah.

Conservative Judaism • a denomination within contemporary Judaism that originated in the nineteenth century as a reaction to Reform Judaism. The Conservative movement maintains that Jewish law is binding but may and should be adapted to new circumstances.

gemara • commentary on the Mishnah developed by amoraic sages in Palestine and Babylonia. Together, the Mishnah and the gemara constitute the Talmud.

halakhah • Jewish religious law. It is also used to refer to the legal portions of rabbinic literature. Halakhah deals with details of how and when commandments are to be observed.

haredim (sg. haredi) • (literally "those who fear God"), ultra-orthodox.

hasidism • a charismatic movement that developed in eastern Europe in the mid-eighteenth century. In response to the focus on Talmud study, it emphasized spirituality and joy as important aspects of Judaism. Hasidism is a part of contemporary haredi Judaism.

haskalah • a late eighteenth-century movement among European Jews adopting Enlightenment values and advocating education in secular studies.

Jesus movement • a movement within Second Temple Judaism whose adherents believed that Jesus was the Messiah. Also non-Jews who believed that Jesus was the Messiah joined the movement.

litvaks (literally "Lithuanians") • opponents of Hasidism, also known as *mitnagdim*. They constitute a group within contemporary haredi society.

mashal • parable.

midrash • rabbinic biblical interpretation based on the assumptions that the biblical text is perfect, relevant to later times and contains hidden meanings beyond the plain contextual meaning. The term can also refer to compilations of biblical interpretations.

Mishnah • one of the earliest works of rabbinic Judaism redacted in the early third century. It consists mainly of legal teachings and traditions attributed to sages who lived before 200 C.E. The Mishnah and its later commentary, the gemara, together form the Talmud. The smallest section of the Mishnah is known also as a *mishnah*.

nimshal • the situation that a mashal (parable) aims to illustrate.

Oral Torah • see Torah below.

Orthodox Judaism • a collective term for modern Orthodox and haredi Jews. While haredi Jews reject modern society, modern Orthodox Jews believe that strict observance of Jewish law can be reconciled with a secular education and integration into modern society.

rabbinic Judaism • the Judaism that emerged after the fall of the second temple in the year 70. A basic tenet of rabbinic Judaism is that the Torah was revealed to Moses at Mt. Sinai in one written (the Bible) and one oral form (rabbinic tradition) and that the written Torah can only be understood through oral tradition (Mishnah, Talmud, midrash).

rabbinic literature • refers primarily to the literature of the Talmudic era (the Mishnah, Talmuds, and classical midrashim), but can also include midrashic anthologies redacted later.

Reconstructionist Judaism • a denomination within contemporary Judaism that originated as a branch within the Conservative movement. Judaism is seen as a progressively evolving civilization and an emphasis is placed on its cultural aspects. Jewish law is not considered binding.

Reform Judaism • a denomination of contemporary Judaism that emerged in the late nineteenth century as a consequence of the attempts to reform and adapt Jewish tradition. Reform Judaism regards Jewish law as a set of guiding principles rather than a binding law code.

Responsa (sing. *responsum*, "answers") • a body of rulings written by legal authorities in response to specific questions addressed to them. The custom of writing responsa began in the early medieval period and continues to the present.

stam ("anonymous") • the latest, anonymous layer of the Talmud.

sugya • a literary unit in the Talmud.

Talmud • a central collection of texts from the rabbinic period. It consists of the Mishnah and its commentary (gemara). The Talmud exists in two versions, the Palestinian Talmud (also known as the Jerusalem Talmud), that originated in the Galilee between 225–400 C.E. and the Babylonian Talmud that evolved in Babylonia between 225–700. The Babylonian one is the most comprehensive and the one still studied by religious Jews.

Tanakh • an acronym for the Hebrew Bible, formed from the first Hebrew letters of the three main units of the Bible: *Torah* (five books of Moses), *Nevi'im* (Prophets), and *Ketuvim* (Writings).

tanna (pl. tannaim) • Aramaic term for sages who flourished during the tannaitic period, from the destruction of the temple until ca. 225 C.E.

targum (literally "translation") • Aramaic translations of the Bible that also include many interpretive traditions.

Torah • In its most restrictive sense, Torah refers to the first part of the Hebrew Bible (the five books of Moses), in a more expanded sense to the Hebrew Bible as a whole (Written Torah), and in an even more expanded sense to the entire body of rabbinic interpretation and legislation (Oral Torah).

Tosefta (Aramaic, literally "addition") • A collection of traditions from the tannaitic period roughly contemporaneous with the Mishnah. The Tosefta is organized according to the same tractates as the Mishnah but includes more traditions.

Written Torah • see Torah above.

Bibliography

Sources and Translations

Bibles, Apocrypha, and Pseudepigrapha

New Revised Standard Version Bible. Nashville: Thomas Nelson, 1990.
Novum Testamentum Graece. Edited by B. and K. Aland et al. 27 ed. Stuttgart: Deutsche Bibelgesellschaft, 2001.
Tanakh: A New Translation of the Holy Scripture according to the Traditional Hebrew Text. Philadelphia: Jewish Publication Society, 1985.
The Old Testament Pseudepigrapha, Volume 2: Expansions of the "Old Testament" and Legends, Wisdom and Philosophical Literature, Prayers, Psalms, and Odes, Fragments of Lost Judeo-Hellenistic Works. Edited by James H. Charlesworth. New York: Doubleday, 1985.

Jewish-Hellenistic Literature

Josephus. Translated by H. St. J. Thackeray et al. 10 vol. Loeb Classical Library. Cambridge: Harvard University Press, 1926–.

Rabbinic Literature

Mishnah

Mishnah: Shishah Sidre Mishnah. Edited by Ch. Albeck. Jerusalem: Mossad Bialik, 1952.

Tosefta

Tosephta: Based on the Erfurt and Vienna Codices with Parallels and Variants by Moses Samuel Zuckermandel. Jerusalem: Wahrmann, 1963.

Babylonian Talmud

Babylonian Talmud. Translated into English with Notes, Glossary, and Indices under the Editorship of I. Epstein. London: Soncino, 1935–1952.

Midrash

Mekhilta de-Rabbi Ishmael: A Critical Edition on the Basis of the MSS and Early Editions. With an English Translation, Introduction, and Notes by Jacob Z. Lauterbach. 3 vols. Philadelphia: Jewish Publication Society, 1976 [1933–1935].

Midrash Pirke de Rabbi Eliezer according to the Text of the Manuscript Belonging to Abraham Epstein of Vienna. Translated and Annotated by Gerald Friedlander. New York: Sepher-Hermon, 1981.

Midrash Rabbah. Translated into English with Notes, Glossary, and Indices under the Editorship of H. Freedman and M. Simon. 10 vols. London: Soncino, 1983.

Midrash Tanhuma. Jerusalem: Eshkol, 1990.

Pesikta de-Rab Kahana: R. Kahana's Compilation of Discourses for Sabbaths and Festal Days. Translated from Hebrew and Aramaic by W. G. Braude and I. J. Kapstein. Philadelphia: Jewish Publication Society, 2002.

Sifra. Edited by I. H. Weiss. Wien, 1862.

Sifre: A Tannaitic Commentary on the Book of Deuteronomy. Translated from the Hebrew with Introduction and Notes by Reuven Hammer. New Haven: Yale University Press, 1986.

Siphre ad Deuteronomium: H. S. Horovitzii schedis usus cum variis lectionibus et adnotionibus edidit Louis Finkelstein. Jewish Theological Seminary: New York, 1969.

Tanna debe Eliyyahu (=Seder Eliahu Zuta). The Lore of the School of Elijah. Translated from the Hebrew by William G. Braude and Israel J. Kapstein. Philadelphia: Jewish Publication Society, 1981.

Targums

Targum Neofiti: The Aramaic Bible—The Targums. Translated with Apparatus and Notes by M. McNamara: Vol. 1A. Edinburgh: T&T Clark, 1992.

Targum Pseudo-Jonathan: The Aramaic Bible—The Targums. Translated with Introduction and Notes by M. Maher. Vol. 1B. Edinburgh: T&T Clark, 1992.

Haggadah

Passover Haggadah. With an Introduction and Commentary by Shmuel and Zeev Safrai. Jerusalem: Karta, 1998 [Hebrew].

Siddur

The Complete Artscroll Siddur: A New Translation and Anthologized Commentary. Rabbi Nosson Scherman. New York: Mesorah, 1988.

Patristic Literature

The Apostolic Fathers. Translated by Bart D. Ehrman. 2 vols. Loeb Classical Library. Cambridge: Harvard University Press, 2003.

SECONDARY LITERATURE

Alexander, P. S. "Jewish Aramaic Translations of Hebrew Scriptures." In *Mikra: Text, Translation, Reading, and Interpretation of the Hebrew Bible in Ancient Judaism and Christianity*, edited by M. J. Mulder, 217–54. Assen: van Gorcum, 1990.

Baumgarten, A. I. *The Flourishing of Jewish Sects in the Maccabean Era: An Interpretation*. Leiden: Brill, 1997.

Berkovits, E. *Not in Heaven: The Nature and Function of Halakhah*. New York: Ktav, 1983.

Bialik, H. Nahman. *Halachah and Aggadah: Translated from the Hebrew by Leon Simon: With an Introductory Note by Ephraim Broido*. London: Education Dept. of the Zionist Federation of Great Britain and Ireland, 1944.

Bokser, B. M. "Rabbinic Responses to Catastrophe: From Continuity to Discontinuity." *American Academy for Jewish Research* 50 (1983): 37–61.

———. "The Wall Separating God and Israel." *Jewish Quarterly Review* 73 (1983): 349–74.

———. "An Annotated Bibliographical Guide to the Study of the Palestinian Talmud." In *Aufstieg und Niedergang der Römischen Welt* 19.2, edited by H. Temporini and W. Haase, 139–256. Berlin: de Gruyter, 1979.

Borowitz, E. B. *Studies in the Meaning of Judaism*. Philadelphia: Jewish Publication Society, 2002.

Boyarin, D. "A Tale of Two Synods: Nicaea, Yavneh, and Rabbinic Ecclesiology." *Exemplaria* 12 (2000): 21–62.

———. *Border Lines: The Partition of Judaeo-Christianity*. Philadelphia: University of Pennsylvania Press, 2004.

———. *Carnal Israel: Reading Sex in Talmudic Culture*. Berkeley: University of California Press, 1993.

———. *Intertextuality and the Reading of Midrash*. Bloomington: Indiana University Press, 1990.

Cohen, S. J. D. "The Significance of Yavneh: Pharisees, Rabbis, and the End of Jewish Sectarianism." *Hebrew Union College Annual* 55 (1984): 27–53.

———. *The Beginnings of Jewishness: Boundaries, Varieties, Uncertainties*. Berkeley: University of California Press, 1999.

———. *From the Maccabees to the Mishnah*. Louisville: Westminster John Knox, 1987.

Cohn-Sherbok, D. *Modern Judaism*. London: Macmillan, 1996.

Davies, P. R. and B. D. Chilton. "The Aqedah: A Revised Tradition History." *Catholic Biblical Quarterly* 40 (1978): 514–46.

Davies, W. D., and D. C. Allison. *A Critical and Exegetical Commentary on the Gospel according to Saint Matthew*. 3 vols. Edinburgh: T&T Clark, 2004 [1991].

Don-Yehiya, E. "Traditionalist Strands." In *Modern Judaism: An Oxford Guide*, edited by N. De Lange and M. Freud-Kandel, 93–105. Oxford: Oxford University Press, 2005.

Dorff, E. N. "A Methodology for Jewish Medical Ethics." In *Contemporary Jewish Ethics and Morality: A Reader*, edited by E. N. Dorff and L. E. Newman, 161–76. New York: Oxford University Press, 1995.

———. *Conservative Judaism: Our Ancestors to Our Descendants.* New York: United Synagogue of America, 1983.

———. *For the Love of God and People: A Philosophy of Jewish Law.* Philadelphia: Jewish Publication Society, 2007.

———. *Matters of Life and Death: A Jewish Approach to Modern Medical Ethics.* Philadelphia: Jewish Publication Society, 1998.

Draper, J. A. "Torah and Troublesome Apostles in the Didache Community." *New Testament Studies* 33 (1991): 347–72.

Drijvers, H. "Syrian Christianity and Judaism." In *The Jews among Pagans and Christians*, edited by J. Lieu, J. North, and T. Rajak, 124–46. London: Routledge, 1992.

Dubin, L. C. "Enlightenment and Emancipation." In *Modern Judaism: An Oxford Guide*, edited by L. De Lange and M. Freud-Kandel, 29–41. Oxford: Oxford University Press, 2005.

Eisenbaum, P. *Paul Was Not a Christian: The Real Message of a Misunderstood Apostle.* New York: HarperOne, 2009.

Ellenson, D. H. "How to Draw Guidance from a Heritage: Jewish Approaches to Mortal Choices." In *Contemporary Jewish Ethics and Morality: A Reader*, edited by E. N. Dorff and L. E. Newman, 129–39. New York: Oxford University Press, 1995.

Elman, Y. "Classical Rabbinic Interpretation." In *The Jewish Study Bible: Featuring the Jewish Publication Society Tanakh Translation*, edited by A. Berlin and M. Zvi Brettler, 1844–63. Oxford: Oxford University Press, 2004,.

Elon, M. *Jewish Law: History, Sources, Principles.* Philadelphia: Jewish Publication Society, 1994.

Eshel, H. "The Bar Kochba Revolt, 132–135." In vol. 4 of *The Cambridge History of Judaism: The Late Roman-Rabbinic Period*, edited by Steven T. Katz, 105–27. Cambridge: Cambridge University Press.

Fish, Stanley. *Is There a Text in This Class? The Authority of Interpretive Communities.* Harvard University Press: Cambridge, 1980.

Fitzmyer, J. A. *The Gospel according to Luke: A New Translation with Introduction and Commentary.* 2 vols. New York: Doubleday, 1981.

Flusser, D. "Paul's Jewish-Christian Opponents in the Didache." In *The Didache in Modern Research*, edited by Jonathan A. Draper, 195–211. Leiden: Brill, 1996.

———. *Die rabbinischen Gleichnisse und der Gleichniserzähler Jesus.* Bern: Peter Lang, 1981.

Fonrobert, C. E. "The Didascalia Apostolorum: A Mishnah for the Disciples of Jesus." *Journal of Early Christian Studies* 9 (2001): 483–509.

Fox, H., and T. Meacham. *Introducing Tosefta: Textual, Intratextual, and Intertextual Studies.* Hoboken: Ktav, 1999.

Fraade, S. D. "Literary Composition and Oral Performance in Early Midrashim." *Oral Tradition* 14 (1999): 33–51.

———. "Hearing and Seeing at Sinai: Interpretive Trajectories." In *The Significance of Sinai: Traditions about Sinai and Divine Revelation in Judaism and Christianity*, edited by G. J. Brooke, H. Najman, and L. T. Stuckenbruck, 247–68. Leiden: Brill, 2008.

———. "Rabbinic Views on the Practice of Targum, and Multilingualism in the Jewish Galilee of the Third–Sixth Centuries." In *The Galilee in Late Antiquity*, ed. L. I. Levine, 253–86. Cambridge: Harvard University Press, 1992.

———. From Tradition to Commentary: Torah and Its Interpretation in the Midrash Sifre to Deuteronomy. Albany: SUNY Press, 1991.

Fraenkel, J. *Darkhe Haaggadah Vehamidrash*. Givatayim: Massadah, 1991.

Freud-Kandel, M. "Modernist Movements." In *Modern Judaism: An Oxford Guide*, edited by L. De Lange and M. Freud-Kandel, 81–92. Oxford: Oxford University Press, 2005.

Friedman, S. "A Good Story Deserves Retelling: The Unfolding of the Akiva Legend." In *Creation and Composition: The Contribution of the Bavli Redactors (Stammaim) to the Aggada*, edited by L. R. Jeffrey, 71–100. Tübingen: Mohr Siebeck, 2005.

Gafni, I. M. "Rabbinic Historiography and Representations of the Past." In *The Cambridge Companion to the Talmud and Rabbinic Literature*, edited by C. E. Fonrobert and M. S. Jaffee, 295–312. Cambridge: Cambridge University Press, 2007.

———. *Land, Center, and Diaspora: Jewish Constructs in Late Antiquity*. Sheffield: Sheffield Academic, 1997.

Gager, J. G. *Reinventing Paul*. Oxford: Oxford University Press, 2000.

Gaston, L. *Paul and the Torah*. Vancouver: University of British Coumbia Press, 1987.

Gillman, N. *Sacred Fragments: Recovering Theology for the Modern Jew*. Philadelphia: Jewish Publication Society, 1990.

Goldberg, A. "The Babylonian Talmud." In *The Literature of the Sages*, edited by Schmuel Safrai et al., 323–66. Assen: van Gorcum, 1987.

———. "The Mishna—A Study Book of Halakha." In *The Literature of the Sages*, edited by Schmuel Safrai et al., 211–51. Assen: van Gorcum, 1987.

———. "The Palestinian Talmud." In *The Literature of the Sages*, edited by Schmuel Safrai et al., 303–22. Assen: van Gorcum, 1987.

———. "The Tosefta–Companion to the Mishna." In *The Literature of the Sages*, edited by Schmuel Safrai et al., 283–302. Assen: van Gorcum, 1987.

Goldenberg, R. "Talmud." In *Back to the Sources: Reading the Classic Jewish Texts*, edited by W. B. Holtz, 129–75. New York: Summit, 1984.

———. "The Deposition of Rabban Gamliel II." *Journal of Jewish Studies* 23 (1972): 167–90.

Goodblatt, D. "The Babylonian Talmud." In *Aufstieg und Niedergang der Römischen Welt* 19.2, edited by H. Temporini and W. Haase, 257–336. Berlin: de Gruyter, 1979, 257–336.

———. "The Political and Social History of the Jewish Community in the Land of Israel, c. 235–638." In vol. 4 of *The Cambridge History of Judaism: The Late Roman-Rabbinic Period*, edited by Steven T. Katz, 404–30. Cambridge: Cambridge University Press, 2006.

———. "Toward the Rehabilitation of Talmudic History." In *History of Judaism— The Next Ten Years*, edited by B. M. Bokser, 31–44. Atlanta: Scholars, 1981.

———. *The Monarchic Principle: Studies in Jewish Self-Government in Antiquity*. Tübingen: Mohr Siebeck, 1994.

Goodman, M. "The Place of the Sadducees." In *Redefining First-Century Jewish and Christian Identities: Essays in Honor of Ed Parish Sanders*, edited by F. E. Udoh, S. Heschel, M. Chancey, and G. Tatum, 139–52. Notre Dame: University of Notre Dame Press, 2008.

———. "The Roman State and the Jewish Patriarch in the Third Century." In *The Galilee in Late Antiquity*, edited by L. I. Levine, 127–39. New York: Jewish Theological Seminary of America, 1992.

Gray, A. M. *A Talmud in Exile: The Influence of Yerushalmi Avodah Zarah on the Formation of Bavli Avodah Zara*. Providence: Brown University, 2005.

Green, W. S. "What's in a Name? The Problematic of Rabbinic 'Bibliography.'" In *Approaches to Ancient Judaism*, edited by W. S. Green, 77–96. Missoula: Scholars, 1978.

Greenberg, B. "The Theoretical Basis of Women's Equality in Judaism." In *Contemporary Jewish Ethics and Morality*, ed. E. N. Dorff and L. E. Newman, 315–26. New York: Oxford University Press, 1995.

Greenberg, S. *Wrestling with God and Man: Homosexuality in the Jewish Tradition*. Madison: University of Madison Press, 2004.

Grossfeld, B. *The Targum Onqelos to Genesis: Translated with a Critical Introduction, Apparatus, and Notes by Bernard Grossfeld*. Wilmington: Michael Glazier, 1988.

Halbertal, M. *People of the Book: Canon, Meaning, and Authority*. Cambridge: Harvard University Press, 1997.

Halivni, D. "Aspects of the Formation of the Talmud." In *Creation and Composition: The Contribution of the Bavli Redactors (Stammaim) to the Aggada*, ed. J. L. Rubenstein, 339–60. Tübingen: Mohr-Siebeck, 2005.

———. *Midrash, Mishnah, and Gemara: The Jewish Predilection for Justified Law*. Cambridge: Harvard University Press, 1986.

———. "Reflections on Classical Jewish Hermeneutics." *Proceedings of the American Academy for Jewish Research* 62 (1996): 21–127.

———. *Peshat and Derash: Plain and Applied Meaning in Rabbinic Exegesis*. New York: Oxford University Press, 1991.

Hammer, R. Sifre. *A Tannaitic Commentary on the Book of Deuteronomy: Translated from the Hebrew with Introduction and Notes*. New Haven: Yale University Press, 1986.

Harris, J. M. "Midrash Halachah." In vol. 4 of *The Cambridge History of Judaism: The Late Roman-Rabbinic Period*, ed. Steven T. Katz, 336–68. Cambridge: Cambridge University Press, 2006.

Hartman, D. *A Living Covenant: The Innovative Spirit in Traditional Judaism*. Woodstock: Jewish Lights, 1997 [1985].

Hauptman, J. *Rereading the Mishnah*. Tübingen: Mohr Siebeck, 2005.

———. *The Development of the Talmudic Sugya: Relationship between Tannaitic and Amoraic Sources*. Lanham: University Press of America, 1987.

Hayes, C. E. *Between the Babylonian and Palestinian Talmuds*. New York: Oxford University Press, 1997.

Hays, R. B. *The Faith of Jesus Christ: The Narrative Substructure of Galatians 3:1–4:11*. Grand Rapids: Eerdmans, 2002 [1983].

Hayward, R. "The Present State of Research into the Targumic Account of the Sacrifice of Isaac." *Journal of Jewish Studies* 32 (1981): 127–50.

Hedner Zetterholm, K. *Portrait of a Villain: Laban the Aramean in Rabbinic Literature.* Leuven: Peeters, 2002.

Heilman, S. *Defenders of the Faith: Inside Ultra-Orthodox Jewry.* New York: Schocken, 1992.

Hengel, M. *Judaism and Hellenism: Studies in their Encounter in Palestine during the Early Hellenistic Period.* 2 vols. London: SCM, 1974.

Heschel, Abraham J. *God in Search of Man: A Philosophy of Judaism.* New York: Farrar, Straus and Giroux, 1989 [1955].

Hezser, C. "Social Fragmentation, Plurality of Opinion, and Nonobservance of Halakhah: Rabbis and Community in Late Roman Palestine." *Jewish Studies Quarterly* 1 (1993/94): 234–51.

———. *The Social Structure of the Rabbinic Movement.* Tübingen: Mohr Siebeck, 1997.

Hirshman, M. "Rabbinic Universalism in the Second and Third Centuries." *Harvard Theological Review* 93 (2000): 101–15.

———. *A Rivalry of Genius: Jewish and Christian Biblical Interpretation in Late Antiquity.* Albany: SUNY Press, 1996.

Holtz, B. W. "Midrash." In *Back to the Sources,* edited by B. W. Holtz, 177–211. New York: Summit, 1984.

Iser, W. *The Act of Reading: A Theory of Aesthetic Response.* Baltimore: Johns Hopkins University Press, 1991.

Jaffee, M. S. "Oral Tradition in the Writings of Rabbinic Oral Torah: On Theorizing Rabbinic Orality." *Oral Tradition* 14 (1999): 3–32.

Johnson Hodge, C. *If Sons, Then Heirs: A Study of Kinship and Ethnicity in the Letters of Paul.* Oxford: Oxford University Press, 2007.

Kalmin, R. L. "The Formation and Character of the Babylonian Talmud." In *The Cambridge History of Judaism: The Late Roman-Rabbinic Period,* edited by Steven T. Katz, 840–76. Cambridge: Cambridge University Press, 2006.

———. "Rabbinic Literature of Late Antiquity as a Source for Historical Study." In *Judaism in Late Antiquity,* vol. 3, edited by Jacob Neusner, Bruce Chilton, and Alan J. Avery-Peck, 187–99. Leiden: Brill, 2000.

———. *Sages, Stories, Authors, and Editors in Rabbinic Babylonia.* Atlanta: Scholars, 1994.

Kaplan, M. *Judaism as a Civilization: Toward a Reconstruction of American-Jewish Life.* New York: Macmillan, 1934.

Kelley, N. *Knowledge and Religious Authority in the Pseudo-Clementines.* Tübingen: Mohr Siebeck, 2006.

Kimelman, R. "Identifying Jews and Christians in Roman Syria-Palestine." In *Galilee through the Centuries: Confluence of Cultures,* edited by E. M. Meyers, 301–33. Winona Lake: Eisenbrauns, 1999.

Klein, M. L. *The Fragment-Targums of the Pentateuch according to Their Extant Sources.* Rome: Biblical Institute Press, 1980.

Kloppenborg, J. S. *The Tenants in the Vineyard: Ideology, Economics, and Agrarian Conflict in Jewish Palestine.* Tübingen: Mohr Sieneck, 2006.

Kraemer, D. "Rabbinic Sources for Historical Study." In *Judaism in Late Antiquity*, edited by Jacob Neusner and Alan J. Avery-Peck, 201–12. Leiden: Brill, 2000.

———. *The Mind of the Talmud: An Intellectual History of the Bavli*. New York: Oxford University Press, 1990.

———. "The Mishnah." In vol. 4 of *The Cambridge History of Judaism: The Late Roman-Rabbinic Period*, edited by Steven T. Katz, 299–315. Cambridge: Cambridge University Press, 2006.

Kugel, J. L. *The Bible as It Was*. Cambridge: Belknap, 1997.

———. In *Potiphar's House: The Interpretive Life of Biblical Texts*. New York: HarperCollins, 1990.

———. "Two Introductions to Midrash." *Prooftexts* 3 (1983): 131–55.

Lapin, H. "The Origins and Development of the Rabbinic Movement in the Land of Israel." In vol. 4 of *The Cambridge History of Judaism: The Late Roman-Rabbinic Period*, edited by Steven T. Katz, 206–29. Cambridge: Cambridge University Press, 2006.

Larsson, G. *Bound for Freedom: The Book of Exodus in Jewish and Christian Traditions*. Peabody: Hendrickson, 1999.

Le Déaut, R. *La nuit pascale: Essai sur la signification de la Pâques juive à partir du Targum dÉxode XII 42*. Rome: Institut biblique pontifical, 1963.

Leibowitz, N. *Torah Insights*. Jerusalem: Eliner Library, 1995.

Levenson, J. D. *The Death and Resurrection of the Beloved Son: The Transformation of Child Sacrifice in Judaism and Christianity*. New Haven: Yale University Press, 1993.

Levine, L. I. *Judaism and Hellenism in Antiquity: Conflict or Confluence*. Seattle: University of Washington Press, 1998.

———. "The Sages and the Synagogue in Late Antiquity: The Evidence of the Galilee." In *The Galilee in Late Antiquity*, edited by L. I. Levine, 201–22. New York: Jewish Theological Seminary of America, 1992.

———. "The Status of the Patriarch in the Third and Fourth Centuries: Sources and Methodology." *Journal of Jewish Studies* 47 (1996): 1–32.

Licht, C. *Ten Legends of the Sages: The Image of the Sage in Rabbinic Literature*. Hoboken: Ktav, 1991.

Lieberman, S. *Greek in Jewish Palestine/Hellenism in Jewish Palestine*. New York: Jewish Theological Seminary of America, 1994.

———. *Hellenism in Jewish Palestine with a New Introduction by Dov Zlotnick*. New York: Jewish Theological Seminary of America, 1994.

Mandel, P. "The Tosefta." In vol. 4 of *The Cambridge History of Judaism: The Late Roman-Rabbinic Period*, edited by Steven T. Katz, 316–35. Cambridge: Cambridge University Press, 2006.

McNamara, M. *Targum Neofiti 1: Genesis*. Translated with Apparatus and Notes by Martin McNamara. Edinburgh: T&T Clark, 1992.

Milavec, A. A. "A Fresh Analysis of the Parable of the Wicked Husbandmen in the Light of Jewish-Catholic Dialogue." In *Parable and Story in Judaism and Christianity*, edited by C. Thoma and M. Wyschogrod, 81–117. New York: Paulist, 1989.

Miller, S. S. *Sages and Commoners in Late Antique Erez Israel: A Philological Inquiry into Local Traditions in Talmud Yerushalmi*. Tübingen: Mohr Siebeck, 2006.

Moscovitz, L. "The Formation and Character of the Jerusalem Talmud." In vol. 4 of *The Cambridge History of Judaism: The Late Roman-Rabbinic Period*, edited by Steven T. Katz, 663–77. Cambridge: Cambridge University Press, 2006.

Murray, M. *Playing a Jewish Game: Gentile Christian Judaizing in the First and Second Centuries* C.E. Waterloo: Wilfred Laurier University Press, 2004.

Nanos, Mark D. *The Irony of Galatians: Paul's Letter in First-Century Context*. Minneapolis: Fortress Press, 2002.

———. *The Mystery of Romans: The Jewish Context of Paul's Letter*. Minneapolis: Fortress Press, 1996.

Neusner, Jacob. *Comparative Midrash: The Plan and Program of Genesis Rabbah and Leviticus Rabbah*. Atlanta: Scholars, 1986.

———. *Development of a Legend*. Leiden: Brill, 1970.

———. *Invitation to the Talmud*. New York: Harper & Row, 1989.

———. *Judaism and Scripture: The Evidence of Leviticus Rabbah*. Chicago: University of Chicago Press, 1986.

———. *Making the Classics in Judaism: The Three Stages of Literary Formation*. Atlanta: Scholars, 1989.

———. *Midrash in Context: Exegesis in Formative Judaism*. Atlanta: Scholars, 1988.

———. *The Rabbinic Traditions about the Pharisees before 70*. Leiden: Brill, 1971.

Newman, L. E. "Woodchoppers and Respirators: The Problem of Interpretation in Contemporary Jewish Ethics." In *Contemporary Jewish Ethics and Morality: A Reader*, edited by E. N. Dorff and L. E. Newman, 140–60. New York: Oxford University Press, 1995.

Overman, A. J. *Matthew's Gospel and Formative Judaism: The Social World of the Matthean Community*. Minneapolis: Fortress Press, 1990.

Rapoport, C. *Judaism and Homosexuality: An Authentic Orthodox View*. London: Valentine Mitchell, 2004.

Roth, Joel. *The Halakhic Process: A Systemic Analysis*. New York: Jewish Theological Seminary of America, 1986.

Rubenstein, J. L. "Social and Institutional Settings of Rabbinic Literature." In *The Cambridge Companion to the Talmud and Rabbinic Literature*, edited by C. E. Fonrobert and M. S. Jaffee, 58–74. Cambridge: Cambridge Universiry Press, 2007.

Rubenstein, Jeffrey L. *Rabbinic Stories*. New York: Paulist, 2002.

———. *Stories of the Babylonian Talmud*. Baltimore: Johns Hopkins University Press, 2010.

———. *Talmudic Stories: Narrative Art, Composition, and Culture*. Baltimore: Johns Hopkins University Press, 1999.

———. *The Culture of the Babylonian Talmud*. Baltimore: Johns Hopkins University Press, 2003.

Runesson, A. "Judging Gentiles in the Gospel of Matthew: Between 'Othering' and Inclusion." In *Jesus, Matthew's Gospel, and Early Christianity: Studies in the Memory of Graham N. Stanton*, edited by R. A. Burridge, J. Willits, and D. M. Gurtner, 133–51. London: T&T Clark, 2011.

————. "Re-Thinking Early Jewish-Christian Relations: Matthean Community History as Pharisaic Intragroup Conflict." *Journal of Biblical Literature* 127 (2008): 95–132.

Safrai, Schmuel. "Halakha." In *The Literature of the Sages. First Part: Oral Tora, Halakha, Mishna, Tosefta, Talmud, External Tractates*, edited by Schmuel Safrai et al., 121–207. Assen: van Gorcum, 1987.

Saldarini, Anthony J. "The Gospel of Matthew and Jewish-Christian Conflict in the Galilee." In *The Galilee in Late Antiquity*, edited by L. I. Levine. Cambridge: Harvard University Press, 1992.

————. *Matthew's Christian-Jewish Community.* Chicago: University of Chicago Press, 1994.

Sanders, E. P. *Judaism: Practice and Belief 63 B.C.E.–66 C.E.* London: SCM, 1994.

————. *Paul and Palestinian Judaism.* Philadelphia: Fortress Press, 1977.

Sandt, H. V. D., and D. Flusser. *The Didache: Its Jewish Sources and Its Place in Early Judaism and Christianity.* Assen: van Gorcum, 2002.

Satlow, M. L. *Jewish Marriage in Antiquity.* Princeton: Princeton University Press, 2001.

Schäfer, P. "The Causes of the Bar-Kokhba Revolt." In *Studies in Aggadah, Targum, and Jewish Liturgy in Memory of Joseph Heinemann*, edited by J. J. Petuchowski and E. Fleisher, 74–94. Jerusalem: Magnes, 1981.

————. *Jesus in the Talmud.* Princeton: Princeton University Press, 2007.

Schwartz, S. *Imperialism and Jewish Society, 200 B.C.E. to 640 C.E.* Princeton: Princeton University Press, 2001.

————. "The Patriarchs and the Diaspora." *Journal of Jewish Studies* 50 (1999): 208–22.

Segal, A. *The Other Judaisms of Late Antiquity.* Atlanta: Scholars, 1987.

Shanks-Alexander, E. *Transmitting Mishnah: The Shaping Influence of Oral Tradition.* New York: Cambridge University Press, 2006.

Shinan, A., and Y. Zakovitch. "Midrash on Scripture and Midrash within Scripture." *Scripta Hierosolymitana* 31 (1986): 257–77.

Sim, D. C. *The Gospel of Matthew and Christian Judaism: The History and Social Setting of the Matthean Community.* Edinburgh: T&T Clark, 1998.

Simon, M. *Verus Israel: A Study of the Relations between Christians and Jews in the Roman Empire (A.D. 135–425).* London: Vallentine Mitchell, 1996.

Solomon, M. "Sexuality." In *Modern Judaism: An Oxford Guide*, edited by L. De Lange and M. Freud-Kandel, 401–12. Oxford: Oxford University Press, 2005.

Soloveitchik, J. B. *Halakhic Man.* Philadelphia: Jewish Publication Society, 1983.

Spiegel, S. *The Last Trial: On the Legends and Lore of the Command to Abraham to Offer Isaac as a Sacrifice: The Akedah.* Woodstock: Jewish Lights, 1993 [1950].

Steinmetz, D. "Must the Patriarch Know Uqtzin? The Nasi as Scholar in Babylonian Aggada." *AJS Review* 23 (1998): 163–90.

Steinsaltz, A. *The Talmud: A Reference Guide—The Steinsaltz Edition.* New York: Random, 1989.

Stemberger, G. *Introduction to the Talmud and Midrash: Translated and Edited by Markus Bockmuehl.* Edinburgh: T&T Clark, 1996.

Stern, D. "Jesus' Parables from the Perspective of Rabbinic Literature: The Example of the Wicked Husbandmen." In *Parable and Story in Judaism and Christianity*, edited by C. Thoma and M. Wyschogrod. New York: Paulist, 1989, 42–80.

———. "Midrash and Jewish Interpretation." In *The Jewish Study Bible: Featuring the Jewish Publication Society Tanakh Translation*, edited by A. Berlin and M. Z. Brettler, 1863–75. Oxford: Oxford University Press, 2004.

———. *Midrash and Theory: Ancient Jewish Exegesis and Contemporary Literary Studies*. Evanston: Northwestern University Press, 1996.

———. *Parables in Midrash: Narrative and Exegesis in Rabbinic Literature*. Cambridge: Harvard University Press, 1991.

Sternberg, M. *The Poetics of Biblical Narrative: Ideological Literature and the Drama of Reading*. Bloomington: Indiana University Press, 1987.

Stowers, S. K. *A Rereading of Romans: Justice, Jews, and Gentiles*. New Haven: Yale University Press, 1994.

Swetnam, J. *Jesus and Isaac: A Study of the Epistle to the Hebrews in the Light of the Aqedah*. Rome: Biblical Institue Press, 1981.

Tomson, Peter J. *"If This Be from Heaven": Jesus and the New Testament Authors in Their Relationship to Judaism*. Sheffield: Sheffield Academic, 2001.

———. *Paul and the Jewish Law: Halakha in the Letters of the Apostle to the Gentiles*. Assen: van Gorcum, 1990.

Tucker, J. B. *"Remain in Your Calling": Paul and the Continuation of Social Identities in 1 Corinthians*. Eugene: Pickwick, 2011.

Vermes, Geza. *Scripture and Tradition in Judaism: Haggadic Studies*. Leiden: Brill, 1961.

Wahrman, M. Z. *Brave New Judaism: When Science and Scripture Collide*. Hanover: Brandeis University Press, 2002.

Walfish, A. "The Poetics of the Mishnah." In *The Mishnah in Contemporary Perspective: Part Two*, edited by Alan J. Avery-Peck and Jacob Neusner, 153–89. Leiden: Brill, 2006.

Yadin, A. "Resistance to Midrash? Midrash and Halakhah in the Halakhic Midrashim." In *Current Trends in the Study of Midrash*, edited by Carol Bakhos, 34–58. Leiden: Brill, 2006.

———. *Scripture as Logos: Rabbi Ishmael and the Origins of Midrash*. Philadelphia: University of Pennsylvania Press, 2004.

Young, B. H. *The Parables: Jewish Tradition and Christian Interpretation*. Peabody: Hendrickson, 1998.

Zetterholm, Magnus. "'And Abraham Believed.'" In *From Bible to Midrash: Portrayals and Interpretative Practices*, edited by H. Trautner-Kromann, 109–21. Lund: Arcus, 2005.

———. *Approaches to Paul: A Student's Guide to Recent Scholarship*. Minneapolis: Fortress Press, 2009.

———. "The Didache, Matthew, James—and Paul: Reconstructing Historical Developments in Antioch." In *Matthew, James, and Didache: Three Related Documents in Their Jewish and Christian Setting*, edited by Huub van de Sandt and Jürgen Zangenberg, 73–90. Leiden: Brill, 2008.

———. *The Formation of Christianity in Antioch: A Social-Scientific Approach to the Separation between Judaism and Christianity.* London: Routledge, 2003.

———. "Jews, Christians, and Gentiles: Rethinking the Categorization within the Early Jesus Movement." In *Reading Paul in Context: Explorations in Identity Formation: Essays in Honour of William S. Campbell*, edited by K. Ehrensperger and B. J. Tucker, 242–54. London: T&T Clark, 2010.

———. "Paul and the Missing Messiah." In *The Messiah in Early Judaism and Christianity*, edited by Magnus Zetterholm, 33–55. Minneapolis: Fortress Press, 2007.

INTERNET SOURCES

Adlerstein, Y. "Dawn of the Orthodox Celebs." *Jewish World Review*, 2000. www.jewishworldreview.com/0900/ortho.celebs.asp.

Artson, B. S. "Gay and Lesbian Jews: An Innovative Jewish Legal Position." *Jewish Spectator*, 1990. www.ajula.edu/Media/Images/SCM/ContentUnit/4382_9_7828.pdf.

Boteach, S. "Dr. Laura Misguided on Homosexuality." *The Jewish Week*, May 26, 2000. www.highbeam.com/doc/1P1-79391426.html.

Central Conference of American Rabbis (CCAR). "Report of the Ad Hoc Committee on Homosexuality and the Rabbinate," 1990. http://data.ccarnet.org/cgi-bin/respdisp.pl?file=hs6year=1990.

Central Conference of American Rabbis (CCAR). "On Homosexual Marriage" (5756.8), 1996. http://data.ccarnet.org/cgi-bin/respdisp.pl?file=86year=5756.

Central Conference of American Rabbis (CCAR). "Resolution on Same Gender Officiation," 2000. http://data.ccarnet.org/cgi-bin/respdisp.pl?file=gender6year=2000.

Cohen, U. C. "Bibliography of Contemporary Orthodox Responses to Homosexuality." www.atid.org/resources/ATIDbiblio1.doc.

Dorff, E. N. "Jewish Norms for Sexual Behavior: A Responsum Embodying a Proposal," 1992. www.rabbinicalassembly.org.

Dorff, E. N., D. S. Nevins, and A. I. Reisner. "Homosexuality, Human Dignity, and Halakhah: A Combined Responsum for the Committee on Jewish Law and Standards," 2006. www.rabbinicalassembly.org.

Fine, D. J. "Women and the Minyan," 2002. www.rabbinicalassembly.org.

Lamm, N. "Judaism and the Modern Attitude to Homosexuality," 1974. www.jonahweb.org/sections.php?secId=90.

"Platform on Reconstructionism." www.religiousforums.com/forum/reconstructionist-dir/26348-reconstructionist-judaism.

Rabbinical Council of America (RCA), "Response to Rabbinical Assembly's Decisions regarding Ordination of Gays and Lesbians, and 'Commitment Ceremonies," 2006. www.rabbis.org/news/article.cfm?id=100869.

Roth, J. "Homosexuality Revisited," 2006. www.rabbinicalassembly.org.

Tucker, G. "Halakhic and Metahalakhic Arguments concerning Judaism and Homosexuality," 2006. www.rabbinicalassembly.org.

Index of Ancient Sources

Index of Names and Subjects